*More
Than a
Soldier's
War*

TEXAS A&M UNIVERSITY

47

MILITARY HISTORY SERIES

More Than a Soldier's War

PACIFICATION IN VIETNAM

Edward P. Metzner

Texas A&M University Press
College Station

The paper used in this book meets the minimum
requirements of the American National Standard for
Permanence of Paper for Printed Library Materials,
Z39.48-1984. Binding materials have been chosen for
durability.
∞

Library of Congress Cataloging-in-Publication Data

Metzner, Edward P., 1925–
   More than a soldier's war : pacification in
Vietnam / Edward P. Metzner. — 1st ed.
     p. cm.
   Includes index.
   ISBN 0-89096-666-4 (alk. paper)
   1. Vietnamese Conflict, 1961–1975—Personal
narratives, American. 2. Metzner, Edward P.,
1925– . I. Title.
DS559.5.M49   1995
959.704'3373—dc20   95-18482
                                        CIP

To Alina, *for her inspiration, love, and patience in living and writing about an endeavor we both believed in.*

To Howard, Helen, and Hilton, *so that they might understand more about the people and land of their origin and why Dad was there.*

To Hilary, *born in America, but justly proud of his Asian-American heritage.*

WHEN TWO WATER BUFFALOES
FIGHT, THE MOSQUITOES ALWAYS
GET HURT.

—Old Southeast Asian saying

Contents

Illustrations

Preface

After retiring from the army, I often reminisced about World War II and Korea when some old movie or tune or an old friend gave reason. It was different, however, with memories of my seven years as a pacification advisor in the villages of Vietnam. Those episodes kept returning in bad dreams. I would wince in pain as I once more dove to escape the shells exploding in the center of our small team compound in the middle of the Mekong Delta. One night I must have cried out, because my wife awakened me to ask what was wrong.

Another night, sweat soaked my pillow when I again saw the menacing heights of Da Dung Mountain and the withering fire that rained from its caves and crevices down onto Colonel Tai's brave, struggling provincial soldiers at its base.

A pleasant dream about the Children's Moon Festival parade quickly turned sad as I remembered the normally impeccable Colonel Phuc crying unashamedly as his staff awkwardly looked on. Blood-soaked, we had struggled to carry the broken, lifeless bodies of his personal bodyguards to the province hospital in a tragic ending to an otherwise successful first national election. Then a different memory of Phuc dispelled my sadness: Phuc, the imperturbable, losing his calm and pointing his cocked pistol at the head of the terrified driver whose stalled bus blocked our convoy's escape, as darkness and fear descended on us at "Ambush Alley" on perilous Highway 4.

One particularly detailed nightmare was hard to forget. In it I relived a night loudspeaker helicopter mission over pitch-dark mangrove swamps bordering the South China Sea. To my relief, the dream ended just as streams of Viet Cong (VC) tracers reached up like ghostly fingers to pull us down into the darkness from which they spewed.

Corrupt and incompetent, Colonel Tai played a featured role in many of the disturbing scenes that continued to plague me. I muffled an oft-repeated curse at the bad luck that had matched me with Tai in two provinces, and spat again a string of futile protests at his blunders that cost precious lives—his and mine very nearly included.

The odd mixture of defiance and resignation on the faces of a young American captain and Major Canh's handsome young son again wrenched my heart. They accepted Colonel Tai's indifference but found it difficult to believe that I would join their meager defense of Hon Soc Mountain after radio intercept forewarned of the VC attack order.

Last but not least, the image of Dao often appeared in my dreams. Fierce, plucky, and unpredictable, diminutive Le Minh Dao taught me much about overcoming adversity by applying abundant courage and daring, as he performed the impossible against heavy odds. From Tet of 1968, when we served together in the most insecure province in the country, to 1975, when he became the legendary last defender of Saigon, Dao fought off overwhelming enemy attacks to the very end. Such dreams were pleasant; the sadness came when I awakened to the reality of his tragic fate.

Worried that time would gradually erode the clarity and detail of my memories, I began to write an account of those rewarding and often difficult years. Because my seven years as an advisor in Vietnam had the most profound and irrevocable effect on my remaining life, that was the story I needed to tell. I served with the people of Vietnam. As an advisor, I had the duty to be in their midst—among farmers, merchants, civil servants, and soldiers—starting in the humblest of hamlets, and finishing at the highest levels of authority. I walked the rice paddies, hamlets, villages, and remote mud-walled outposts, witnessing their sorrows, hopes, and pain, and often sharing in them.

Regardless of their initial views, all but a very few advisors came to be motivated by the uncomplicated conviction that freedom was preferable to Communist oppression. We were helping to keep a demonstrated desire for freedom alive. Our country sent us to Vietnam to do a soldier's job, and to do it to the best of our abilities.

Through it all, the bloodshed never stopped—and all too often we were caught in the middle of it. Surrounded as we were by seemingly senseless violence against innocent civilians, it soon became clear that the people and their attitudes were the real targets of the war. In the struggle for popular support, the ultimate aim—and most potent weapon—was to help needy people. Our job was to build, not to destroy; to gain the trust and cooperation of the people, not to occupy real estate or count enemy bodies. This knowledge was comforting, for when confronted with pain and fear, all soldiers need an honest cause, especially when they can't make, change, or even clearly understand the policies they are sworn to enforce.

English author C. V. Wedgewood said that "history is lived forward, but is written in retrospect. We know the end before we consider the beginning and we can never wholly recapture what it was like to know the beginning only." Having been among those who witnessed the beginning, as well as many of the events leading to the conclusion of the Vietnam War, I am obligated to tell the story faithfully and accurately. I hope that, in doing so, I may help place that costly and tragic chapter of history in better perspective.

By the time I came home for the last time in 1974, the Vietnam effort had consumed one-quarter of my total commissioned service and one-fifth of my life. During that time I had been the pupil more often than the advisor, and those emotion-filled days and fright-prone moments are forever etched in my memory. The faces of those who died, as well as of those who survived years of heartbreak, only to be caught up in the disastrous aftermath of that tragic episode, will always remain vivid.

The Vietnam Memorial in Washington, D.C., is a wonderful tribute to the servicemen and women who lost their lives in the war, yet it is also a reminder of the continued mistaken perception that Vietnam exclusively was a soldier's war. The 58,000 names inscribed on the memorial do not include any of the many civilian casualties. At its peak, the pacification program involved one thousand U.S. civilians along with five thousand U.S. military. All were dedicated and shared the danger; all justly can take pride in the program's accomplishments, for Vietnam was more than a soldier's war.

Acknowledgments

This book exists because Col. Tom Jones, U.S. Army (Ret.), recommended that it be written. He and Col. Stuart A. Herrington, U.S. Army, provided much needed advice, critique, and encouragement during work on the first draft. Their unwavering faith and guidance were invaluable. I am grateful also to Lt. Col. Robert Pugmire, U.S. Army (Ret.), who volunteered generous amounts of time and effort in helping me to rein in a tendency to ramble and to perfect my prose as the project neared completion. My gratitude also goes to Lisa O'Brien for her several years spent patiently deciphering my handwriting and turning it into typewritten sense.

*More
Than a
Soldier's
War*

Chapter 1

Getting Educated

The 1963 graduating class of the U.S. Army Command and General Staff College at Fort Leavenworth, Kansas, anxiously awaited orders as the course drew to a close. When assignments finally arrived in June, most were interesting and career enhancing. Mine, however, was a disappointing shock. Despite my field artillery training and experience, I was cross-assigned to the air defense artillery as operations officer of the Kansas City air defense headquarters. Equally unbelievable was the fact that the unit was located at a naval air station in Olathe, Kansas. Although the duty turned out to be much better than I had feared, I enviously read about and followed the important events taking place around the world— events I would have preferred to be involved in.

While on leave visiting my family in June, 1964, I went to the Pentagon to inquire what future assignment was in store for me and how I might speed it up. To my surprise and joy, I found that I already was on orders as part of an emergency requisition for a number of psychological warfare (psywar) officers to be sent to Vietnam. After attending hastily-arranged crash courses to qualify as a psywar officer—conducted at the Civil Affairs School at Fort Gordon, Georgia, and the Special Operations School at Fort Bragg, North Carolina—I was on my way. It was October, 1964, and the odyssey upon which I was embarking would consume seven of the next ten years of my life.

As the plane carrying me to Vietnam descended and the coast changed from indistinct grey to lush green, I thought back to the Southwest Pacific in World War II and to Korea. Remembering other deceptively beautiful places, as well as the warnings I'd recently read about Vietnam, I promised myself that I would be skeptical and careful this time. One recent article I'd read had described Vietnam as a place of beauty, a place of horror, a place of danger, a place of fascination. How true that proved to be.

About twenty-five of us were housed temporarily in Saigon at the Majestic Hotel, situated on the banks of the Saigon River. We received four days of Military Assistance Command briefings, followed by three days at IV Corps headquarters in the Mekong Delta city of Can Tho. These briefings provided information that proved to be as useless as the guidance given us at Fort Gordon and Fort Bragg. While everyone seemed to know what they wanted us to accomplish, none had the vaguest idea how we should go about achieving it. The reason soon became obvious. The farther removed one was from the actual conduct of this strange war in the countryside, the less accurate, more distorted, and more prone to personal interpretation the truth became.

Within two weeks of my arrival in Vietnam, it became painfully apparent that I was not psywar qualified. Obsolete post–World War II military civil government training and Western perceptions of how to communicate with and advise Asians were irrelevant to the job I faced. Still, wasted training time notwithstanding, I was delighted to be in Vietnam.

On my last evening in Saigon, I dined and relaxed at the rooftop restaurant and bar of the Majestic Hotel. As I leaned over the open balcony railing sipping an after-dinner drink, I was startled by the loud *crump* of artillery fire nearby across the river. I dropped my glass. After my drink had been replaced by a smiling, white-coated waiter and the pretty vocalist had resumed singing French ballads to the soft accompaniment of a grand piano, flares again popped in the night sky, and artillery shells once more erupted in the jungle beneath them. Through it all, fast-moving black rain clouds briefly eclipsed the full moon, casting the quiet city into momentary shadow, while the war ground grimly on across the river. Only much later did it become apparent to me that the experience was a fitting introduction to the incongruent realities of Vietnam in 1964. It was also the first of many lessons I needed before I could accomplish the job I had been sent to do. Although I came as an advisor, I would more often be the pupil during that important, formative first year.

My initial assignment was to the Army of the Republic of Vietnam's (ARVN) 7th Infantry Division headquarters in My Tho, the capital city of Dinh Tuong Province, thirty-five miles south of Saigon. When I entered the psywar office, the section chief, Captain Toan, introduced the others. He and his assistant, Lieutenant Det, both spoke English well. Det, with his tousled hair, wide boyish grin, and sincere, friendly welcome, immediately took me under his wing. I later came to appreciate how lucky I had

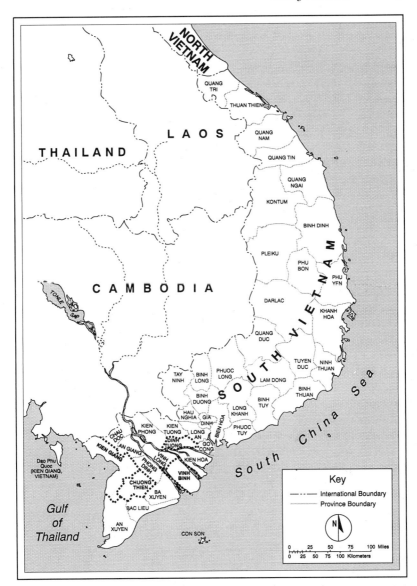

been, for both officers turned out to be honest, patriotic, and dedicated to their country's cause.

We worked hard and well together and tried our best. However, at the outset we were no match for the VC, who were way ahead of us in both the psychological and the shooting wars. For much of that first year, the division ended up chasing but rarely catching a clever, elusive, and deadly main-force enemy across four densely populated provinces in the important and hotly contested rice-producing region south of Saigon.

The second step in my continuing education was to learn some of the language—quickly. Toward this end, my non-English-speaking jeep driver provided both the motivation and the solution. In order to survive his frequent blunders into places where we shouldn't have been, we developed what I called an initial survival vocabulary that expanded each day and with each close call. Lieutenant Det, who rapidly became a close friend, also helped by tutoring me in the use of bilingual pamphlets about his country's history and culture.

The first months were tedious and frustrating for the psywar section, as we alternated among reacting too late to VC initiatives, trying to boost friendly troop morale, and consoling grief-stricken families. Finally, through raw persistence in the face of much well-intentioned bungling, we became the only psywar team in all of Vietnam to achieve some significant victories during a prolonged period of countrywide setbacks.

By persevering in the face of almost uncanny VC skill at beating us to the punch, and by learning from them, we eventually were able to piece together the key to begin chipping away at the enemy's brutally coerced advantage. That critical insight came about as a result of witnessing the suffering of innocent civilians. Such sad circumstances forced us to recognize early on what otherwise might not have been so obvious: we could have more profound, immediate, and lasting impact by changing people's attitudes toward the government than by lining up, counting, and photographing rotting VC corpses. Since we were virtually alone in this recognition, our first success resulted from a secret psywar campaign that Det, Toan, and I aimed at our own senior officers rather than at the VC. We focused on our own side first, because so few in the upper-level civilian and military ranks showed any concern for the welfare of the people caught in the middle of the killing. If we were to begin to persuade the people to support the government, the division's leaders had to become genuinely sensitive to their suffering and do something concrete to stop it.

The plan we decided on was simple, but it took tactful and constant pressure on a worried Toan to get his cautious, nervous, and concealed cooperation. We would subtly introduce modest examples of how the calculated employment of psywar techniques might help increase operational successes while avoiding occasional but predictable and costly mistakes. Since there was mounting emphasis nationwide on producing significant battlefield successes, we would concentrate on showing our superiors how any good result could have been made better, had psywar been used as an effective weapon.

Fortunately, we didn't have too long to wait for the chance to implement our plan. That opportunity stemmed from two concerns at division, one old and one new. The old concern was that, no matter how secretively combat operations were planned, every move we made in preparation for combat broadcast our intentions and alerted the enemy. Civilians inevitably got caught in the middle of the few government-initiated battles. A recent order emanating from Washington and seconded in Saigon, however, had commanded that greater effort be made to reduce the mounting numbers of civilian casualties. This second and more pressing concern would work to our advantage.

Shortly after I cautiously revealed our plan to my boss, the division senior advisor, he found an occasion tactfully to bring the matter of the Saigon order to the attention of his counterpart, the division commander. A staff officer from the division's intelligence section then contacted Captain Toan to gather psywar-related information about an area of current tactical interest. When Toan recovered from his surprise, he carefully initiated our plan. He pointed out that the people's fear of getting caught in the middle of battles was the main reason they communicated and cooperated with the VC; he also noted that friendly air strikes and artillery fire rightfully figured among their greatest fears. Whether or not my boss's prior talk with the division commander had anything to do with the intelligence and psywar sections' discourse that evening, it was an encouraging event in an otherwise lackluster year.

Despite my early anticipation and much finger crossing (which I later found out was an obscene gesture to the Vietnamese), nothing more developed. Two weeks later, when the payoff came, it was of surprising importance.

Psywar finally was to be used in an upcoming operation, and our section at last was being included in the development of details for executing an operation. A deception plan, which was to be almost totally dependent on psywar for execution, also was being considered. The plan's objectives were to try to get the civilians out of harm's way and at the same time to deceive the VC into making a tactical mistake.

The target of the operation was a small village named Ba Dua. Located in the heart of an area in the center of Dinh Tuong Province that had changed hands between the government and the VC over the years, the village and its surrounding area had been under enemy control since November 5, 1963. In the intervening year, its twenty thousand people and four thousand square acres of rich soil had been exploited by the VC, who operated openly, without fear of government interference. It was a difficult region in which to operate, because the thick jungle and coconut groves surrounded open rice paddies.

Recent intelligence revealed that VC battalions and some smaller units had a pattern of movement in the area that cycled them, in roughly predictable timing, through a clockwise series of small base areas. If the pattern held, a VC battalion with attached units would be about two kilometers south of Ba Dua in three days and probably would remain there for three additional days before moving on. Meanwhile, Toan and the division intelligence officer had pieced together information about the population of Ba Dua. The people were dissatisfied with VC rice taxation, the enemy's forced destruction of roads and bridges to isolate the area, the abduction of youth into enemy units, and the assassination of most schoolteachers. It was decided that the people would not be hostile to friendly action and might even welcome the operation, provided that they were not once again caught in the middle. An attack to hit the enemy units was planned on the second day of their predicted stay.

The deception plan Toan and I submitted involved directing the civilians to a specified safe area. A problem we'd never had to face before was how to receive and care for the displaced civilians. If we did the job carefully and effectively, we hoped to demonstrate real government concern for the people, gain a degree of credibility, and expose VC distortions for what they were.

Shifts from the psywar section worked through the night, producing 180,000 leaflets on our old mimeograph machine. After an evening of constant and heavy rain, the morning of the operation, November 19, 1964, dawned with clear skies. We hoped that this was a good omen.

In accord with the deception plan, psywar aircraft broadcast messages and dropped leaflets in the decoy area from 6:45 A.M. to 7:15 A.M., informing the civilians of safe travel routes to protected areas away from the feigned battle zone. False restricted areas and prohibited directions of movement were also given, plus a brief explanation of what was supposed to be happening. The aircraft then headed back toward Can Tho Airfield before abruptly turning northwestward into the actual area of operations. At 7:30 A.M., correct broadcasts and leaflets began instructing the people to move quickly either north to Ba Dua village or south to the My Tho River. All lateral movement to the east or west would be interpreted as hostile and would risk drawing fire from government forces. Observation aircraft reported streams of civilians moving first toward the deception areas, then changing course as directed. The plan was working.

Troop units did not encounter opposition until they closed from both sides on a series of coconut-palm groves about halfway between the Ba Dua marketplace and the river. The area was then sealed off, and fighting grew from occasional sniper fire to a pitched battle. Enemy units had taken the bait and, by following foliage-covered canals out of the deception area, had slipped into the pocket we had hoped they would occupy. All day long the sounds of air strikes and artillery fire vibrated throughout the command post in the nearby town of Cai Lay, as the division pounded the trapped VC.

After the operation, Toan and I put together our separate after-action reports. The deception plan had worked; enemy casualties were heavy, whereas comparatively few friendly troops were killed or wounded. Advisors on the ground took special care to substantiate the reported results, and the action was hailed as a significant victory that had put an enemy battalion out of action.

For me, the best part was that, thanks to psywar participation, only one civilian was killed. Furthermore, thirty-four VC rallied to the government. In the aftermath of the fighting, because of the considerate treatment they received, the Ba Dua villagers convinced the government to remain in the area. Toan and Det's civic action teams reopened schools and dispensaries, and word of the improved living conditions spread throughout the province.

After the Ba Dua operation faded into memory, the tempo of activity in the psywar section slowed. During this quiet time, my friendship with Det grew. He had me to his house for occasional dinners, and I reciprocated by inviting him to the advisors' compound. We discussed our families, past experiences, and future plans, and exchanged stories of our homelands and their histories.

As spring approached, the source of our only other productive psywar achievement was an informant's accurate location of a large VC base area in the central seacoast region of neighboring Kien Hoa Province. Since the base was located in difficult-to-reach coastal mangrove swamps, the division planned an attack launched simultaneously by land, sea, and helicopter.

The assault on the base area of Thanh Phu began March 28, 1965, with intense but selective air strikes, carefully restricted and controlled because many civilians were living on the fringes of the mangrove swamps. At the outset the psywar section was asked to contribute a population protection plan, whereas before we had had to suggest that it might be wise to have one. By operation's end, 3,480 people, representing approximately four hundred families, were safely relocated to Thanh Phu and resettled with considerate, preplanned care. Again, the word spread far and wide.

Since the operation was going to be a long one, the psychological effort was divided between convincing the civilians to evacuate the fringe of the mangroves and trying to lower VC troop morale and generate returnees. When intelligence located a basic training area in the mangroves containing two hundred to four hundred recent VC draftees, the psywar focus quickly shifted back to the enemy. Because of the inaccessibility of the target areas, initially we were restricted to dropping leaflets designed to persuade the conscripts to defect—an improbable expectation, considering how carefully guarded and controlled they were.

We carefully scripted leaflets that would convey special meaning in the precise situation the young VC draftees faced and then laboriously produced about a thousand on our aging mimeograph machine. At the same time, the U.S. Information Service (USIS) and the Vietnamese Political Warfare Directorate in Saigon sent us bale after bale of professionally printed, multicolored, leaflets irrelevant to our situation and most probably unintelligible to the uneducated VC and rural population. Within a week, Toan dutifully dumped over 800,000 pieces of paper on our captive audience in the small area of operations. I learned another important lesson when a U.S. helicopter pilot wryly commented that, regardless of other more significant results, we could claim civic action credit for providing the target hamlets with a two-year supply of toilet paper.

To my surprise and gratification, as the campaign wore on Toan showed the positive effects of my continuing subtle influence to get him to exercise initiative. He went to the division chief of staff and requested permission to conduct a night-time helicopter loudspeaker mission. Almost as astounding, he was given permission. Toan's idea was to appeal to the young inductees at a time when they might be reflecting on their plight and better able to pay attention to our message, in spite of close control by hard-core VC cadre. Toan showed up at the helipad with two young women from the Cultural Platoon fifteen minutes before the scheduled arrival of the helicopter loudspeaker team. He brought them because he reasoned that, if the night mission was going to be effective at all, it would be more so if a young, female voice did the pleading with tender feeling.

The night was beautiful, and a quarter moon was just beginning to rise as Toan, Det, the two women, and I lifted off in the U.S. loudspeaker helicopter. Two accompanying gunships followed close behind, and the command and control chopper was above and behind them. When a thousand stars became visible in the unreal, tranquil atmosphere at two thousand feet, I stared into the ink-black depth and tried to imagine what it was like in the dark, silent, life-and-death struggle below.

Some minutes later, the pilot explained that we were going to continue straight ahead for a few minutes more, then turn left and drop to broadcast altitude. When I shouted for Toan to get ready, he returned a thumbs-up sign and turned his grin from me to his female companions. He spoke to them and then handed one the microphone. I moaned audibly when I saw Det holding a wildly flapping piece of paper in front of the women. Good God! The women hadn't memorized the script. They were going to attempt to read it for the first time and impart sentimental thoughts of home, amid the noise, vibration, and stiff wind enveloping the cabin.

On cue, the one with the microphone nervously started reading, and the loudspeaker mounted directly under us blared out the halting message. After the second or third time through the script, she relaxed and pushed the paper from in front of her face. She knew what she had to say. The pilot had been turning every now and then, with the gunships remaining above and to our rear. The command and control bird followed behind them at a still higher altitude. When the first woman became hoarse from the exertion and the cold, the other one took over.

Suddenly the headset boomed a warning that we were taking a large amount of enemy ground fire. With that, our pilot began a neck-wrenching turn to the right and pulled up so abruptly that I was pinned heavily against the seat bottom as I strained to lean out and look behind us. Several arcs of tracers were pumping upward, then falling in a dying curve beneath us. Something *whooshed* in front of my face and scared the hell out of me. When I regained my composure, I could see in the dim, red glow of the cabin lights that it was the long hair of the women flying wildly back and forth above their heads. Both had lost their hats during the evasive maneuver and were holding on to Toan for dear life. After I told the pilot that we were all okay, he said he'd swing around and try it again.

Shortly into the second pass, the episode repeated itself. Lines of tracers converged in our direction; whoever said that tracer fire at night looks like it's coming right down your throat was right. I caught my breath and braced for the expected impact. Nothing happened. I finally exhaled in relief when I heard the team commander tell the pilots that that was enough for one night.

An effect we hadn't anticipated was that friendly units who heard the messages suffered the great sadness and homesickness we had hoped to inflict on the enemy. Although we continued to try to help the people and change their attitudes, as well as that of the division, the Ba Dua and Thanh Phu episodes were the only tangible results of our year-long effort.

I received orders for reassignment to the Pentagon at the end of August, 1965. As the time for my departure neared, I experienced deep concern and empathy for the dilemma and the suffering of the Vietnamese civilians, accompanied by a strong desire to stay on and try to help. Since I couldn't, I took every opportunity to accompany Toan's military civic action teams into the countryside to find ways to assist them. The memories of terror, death, and disease were best left behind. Besides, I wanted to take away better ones. At the time I didn't know that my exposure to the violence and horror of the war had been relatively distant and restricted.

Det made a special trip to Saigon for my departure, and we met at the bar of the Brinks Hotel officers' quarters. On Christmas Eve the year before, the VC had exploded a large bomb at the Brinks, killing two and wounding fifty-two Americans. The hotel was centrally located and remained a convenient and popular meeting place. On the taxi ride to dinner along broad, tree-lined Tran Hung Dao Boulevard, connecting Saigon with Cholon, I couldn't take my eyes off the rain-dampened street activity beneath glistening trees illuminated by lamp posts. Although I'd driven through the area many times before, I felt a sudden and intense longing to stay, which gave me special cause to notice and appreciate its beauty.

After dinner we went to Det's home to meet his parents, brothers, and sisters, who had assembled for the occasion. Following tea, cake, and a proper period of talk, Det walked with me slowly, silently, arm in arm, down the winding, muddy alley leading to the avenue beyond. He hailed a taxi for me, and we parted quickly, neither wanting to prolong the farewell. At that moment, I knew that I would return.

Later, as I tried to adjust to a Pentagon desk job, my thoughts were never far from the U.S.-Vietnamese team and its efforts. The fact that my job involved reading detailed day-to-day reports of the war and its results fueled my desire to move from behind the desk and return. Det and I had been corresponding, and his latest letter—in response to my telephoning him from the Pentagon communications center—spurred my attempts to escape Washington and return to more worthwhile endeavors.

6-16-66   My Tho

My Dear Brother,

I am very proud and emotional when I spoke with you in telephone. The first time and first advisor did this with a Vietnamese officer. I am very proud to have a brother as you. I never forget, brother! In writing this letter, I cannot help crying because I miss you very much. I hope one day I meet you either at US or Vietnam brother. Hope after some year with your family, you will come back to share with us the sadness and joy. I dream of the day we meet together. I am sure that I must cry in joy. By the way, I sent you my two pictures to remind you of your young brother. I send all my emotion to you and pray God bless you and your family.

Respectfully and sincerely.
Your Young Brother,
Det

Shortly after that, I manipulated an exception to the rule which prevented early release from my three-year assignment to the Pentagon. I was helped by my assignment officer, who was hard-pressed to fill some special-category assignments to Vietnam for which I was qualified, and by my ability to persuade my boss that sending a single man would permit a married man to stay home with his family.

Chapter 2

Optimism Is Its
Own Reward

During the long return flight across the Pacific in January 1967, I thought about developments that had occurred since my departure one year and three months earlier. America had moved from an advisory and combat-support role to employing ground combat units. Air strikes against North Vietnam were a daily occurrence. When I first arrived in Vietnam in October 1964, there were 23,000 American advisors and support troops throughout the country. When I left a year later, the number had been 148,300. Now, at the beginning of 1967, U.S. troop strength had jumped to 389,000. American combat deaths totaled 6,644, and the number of wounded stood at 37,738. While that many casualties was both surprising and disturbing, I still managed to think positively about my return.

As we approached Saigon and banked into the landing pattern for Tan Son Nhut Airport, the planeload of new arrivals fell silent and strained to glimpse the ground. Their tension and my relaxation made me want to say or do something reassuring, since I knew the doubts going through their minds. Turning to the young soldier seated beside me, I tried to comfort him by explaining what he could expect once we were on the ground. Whatever success I achieved was lost when the line of men waiting to depart shouted catcalls and taunts as we filed into the terminal.

Our processing was rapid despite the large number of American troops moving through. My sentimental return to the Two Crabs Restaurant was spoiled by U.S. troops crowding the downtown area, eager for the cheap and noisy new commercialism catering to them.

The next morning I received another disappointment. I was assigned as pacification advisor at II Corps headquarters in Pleiku in the central highlands, far from the Mekong Delta.

The flight north broke through January rain clouds above the flat and rolling central plateau and followed it into Pleiku. As we descended, the town and all that surrounded it looked as bleak as the winter weather. During the short jeep ride to the corps's and the advisor's compounds, the gloomy impression was intensified. Corps headquarters was a drab structure sitting atop a long, barren hill. Perhaps it was the chilly, damp weather, but the headquarters struck me as a dank and somber place regardless of the season. The advisor's compound, situated halfway down the northern slope of the hill in an old French army enclosure, looked no more inviting. Wondering briefly if the population ever compared the French and the Americans, I laughed to myself, knowing the VC would make sure we were both pictured in the same manner—foreigners bent on subjugating and exploiting the people.

As soon as my baggage was in my room, I was directed to the office of the assistant deputy senior advisor. He welcomed me to the team and said he'd have the duty officer contact me later to meet Brig. Gen. Richard Lee, the corps's deputy senior advisor. An hour or so after dinner, a visitor at my door announced that the general was ready to see me.

General Lee was shorter than I, a thin man with delicate, almost fragile features. His smile and greeting were curt and his handshake limp and perfunctory. Inviting me to sit, he expressed surprise and disappointment that I was a major rather than a lieutenant colonel. Wondering why that should be of concern, I explained that I had been selected for promotion and expected to receive it within the next several months. The answer must have satisfied him, because he immediately changed the subject.

For the next half hour I listened to a dissertation on "rural development," which was the new term for pacification. My initial reaction went from uneasiness at his constant references to the importance of our reports to higher headquarters and the emphasis he placed on optimism, to concern that he apparently had the roles of pacification and the shooting war reversed. If I had heard correctly, it sounded like General Lee considered the pacification effort as an adjunct to the destruction of the enemy and not the other way around.

My office occupied the entire space of a recently constructed building situated half way up the hill that separated the compound from the corps headquarters. I introduced myself to my assistant, Maj. James Lord, and he in turn introduced me to a surprisingly large staff consisting of a captain, two sergeants, and a corporal serving as clerk-typist. Everyone in the office was busy starting a monthly three- to five-day effort to put together a lengthy review called "The Revolutionary Development Progress Report." Lord explained that it was the most important of three recurring monthly reports. When I asked about our Vietnamese counterparts, our duties and relationships with them, and the field trips we were required to accompany them on, Lord, a Georgia farm boy, just smiled, shrugged, and drawled that what the staff was doing now was about as far as our involvement went. Two Vietnamese counterpart staff sections at corps operated pretty much on their own and just fed us information. Once in a while they came to us when they needed air transportation, but that was about it.

As we climbed the hill to corps headquarters, I pressed for more information. Lord confided that the advisory headquarters was run like a spit-and-polish U.S. troop unit instead of like an advisory team. The general had even tried to get authorization for all advisors to wear U.S. Army General Staff insignia, but his request had been refused. Despite his matter-of-fact tone, I understood the significance of what Lord was telling me. The general saw our function more as being his personal staff than as being advisors to the Vietnamese staff. While it all sounded incredible and gave me a dull, sinking feeling, I pushed for more. Lord then related how my predecessor was a favorite of the general's, a master at turning out artful but questionable reports, the substance of which came almost exclusively from unverified information and statistics provided by the Vietnamese. The previous pacification advisor had known exactly what the general wanted to report and how he wanted it reflected. The man rarely, if ever, traveled to the field. In fact, few on the team ever went to the field. At this point, I almost was not listening. Knowing that I could never be content in such a futile situation, I was going over in my mind how I could approach the general to try to impress on him the need and the importance of going out to get the facts. Even though I didn't think I would convince him, I knew I had to try.

The first of my two Vietnamese counterparts introduced by Major Lord was the corps psywar officer, who gave a glib, well-rehearsed briefing obviously meant to impress visitors. After learning that my second counterpart, Lt. Col. Nguyen Ba Lien, the deputy to the corps commander for revolutionary development (RD), was away in Nha Trang on business, we returned to the office. Near the end of the afternoon, which I spent reading through the reports of the last three months and starting to digest the current one, I was in a sullen mood. Turning to Lord, I asked if he could take me for a quick tour of Pleiku before supper. As he drove the jeep through the gate and toward the line of rising dust that I knew must be the main road, he remarked that the captain would make up some story to cover for us if the general called while we were gone. We were expected to be available on call and could get in trouble if we weren't. When he added that his efficiency reports didn't make a difference anymore, since he'd already been passed over for promotion twice, I wondered if assignment to advisory duty held the same priority and was based on the same selectivity I earlier had been led to believe. It didn't. The reason was that the United States was involved in the combat war, and troop duty thus got priority.

Seeing Pleiku didn't shake off my discouragement or raise any enthusiasm. It was a small, shabby, dirty town crisscrossed by endless lines of convoys rolling in from Qui Nhon to the east and Ban Me Thuot to the south. Days dragged into weeks, and my frustration turned into misery. The overweening preoccupation with reports and the restrictions on our travels compounded the affects of abysmal weather. Maybe I wouldn't have been so depressed if thoughts of My Tho and the gratifying joint effort I'd known there hadn't kept returning. Even General Lee seemed to suffer a great deal of frustration in his attempts to influence the Vietnamese corps commander, Lt. Gen. Vinh Loc. When I understood the complicated circumstances and relationships that existed in the corps, I saw why things here could never work as they did in the Delta. The entire arrangement between the Americans and Vietnamese in the corps was predisposed to unilateral action and polite, mutual tolerance. The senior U.S. commander, a three-star general, was located 150 miles away in Nha Trang and held the title of senior corps advisor. His counterpart, Vinh Loc, who also wore three stars, was in Pleiku—where General Lee with his one star was supposed to deal with him effectively. Even General Lee's title, deputy senior advisor, diminished him in the eyes of the Vietnamese, since Vinh Loc knew that General Lee had to answer to the three-star in Nha Trang and couldn't make substantive decisions on his own. Complicating matters, there was a two-star general commanding the U.S. 4th Division five miles south of Pleiku. Like other American combat units in the vast corps area, the division operated independently in its given zone. The size of the corps itself contributed to the problems of coordination and communication. It stretched three hundred miles from its northern to its southern borders and was about a hundred miles across, from the Cambodian border to the beaches of the coastal lowlands on the South China Sea in the east. Those coastal lowlands contained the bulk of the population, mostly ethnic Vietnamese. The remaining nine-tenths of the zone lay in the mountains and high plateau, with their sparse spread of Montagnard tribes and a sprinkling of Vietnamese. The tribes, because of their vastly different dialects, couldn't even speak to each other. The city of Pleiku boasted only fifteen thousand.

I could have tried to accept the situation after seeing the complicated problem, except for one overriding irritation. There was so much pressure to reflect pacification progress that our reports purposely were made overly optimistic. Any criticism that survived, no matter how diplomatically or cautiously presented, had to be followed by a neutralizing statement. General Lee personally went over my draft reports in detail, editing them until much of the content bore little resemblance to my original thoughts. I tried unsuccessfully to convince him of the necessity for me to get out and verify the facts and figures fed to us by the Vietnamese, or even just be able to put them into perspective. He didn't agree. I don't believe he or his assistant deputy understood how an advisor was supposed to function or that one of the best ways to apply leverage to our counterparts was to gather the facts personally and then forward the truth to higher authority for resolution of the discrepancies.

After I met and got to know Lieutenant Colonel Lien, my situation began to take a slight turn for the better. Lien was a fierce patriot and a respected officer who was delighted that I had volunteered to return for a second tour, knew a little of his language, and was conversant with the history of his country. Even so, it became evident in our conversations that Lien saw America's presence in Vietnam as a means to an end. While he respected the strength we represented, we were still unwanted foreigners. We had long talks about the war, problems, possible solutions, and what turns the future might take. About a month after we met, he started to invite me on trips. When General Lee learned that Lien had called for me to be with him, the general tolerated my short absences, perhaps due to Lien's influence. Gen. Vinh Loc liked and respected Lien, probably in part because it was rumored that Lien had highly placed connections in Saigon.

As the rains subsided and the weather began to warm, Lien's friendship and his indifference to the blustering of my bosses brought about a slight relaxation of my restriction to Pleiku. Matching my celebratory mood, in the spring of 1967, millions of small, white butterflies began a migration over the plateau. Moving from east to west, the flight lasted for more than two weeks and must have gone on around the clock, because I could see the fragile insects flittering past on moonlit nights when I went for a walk before going to bed.

I was promoted to lieutenant colonel in mid-April. Lien and I were traveling together about every two weeks, and the trips kept me motivated and in touch with the realities of the war. Not only did they get me away from the stifling and frustrating paperwork in the office, but every place we visited had a unique and striking beauty. Lien's official purpose was to inspect the fifty-nine-man RD cadre teams working in the villages. The teams were made up of young men and women recruited and trained to work and live with the people of the hamlets and villages in order to provide constructive, grassroots governmental presence and assistance. Our visits required prior clearances from provincial chiefs and also required preliminary stopovers at district headquarters, in which the teams were located. While such protocol was irksome to Lien, it provided a great opportunity for me to see much of the corps area. After rehearsed briefings by each RD team chief, Lien would ask them to take him into the villages so he could see the team in action and talk with both team members and villagers. Almost invariably, there was some time available to tour the vicinity. The few times when there wasn't, I left the inspection party to tour on my own. While each visit was tensely quiet, evidence of violence, pain, and sadness was never far away. Underlying fear and strain always emerged in any conversation lasting more than five minutes, and the lingering stench of death was always close.

Our travels took us to the seacoast town of Phan Rang in Ninh Thuan Province. Lush tropical foliage surrounded the picturesque beaches, but the terrain a short way inland unexpectedly turned into a semidesert somewhat reminiscent of southwestern Texas. This was the land of the once-powerful Champa race. The ruins of ancient temples still protruded from the bare hilltops. Their design reminded me of pictures I'd seen of the temples of Angkor Wat in Cambodia—tall, beautiful, and full of silent history. The estimated thirty thousand Chams who remained still struggled to preserve their language and culture despite the pressures on them as a declining minority.

Nha Trang, farther north in Khanh Hoa Province, once had been a bustling coastal resort. Whereas the bays and coves on either side of the city were breathtaking in their beauty, with thick jungles enclosing white sand beaches washed by sparkling blue water, Nha Trang's beachfront was shabby, dirty, and stained with oil by the large ships riding at anchor out in the bay. Hotels, restaurants, and the kiosks and bars lining the beach had become tacky and seedy as a result of time and the war. American soldiers and airmen from the bases and airfields nearby had replaced the vacationing Vietnamese families, fueling a new business boom.

Still another trip took us to the quaint fishing town of Phan Thiet in Binh Thuan Province at the southern extremity of the corps. Lien awakened me at dawn to go to the beach, where small boats were unloading their catches from the night before. The number, size, and variety of fish netted from the sea by the small, leathery fishermen was staggering. While Lien thought I would enjoy the scene, his motive was more practical. He was taking some of the catch back home to his family in Pleiku.

Farther to the north, Binh Dinh Province, with its sprawling coastline, jungles, and mountains, was as deadly as it was lush and beautiful. A large concentration of U.S. and Vietnamese forces were locked in battle with the Communists, trying to retain control of the rich, densely populated areas paralleling the sea. We never stayed in Binh Dinh long because few of the population would or could make a commitment, one way or the other. Therefore, the efforts of the RD teams were of questionable value.

In all our travels, our security was overtly threatened only once. While danger surely always was there, the respect local officials held for Lien as a person, mixed with the fear they had of his authority and influence, prompted great precautions to ensure his safety. Our one brush with the enemy happened on our visit to the small, fairy-book town of Bao Loc, nestled in the mountains of Lam Dong Province on the southcentral border of the corps. Blau, as the Montagnards called Bao Loc, was a small, neat, and attractively overgrown village lying on the hillsides of the receding main mountain range that split the corps from north to south. Our flight south from Pleiku followed those mountains, as we dodged late rain squalls and dark, low, rolling clouds all along the way. As we neared our destination, the dark green foothills and valleys of the gently receding mountains led us to the tiny dirt landing strip that looked like an extension of one of the town's muddy roads. Neat rows of tea bushes covered the hills passing to our right and left as the plane settled past the slopes of the French-built plantations that followed every twist and turn of the hillsides. As a light rain fell on the landscape and grey-blue clouds drifted over the plantations, it occurred to me that this was how China must look.

After the normal series of briefings and visits, Lien excused himself so he could discuss where we would spend the evening with the district chief. When the decision was made, our jeeps followed the steep dirt roads in town to a neighborhood of neat and comfortable houses roofed in red tile. Our destination was a large home near the center of the group. Our host for the evening was a tea plantation owner and previous acquaintance of Lien's from Saigon. As Lien and our host talked after dinner, I wandered outside to stretch and relax before bed. In the settling dusk and fog of the high altitude, I glimpsed the movements and heard the muffled sounds of soldiers and the RD cadre camped around the yard and huddled over two radios at the rear of the house. One was monitoring the perimeter positions, and the other was tuned to the district security net. Reassured by the precautions I saw, I returned and prepared to turn in.

As I started to undress, a jeep pulled up in the dark, and the district chief rushed in to confer with Lien in the flickering shadows of a kerosene lamp. When they finished, Lien said that we were moving to another location. Two other jeeps arrived, and we moved through the darkness using flashlights in place of headlights. Ten minutes later we arrived at a thatched farmhouse partially built into a steep hill at its rear. Lien was busy and didn't explain the move, so I didn't ask him, trusting that there had to be a good reason. The light rain on the thatch should have made sleeping easy. Yet, although I was tired, I couldn't doze off. The combination of the hard and damp dirt floor and the buzzing mosquitoes made early sleep out of the question.

I lay listening to the hungry insects and the crackling radio beneath the wooden, boarded window above me until small-arms and automatic-weapons fire, followed by grenade explosions, erupted somewhere nearby. The luminous dial of my watch showed 1:30 A.M. as the radio outside came to life and blurted out a rapid string of high-pitched words. When the soldiers outside the window answered in hushed tones, I groped in the darkness to find my pants and my pistol and pulled them closer. As the firing rattled on, Lien and the others around me continued to snore peacefully, only grunting or turning over when a grenade went off. I pushed back the urge to awaken them until the distant firing trailed off to an occasional burst and finally stopped. It was 2:00 A.M., and I counted as three, four-thirty, and five o'clock passed before I finally fell into a fitful sleep.

On the jeep ride to the airfield, Lien casually explained what had happened during the night. An informant of the district chief's had told the chief that the VC had learned through their informants that Lien was at the first house. Certain that the VC would try to get rid of Lien, the district chief arranged for a quiet change of location. The security force at the first house was left in place to deceive the VC and caught them in a trap.

On one of the few occasions when I was permitted to attend the monthly psywar advisors' conference in Saigon, I met the deputy chief of the Office of Civil Operations, Brig. Gen. William A. Knowlton. Since I doubted that I'd get to attend any future conferences because General Lee didn't think they contributed anything concrete to our mission, I decided to take advantage of the present opportunity to inquire discreetly about the possibility of transferring out of Pleiku. The general knew of me from reports through his Nha Trang headquarters staff and dumbfounded me when he said the province senior advisor's job in Dinh Tuong would be vacant in six weeks and asked if I would accept it. He added that I would have extend my tour an additional six months, and I almost shouted my agreement.

It was the first week of June, 1967, and the southern monsoons were just beginning, but the weather in Saigon seemed beautiful. Within a week, orders arrived directing me to be in My Tho no later than July 6. Colonel Lien was happy for me but also said he was sorry he was losing "his advisor"—the first time he had used the phrase. Since I really hadn't done any advising, the veiled compliment touched me, and I asked him to break his habit of refusing to join me in having a drink. He replied that he didn't want to go to the club, but if I had a bottle in my room, he'd be glad to. While we were there, he handed me an envelope and asked me to take time to read its contents when I had a quiet moment. After I did so, he wanted my frank and honest opinion. When he left, I read the cover to six pages neatly typed in English: "Would There Be Another Dien Bien Phu?" Then, handwritten beneath, "Turn the pages with a constructive hand. Read the verses with an open heart. Judge the ideas with the mind of a soldier fighting for victory." A note was at the bottom, "Dear Lieutenant Colonel Metzner,—This is what I think of the RD program. I would very much like to have your comments before I submit it to our respected Commanding Generals, General Loc and General Lee.—Thanks, Nguyen Ba Lien."

That night I lay on my bed and read an amazing indictment of the RD program. Lien had constructed a case opposing the program and documented why, in his opinion, it would never work and should be discontinued. He began by recalling the mistakes of the French when they built their network of forts and watchtowers. Then he moved on to the similar failure of President Diem's Strategic Hamlet Program and the problems of the present concept of New Life Hamlets. The first two had failed, and Lien claimed that the current program—and any other attempt to protect the people from the VC—also would be doomed to failure. The cause for such mistaken strategy stemmed from Mao Tse Tung's theory that "the people are the water, and the guerrillas are the fish."

Lien further reasoned:

> Since fish must live in water, the authors of the programs designed them to protect the people from the VC, simply concluding that the enemy would be caught when the water dried up. Drying up the water meant to control the people and separate them from the VC. While I once agreed completely with this theory, I now realize the idea was a mistake. Mao didn't say how big a body of water there was, a pond, a stream, river, lake or ocean. Trying to protect from the VC is like trying to dry up rivers and oceans and this cannot be done. Numerous as we are, we will never be able to dry the oceans. Strong as we are, we will never be able to protect the people. That old concept of protecting the people, dating from the French regime, has been nothing other than a suicidal method that the Communists have wisely devised and canalized us into accepting as our own national policy. By killing their own people, burning their houses, the VC caused the gallant French, heroic Americans, and peace-loving Vietnamese to rush to the people's rescue, becoming the trapped "Defenders of the People" and thus leaving the initiative of attack to the Communists.

Lien then cited Napoleon's and Hitler's attacks into Russia and the resulting success of Russia's scorched-earth policy that contributed to their respective defeats, as examples of how best to defeat an enemy like the VC, "who is all around you." Finally, he elaborated on his main arguments:

> —South Vietnam has more than 2,000 villages and 13,000 hamlets and the mission is impractical for the Armed Forces. We are pouring much of our military and civil resources into a program that is easy for the VC to sabotage.

—The program's only real benefit is that it is a Vietnamese and U.S. government show for others to see.

—Many of the RD Cadre are not dedicated to the program and joined only to avoid being drafted into the Armed Forces.

—The people in the countryside are indifferent to the program and go along only for the cement, roofing, wheat flour, rice, and other gifts from the generous Americans.

—The RD program is beneficial to the enemy because it creates more political and military objectives for them to attack. It maintains most of the army units in a defensive status and provides supplies for the VC and their families. The VC only harass the New Life Hamlets and never mount a concentrated effort to sabotage the program in order to keep us from becoming suspicious about their tolerance of it. The program is not a threat to the VC, but instead a help.

—The VC want and need the RD program to expand until the day we are engaged deeply in the program. Then, and only then, will they launch an all-out offensive campaign to destroy the hamlets. We would be in a very embarrassing position. To go on with the program means to waste away our time and our resources. To quit the program means to lose prestige and to accept our defeat. Therefore, a saving-face exit naturally would be for a Geneva-type conference table.

Thus, unable to defeat the Americans on the military front, this is the type of a second Dien Bien Phu that the VC want to trap the Americans in and destroy them just like they did with the French in 1954.

Lien's ideas were sure to be viewed as controversial, if not radical, and perhaps even as Communist inspired, by the paranoid political regime in Saigon. In any case, I felt that he was sticking his neck out and felt gratified that he trusted me enough to share his ideas with me. Lien had a reputation as a political activist and had stuck his neck out before, as one of the key conspirators in the 1963 coup that overthrew President Diem. Still, I found myself unable easily to dismiss many of the points Lien made and wanted to go and discuss the paper with him right away. Since it was already late Friday night, however, I would have to wait until Monday.

Monday morning, I bounced through our team calisthenics with light-hearted energy, knowing that only three days remained before I'd be saying good-bye to Pleiku. I spent the rest of the morning making certain that the final draft of the monthly RD progress report would turn out to be at least as accurate as it was impressive. Each paragraph I read that told of progress made me think back to Lien's arguments about the futility of the RD effort, and I was tempted to inject a comment. But I didn't, because I knew it would be deleted. Captain Si, Lien's deputy, came by shortly before noon with an invitation from Lien for a farewell dinner at his house that evening.

Lien and his wife met me at the door and, after introducing their four children, she shyly accepted the artificial flowers and cut-glass vase I had brought.

The gathering, which included Si and two other captains who worked for Lien, grew more comfortable when everyone joined the conversation during dinner. Maybe it was because the menu was so obviously special—perhaps a little *too* special, in view of the high cost of food in Pleiku. After coffee and dessert, Si leaned across the table and quietly asked if I could find my way back to the compound by myself; then he and the other captains excused themselves and left. Lien picked up the cognac bottle and invited me to bring my glass and sit with him in the living room. His wife must have taken that as a cue, because she withdrew to the kitchen.

Lien refilled our glasses and said he was sorry to see me go but that he understood my desire to return to the Delta. Before I could answer, he added that he had just received word that he also would be leaving soon. He was moving to Kontum to become commander of a new special zone being formed of Kontum and Pleiku Provinces; he was being promoted to colonel in the process. I raised my glass and held it toward him, offering a toast to his success in the new job. He returned a tired smile and emptied his glass. I did the same. Without answering, Lien went and brought back more coffee, refilled our cognac glasses, and contemplated a moment before speaking again. To my utter surprise, he said he would like it very much if I would accompany him to Kontum. His offer was tempting, and I groped for the right thing to say. I finally replied that, while he had paid me a great compliment and I felt humble and appreciative, I felt that I belonged back in the Delta. I added truthfully that this was a difficult decision because it was such a great honor. While we made a good team, I doubted that Saigon would approve another transfer for me so soon. Lien interrupted me to say that he agreed the position of senior advisor in Dinh Tuong was a great opportunity. He recommended that we keep in touch. Then he handed me a folded piece of paper with his home address in Saigon, said I'd be welcome there any time, and changed the subject.

I still wanted to discuss his paper on the RD program, but I wondered if this was an appropriate time, in view of my rejection of his offer. I decided to go on with it anyway, and for over an hour we covered each point in his argument. Since I had carefully reread the paper several times, I was able to discuss it from memory. I thought that would please him, and it did. While he also was pleased that I agreed with many of his arguments, he was more interested in hearing about those I *disagreed* with. My summation keyed on the fact that he had said the people didn't want to be the object of the war, when the truth of the matter was that the war had made them its object. If we didn't realize and respond to that, we might never end the war favorably. I explained that I was convinced that the side that finally receives the support and trust of the people would be the side in control at the end. While Lien was convinced that RD efforts in the villages play into the hands of the VC and would ultimately fail, I maintained that correcting and redirecting the program would be better than disbanding it, as he suggested. Our only point of agreement was an important one: herding the people together, far from their home villages, to protect them and earn their gratitude and loyalty had proven to be counterproductive.

Thanks to the help of another large cognac, I was about ready to get into the sensitive issue of the need for some honest social and political reforms, combined with protecting the people, when his wife reappeared to remind us of curfew. Instead, I settled for a less contentious final statement: "Colonel, you certainly know your own people and the enemy as I will never come to know them. I hope you will let me keep your paper, because I've wondered so many times, after all the energy and effort, time and money, pain and blood, we've invested in the New Life Hamlets, what does it get us when the sun goes down and the VC come out?" That delighted him. After slapping his leg a couple of times as he laughed, he tried to pour me another cognac, but I put my hand over the glass. He poured a short one for himself and urged me to continue. It was getting late and I was tired, but I still had to caution him that I considered him my good friend and that we were talking openly and in confidence.

"I have to tell you that I seriously doubt that General Lee would react favorably to your paper. Even if he agreed on the points you make, which I don't think he would, he wouldn't openly support your conclusions. As for General Loc, I would be surprised if he took the time to read it. If he did read it and agreed, I would be more surprised and happy for you. If he agreed and proposed that Saigon do something about it, I would be amazed." The cognac had made me bold. "Even if he made some proposals to Saigon, I doubt that the government would pay any serious attention to him. Why else was General Loc stuck in Pleiku?" Lien had been leaning forward to listen, but when I said that, he fell backward in his chair, threw his head up and let out a long laugh. Before leaving I added, laughing with him, "You might have to wait until you're a general in Saigon yourself, an event I hope will happen soon." Lien and his wife saw me to the door, then accompanied me out to my jeep to say a final good-bye. On the drive back to the compound, I felt depressed because of Lien's doubts about the pacification effort, even though in two more days this unhappy time would be behind me.

It was 7:30 A.M. when Captain Si tapped me awake again. I jumped up in panic because the flight left at nine and only half of my things were packed. Si had come with a farewell gift, a brass Champa bracelet. As he

solemnly placed it on my wrist, he explained that the bracelet would provide me protection from all harm, including VC bullets, mortars, and
mines. While he talked, I put him to work helping me cram items from
drawers, closets, shelves, and the desk into already half-full footlockers.
Although my head was aching, I was moving at top speed. Nothing was
going to keep me from getting on that 9:00 A.M. flight.

Chapter 3

Return to the Delta

Stopping in Saigon only long enough for an intelligence update on Dinh Tuong Province, I eagerly pressed on. As we approached the My Tho helipad, familiar sights brought back half-forgotten memories. Fishermen were still casting their circular nets into the freshwater pond to the right of the landing pad, and in the morning sunshine the white crosses of the French cemetery on the opposite side stood out in stark contrast to the drab background of age-worn houses. The helicopter had radioed for a jeep to pick me up. When it arrived, the officer who bounced out to greet me introduced himself as Maj. Carroll Papajohn, the deputy province senior advisor. As we bumped down the busy side streets to the main avenue, we were slowed by the tail end of the morning procession of students on their way to school. The scene was exactly as I remembered it from my first arrival almost three years before. Finally I was back.

Carroll turned into the two-story villa that served as the team house, and a greying, older officer came out to the jeep, grabbed my hand, and welcomed me. Col. Bob Brown was the man I was replacing, and my first impression was that his shoes would be hard to fill. The morning briefing Bob promised never took place. When I came out for breakfast, the team house was deserted except for the acting first sergeant and the clerk. The first sergeant introduced himself and shook his head, saying that the VC really had given me a whale of a welcome during the night. They had mined Highway 4 in many places west of Cai Lay. Most of the team members had

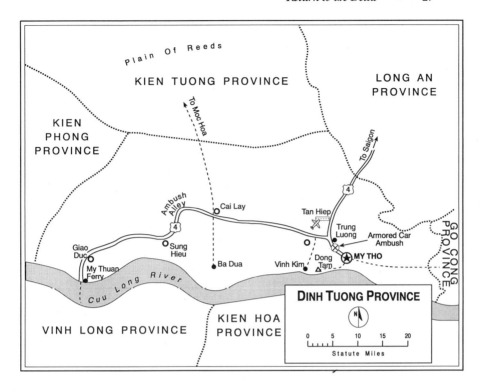

left around 5:00 A.M., and Colonel Brown had left word that he'd see me sometime later but couldn't say when.

After gulping down my coffee, I jumped in the jeep left for me and headed for the province operations center. It was in a state of chaos. The American sergeant on advisor duty briefed me at the operations map, interrupted by three or four phone calls. The VC had detonated approximately thirty mines, cutting the highway between Cai Lay town near the center of the province and the My Thuan ferry, which linked the province's western end with Vinh Long Province and the rest of the Delta. The highway was the major land artery south of Saigon, and both military and economic traffic depended on it; if it remained closed for any appreciable length of time, there would be serious military, economic, and political repercussions.

With the limited road repair resources available in the province, quickly getting the road back in operation would be difficult. The sergeant finished his briefing with some comments of his own to the effect that traffic was piling up on both sides of the closure and that it would be a monumental mess and a tempting target by nightfall. The Vinh Long ferry was shut down, and it looked like every government official from Saigon to Can Tho had descended on the province since sunup. Colonel Brown had gone out there with the province chief, Col. Tran Van Phuc, about an hour and a half before my arrival.

The helicopters had been droning overhead since I got up at 6:00 A.M. They sounded like they were flying in and out of the soccer field, so I drove in that direction to get a ride out to the site of the minings. The situation there was utter confusion. As each empty helicopter returned to pick up a new load, it was mobbed by police, soldiers, and civilian officials trying to get a place on board. Fighting my way through the crowd to the next helicopter that came in, I jumped on the landing skid next to the pilot and shouted out who I was. He shouted back that every available helicopter in the corps area was involved and that nobody was controlling the action. Shouting so as to be heard over the noise of the engine, I explained that I was in charge and told him to stay put. I then grabbed the nearest policeman by his shoulder. Hoping he would understand my Vietnamese, I yelled in his ear for him to get his superior and bring him to me. When he came back with a police lieutenant who froze at attention and saluted, I bellowed for him to line up his men and wait until I told him to come. As he started to run off, I grabbed him and added that I needed two or three of his people around each helicopter to keep everybody away until I called for them.

Feeling certain that traffic control was the greatest need at the mining sites, I moved all of the police out first. What I hadn't taken into consideration was that when the last load lifted off, I lost control of the remaining crowd. As a large number of small children charged in to whirl and dance in the downwash of wind from the next landing helicopter, a group of soldiers raced to climb aboard. I grabbed a province captain from the mass of bodies and told him to help me restrain the pressing mob. He returned a blank stare and tried to scramble back on the departing helicopter, which was already a few feet off the ground, but I grabbed him by his belt and yanked him off. Howling in his face that I was the new province senior advisor, I repeated my request. My look must have been menacing, because he just stood there until I shoved him toward the surging mass of oncoming bodies. Both of us manipulated the crowd into groups of tens and brought some semblance of order to the turmoil. When most of the crowd had been flown out and the helicopters were returning less frequently, I motioned the captain aboard the next one and jumped in behind him. Any other helicopters would just have to manage as best they could.

The pilot flew out on a line south of the road. As reported, the highway was a mess, starting two miles east of Cai Lay. From that point west, traffic was at a standstill, including buses, trucks, military vehicles, Hondas, Vespas—everything. The holes blown in the highway west of Cai Lay ranged in size from small ones to craters two-thirds as wide as the road. We landed about midway between Cai Lay and the ferry. When everyone was out of the helicopter, the pilot lifted off and swung back toward My

Tho. I silently wished him good luck and walked toward a group of soldiers and civilians who were organizing the large numbers of villagers arriving to help with the repair work.

Somebody waved at me, and when I squinted in the sun I saw it was Mr. Hoi, the province deputy for administration. Hoi was a rotund man with a reputation for ruthless efficiency hidden behind benevolent tact; I was relieved to see him. We had met during my earlier tour and had gotten along well. Hoi welcomed me back and said the province chief was somewhere nearby rounding up villagers to help repair the road. I jogged off in the direction he pointed, but after fifteen or twenty minutes of trying to find Phuc, I busied myself helping to direct the horde of villagers carrying baskets of rice paddy mud to fill in the holes.

The bedlam calmed after several hours, and work began moving in an orderly way, allowing me to sit down and catch my breath. In the far distance, the police had started directing traffic slowly around or through the partially filled holes, to begin thinning out the traffic backup. That and the dwindling crowd of visitors, inspectors, and province officials seemed to signal that the emergency was over. When another hour had passed and several helicopters arrived empty to load for the return trip, I went back with one.

As things turned out, rather than spoiling my arrival with the minings, the VC had made it auspicious. I went directly from the soccer field to Colonel Phuc's office; his secretary recognized me and bounded out of his chair to greet me. After knocking gently on Phuc's door, the secretary leaned in to say something, then quickly waved me inside. Phuc beat me to the door. His warm smile and welcome took away some of the fatigue I was beginning to feel. Phuc was an educated and sensitive man who combined being a talented administrator with the qualities of a good soldier. If he hadn't been so well-rounded and adept, he wouldn't have remained chief of a province of Dinh Tuong's importance for as long as he had.

We conversed politely until the secretary tiptoed in and put a large pile of dossiers on Phuc's desk. Glancing at my watch and realizing how long we'd been chatting, I rose and acknowledged that my unannounced visit had interrupted him at a busy time. I asked that he tell me about the day's minings when we next met. Phuc's broad, impish smile returned as he replied that his staff had told him how much I'd helped that morning and how much he appreciated it. Leaning over to shake my hand, he raised his eyebrows high and, feigning seriousness, asked softly in Vietnamese if I understood what he was saying. I understood he was complimenting me on my attempted use of his language at the soccer field, and I replied in Vietnamese that I was glad I had been able to help in some small way.

The biggest surprise of Bob Brown's briefings was learning that four main-force VC battalions were operating in the province. Major enemy units had doubled, while many active local platoons and squads had expanded. Bob was unhappy with the way the province forces were operating and with the lack of coordination between the division and the province. Military support for pacification remained mostly verbal, and the VC still had free rein at night in all the contested areas. Civil programs, though, were advancing and were being run as well as could be expected, under the able direction of Mr. Hoi and Colonel Phuc. Bob was convinced that Phuc was scrupulously honest, an assessment that coincided with my previous impression of the province chief. Brown considered Phuc aloof and reserved when it came to accepting advice, but he added that many advisors on the team complained of similar problems with their counterparts.

During Phuc's farewell party for Bob Brown, I remembered that I had been in My Tho several days and had not yet seen Det. After the party, I went to the psywar section and found Det busy at his desk. I announced softly in Vietnamese that his brother was back. Det knew my voice and stood up slowly, tears welling in his eyes. Extending his arms toward me, he came quickly around the desk, and we hugged for a long time. He cried openly, even though several sergeants were in the office. Most of those present had been there during my previous tour, and they responded by applauding. We talked for only a few minutes before Det put on his hat and said he had to leave. His wife had been planning a dinner all week, and she would need help preparing it. I was to be there at seven.

The reunion and the meal were wonderful. When I finally summoned my jeep driver, it was almost 11:00 P.M. As we drove back to the advisory team house through the quiet and deserted streets, artillery fire was rumbling from three directions out in the darkness. Things obviously were not as quiet as Colonel Phuc had hoped they might be following the quick reaction to the road minings.

With each passing day, Colonel Phuc and I became closer, our relationship more trusting and confidential. Much of our early trust probably stemmed from the fact that I was a known quantity, with a reputation for keeping my word. This eliminated Phuc's need to go through the normal initial period of feeling out and evaluating a new advisor. For both of us, it was almost as if my presence was an extension of my earlier tour. For the first time, I realized what the Vietnamese went through in getting a new and eager but inexperienced advisor each year.

While advisors were counseled to be patient and tactful, those qualities probably were more essential in their Vietnamese counterparts. Each new advisor had to be exposed slowly and diplomatically to the realities of a grim war, while he struggled to come to grips with a vastly different culture. Even if there hadn't been a shooting war to contend with, differing cultural attitudes were more apt to clash than to harmonize. The difficulty was exacerbated by the brevity of the standard U.S. one-year tour. A previous 7th Division senior advisor, John Paul Vann, when later asked about our experience, answered that we didn't have twelve years' experience in Vietnam, we had one year's experience twelve times over. Although we never discussed it, Phuc and I both appreciated being spared the awkward preliminary period of waiting to see what kind of person fate had dealt us.

While my rapid bonding with Phuc helped in the daily transaction of sensitive matters, it had an equally important and profound effect on the entire province advisory team. Things had not been running smoothly for the team before my arrival, and morale was visibly low. Besides the problems the team members had been experiencing with their obstinate counterparts, there was widespread internal dissension between civilian and military personnel. An underlying cause was the separation of responsibilities and authority between military and civilian agencies, starting in Washington and reaching down through Saigon into the province. There were even serious coordination problems among the civilian agencies themselves. Advisors and operators from the Agency for International Development (AID), U.S. Information Service (USIS), the Central Intelligence Agency (CIA), and the State Department operated independently, answered only to their respective chiefs in Saigon, guarded their own prerogatives, and were loosely held together at province level by an ad hoc organization lacking any authority or power. Day-to-day activities were uncoordinated and relied only on willing cooperation.

By a stroke of good timing, this tangled mess was altered three weeks after I arrived. Robert W. Komer recently had been sent to Saigon by President Johnson to create and direct one organization that brought together all segments of the struggling pacification program. This meant that he also had to energize the Vietnamese side of operations. Komer conceived and implemented Civil Operations and Rural Development Support (CORDS), an organization that placed the U.S. civilian and military pacification efforts under one unified chain of command. All advisors worked for Komer, who was the deputy for CORDS to the commander of the Military Assistance Command, Vietnam (MACV), with the civilian rank of ambassador. From top to bottom, military personnel found themselves working for civilians, and civilians were commanded by military officers. Responsibility and authority at each advisory level down through district rested solely in the hands of the senior advisor, whether civilian or military. For the Dinh Tuong Province team, I had that responsibility and authority.

On the day the team was merged under the new organization, I called the entire group together to announce the new arrangement and set forth my own personal ground rules. Luckily, two recent events made relatively easy a task that otherwise could have been most difficult. First, I recently had been assigned a civilian deputy named Peter Brownback, who turned out to be a dynamic, competent, pleasant blessing. Pete was a large hulk of a man with a quiet disposition, whose no-nonsense efficiency had been gained during a long career as a State Department foreign service officer. Second, the team's ability to deal effectively with its various counterparts had been steadily improving, due to my own ability to intercede diplomatically in their behalf behind the scenes with Phuc.

After announcing that we were to have open, clear, and honest communication at all times, I insisted that all egos be set aside and that we all play our roles in a low-key manner, keeping U.S. assistance in the background and making it appear to the population that it was the Vietnamese government that deserved their confidence and support. Then, according to a plan I'd previously arranged with Pete, I got everyone involved in preparing a report for me showing why pacification was not getting the military support it should and how we could begin to correct the problem. Saying I needed the answers in two days, I left—taking Pete with me, on the pretext that we had a meeting with Mr. Hoi. As we walked out, the others already were discussing the problem.

Chapter 4

Honest Deception

The finished team report contained just the information I needed to approach Colonel Phuc about the lack of military support for pacification. My rushed deadline had made it impossible for the team members to try to protect previously sacrosanct agency prerogatives. What began as compelled and grudging cooperation blended smoothly into a first cooperative undertaking.

While the reported causes of lack of pacification progress in the province were many, the predominant one mentioned was lack of cooperation and coordination between division and province operations. Since the report blamed the bulk of the problem on the Vietnamese 7th Division, trying to correct it would be a difficult and sensitive task, as I had no direct influence with the division or the division senior advisor.

The Vietnamese 7th Division had reverted back to an emphasis on enemy body counts—understandably, given the four main-force VC battalions operating in the province. But with the division concentrating almost exclusively on the enemy main-force battalions, province territorial forces were left on their own. Not too surprisingly, that same concern over the larger and more potent enemy units caused the province forces' so-called "security sweeps," intended to protect the pacified areas, to end up providing only local security for their own outposts. Any genuine contact with the enemy probably occurred only by chance or as a result of mixed signals. More and more, outright collusion with the enemy, or a tacit agreement to leave each other alone, lay behind the lack of accomplishments by many of the province operations. The VC, however, shrewdly were getting the better of the bargain, since public confidence and support for the government steadily were undermined. On paper the daily number of territorial force operations looked good. Corps then encouraged the deception by failing to question the reported figures, despite the absence of any positive results. To cap it all, as the enemy threat intensified, the division didn't trust province forces to assist them by providing screening and blocking units on division operations. Providing those forces from its own units, the division took sizable numbers of troops away from its primary role—aggressively seeking out and engaging the enemy main-force units.

I confronted Phuc with the report's findings, and he answered with a weary smile that I was exactly correct. He added that he worked for the division commander, General Thanh, and that the general didn't listen to Phuc, Phuc listened to him. I acknowledged his predicament and wondered a loud what might happen if I went to see my old friend Colonel Ngo Le Tue, the division chief of staff. I could tell him that I was there on my own account to discuss the problem with him and that Phuc knew nothing about my visit. Phuc was showing no reaction, so I asked if he would agree for me to try to convince Tue that the division would profit from using province forces to block and screen for them. Phuc leaned back and put his hands beside his nose, fingers resting over his eyes, but still he said nothing. He was thinking, though, so I pressed on, emphasizing that he too would benefit, because, if division agreed, any such operations would have to be carried out near where his province force units were stationed. Since province forces have little transportation, they would have to deploy on foot. As a result, if division would agree to use province forces to screen or block, any such operations would take place near pacified areas. Undoubtedly such maneuvers would keep the VC on the move and help take some pressure off the people. When I finished, Phuc took his hands from his face and looked at me as if surprised that my last remark came from a military man, especially an American.

Seeing his reaction and sensing a mutual concern for the people out in the countryside, I injected something I had intended to hold back for a later time. I told him that I was firmly convinced that neglecting now to take enemy pressure off the people would hurt our efforts in the future, no matter how many VC we killed out in the jungle. The most important objective of the war right now was for us to gain the support of the people for the government—their government. After a little thought, Phuc agreed that the idea could help the province and the division, and he said he'd think about it. He cautioned that if I did go to see Colonel Tue, it would have to be in the strictest confidence. He didn't want General Thanh to think he was being insolent.

Then I took a gamble calculated to accomplish three ends: first, to prod

Phuc to support the plan; second, to give Tue reason to trust province forces; and last, to give me a means to begin making territorial force units more effective. I made a commitment to send a team of advisors with a radio along on each operation conducted by one or more province companies, if Phuc agreed. That caught him by surprise. Though division advisors went along on operations with division units as part of their job, province advisors rarely did so. Encouraged by his look and silence, I continued: with advisors and a radio present and another team of advisors at the command post of each operation, we would gain better control of the units and also be able to get quicker and more accurate helicopter gunship and medical evacuation support when we needed it. Phuc began to smile. He knew well that, while the presence of advisors with his territorial force companies would give inexperienced or incompetent commanders instant advice and assistance, it also would help him. The advisors would know what the mission was, where the unit was supposed to be at any given time, and what it should be doing. All instructions passed from the field command post to the unit commanders also would be given to the advisors. This would make it impossible for Phuc's commanders to disregard or violate orders, or to lie about their locations or actions. Any results also would be confirmed by the accompanying advisors. If the double reporting chain worked carefully and delicately, as Phuc and I would make it do, control and correction could be applied in a face-saving manner—a point important to Phuc and one that he was sure not to miss. He thought a moment more, then stood up, extending his hand. He agreed that I could go and see Colonel Tue and even thought that the whole arrangement just might work.

I used a different approach with Tue. I wanted to put more pressure on him than I had on Phuc, while still keeping our friendship intact. After securing his promise of confidentiality, I lied, saying that I was seeing him because I had a big problem. The corps senior advisor was putting extreme pressure on me to try to get more cooperation between province and division forces. He wasn't happy with military support for pacification in the province and wanted it improved. I explained that I hadn't discussed the problem with Colonel Phuc yet, but now I was caught in the middle because my report to corps was due the following week. The general expected the report to show some action, and I needed Tue's advice.

Tue sat stolid and silent as I reached down and opened my briefcase. Pulling out a counterfeit typewritten report, I handed it to him, saying that it was what I was considering sending and asking his reaction to it. The fake report outlined my recommendation that the division should use province units for the simpler and less exacting missions of blocking and screening on operations conducted near pacified areas. Included was my intention to offer advisors with radios to accompany all province units so used. Tue read slowly and intently, stopping every now and then to gaze out the window and tap the report with his finger. I knew Tue was smart enough to understand that, if advisors accompanied the province companies, their presence would give some guarantee of dependability. My bogus report also emphasized that, by including territorial forces on such operations, sizable numbers of division troops would be freed for more appropriate employment. I further hoped that the combined guarantees of improved territorial force effectiveness and additional availability of division units would impress Tue. If he balked, I was prepared to tell him bluntly that the matter was so important to the corps senior advisor that he was sure to discuss my recommendations with the corps commander. Consequently, the division commander, General Thanh, probably would hear about it soon after. If all else failed, I intended actually to submit my report. I would tell Phuc before I did and was prepared to accept the fact that doing so might hurt my relationships with both Phuc and Tue.

When Tue finished reading the report, he put it down on his desk and thought silently for a long time. Although I knew I probably should let him be the first to speak, I went ahead and broke the silence, stating that I was convinced that trying this kind of cooperation would be good for the division and the province and be bad for our enemy. Tue gave a hint of a smile and chuckled, saying that he hoped it would. He began to hand the report back to me, indicating that he would have to discuss this with General Thanh and would talk with me again about it. I told him to keep that copy of the report, but asked him to remember that I had to send the original in four or five days. As I left, I reminded Tue not to mention to Phuc that I had come to see him.

About five days later, Phuc told me that General Thanh had called him to his office to discuss an idea Colonel Tue had. The idea was for using Phuc's units on selected division operations. The general thought the idea might be worth a try—if, of course, Phuc agreed.

Nothing changed for three weeks, but that was the way things normally went in Vietnam. Instant change happened only when catastrophic results clearly would follow inaction. In such cases, the change made probably would be discarded after the crisis passed. Long-lasting or permanent change came about only after long periods of cautiously and reluctantly taking one small step at a time. I had come to accept that the Vietnamese really didn't want to change much of anything, because most practices were connected in some manner to their traditions. And if change challenged tradition, it was bad. Advisors were there to create constructive change—to force it if necessary—but our counterparts weren't convinced that we had much of a culture of our own. I felt certain that, beneath all their show of agreeing and understanding, the Vietnamese resented our mission to bring about change. If all the advisors suddenly disappeared, most of the changes we had brought certainly would disappear with us. In this case, however, the division did start to combine use of Phuc's units on some operations.

Two such operations were conducted using province companies as blocking units before I found out about it. I guessed that Phuc had planned things that way, to see how events would work out, prior to allowing advisors to witness inevitable mistakes. Colonel Tue probably was in on the deal, too. To prompt Phuc to include advisors soon, I asked the province deputy for security for the results of operations. I wasn't interested so much in his answer as in the fact that word was certain to get back to Phuc that I had asked. Shortly there after, we were included.

Colonel Phuc missed going on the first several operations, so I made a special point of going over the results with him shortly after I returned from the field command post. Since I already had covered the mistakes made with his deputy for security before returning, I restricted my comments to Phuc to those things that did go well. It wasn't long before Phuc started going along to direct the operations, seeming to enjoy the brief escapes from the mounds of paperwork and administrative entanglements of My Tho.

Only once did I see Colonel Phuc reveal any outward sign of anger. In Giao Duc, the westernmost district of the province, four local territorial force companies had been blocking for a division search-and-clear operation in a troublesome area near the place where Highway 4 turned south to the ferry to Vinh Long Province. Little of consequence had resulted from the operation, but it had taken much longer to complete than planned. The only reason offered was that the day was particularly hot and humid, and the troops were moving slowly.

Phuc returned to the command post around 3 P.M. from visiting surrounding hamlets. He showed initial signs of irritation when he learned that the operation was behind schedule and would drag on for another hour or more. The later it got, the shorter Phuc's temper became. By the time all the companies were finally released, it was after 6 P.M. A short while earlier, I had realized the reason for Phuc's concern and had begun to share it. It wasn't healthy for any small convoy to be on the road west of Cai Lay, nicknamed "Ambush Alley," near sundown—especially a small command group easily identified by its many tall, waving radio antennas. The four or five kilometers west of Cai Lay were the worst stretch of all, as this was a favorite crossing place for VC units moving between the northern and southern halves of the province. If any enemy unit was going to operate anywhere in the southern part of the province during the night, it would be in position north of the highway around dusk to observe its selected crossing point. We would be traveling that area just about dusk, and the small province command post convoy would be an inviting target.

Moreover, none of the troop units would be with us to provide protection, as they would have turned off the highway to return to their nearby home outpost locations before we reached "Ambush Alley."

For an hour before the companies were released, Phuc paced continuously between the command tent and the radio truck. At 5:30, he ordered everything packed and loaded and the vehicles lined up. He monitored his units from the radio truck, and I used my jeep radio to stay in touch with the advisors. When the operation finally ended, he urged his commanders to hurry from their blocking positions to areas of relative safety—ordinarily not a prudent thing to do. It was hard enough normally to get the units to stay alert and be concerned with point, flank, and rear security as they started home to families and supper. Now, in view of their boss's order to speed things up, even small precautions undoubtedly would be totally disregarded. If the enemy were listening to our radio transmissions, as often happened, and if enemy troops could move to take advantage of the situation, as often was possible, serious consequences could follow.

I radioed the advisor teams with the companies, cautioning them to stay alert and press their counterparts to maintain adequate security on the move. For the benefit of any VC commander who might be listening in, I added the lie that I was in radio contact with a team of helicopter gunships operating across the river in Vinh Long and could have the team over the units in ten minutes. All units made it in without incident. When the convoy finally did get rolling down the highway, long shadows were cast in the waning daylight.

All proceeded tensely but quietly until we were about four kilometers west of Cai Lay—exactly where we didn't want any problems. At that point, the convoy ground to a halt. My jeep was three vehicles behind Colonel Phuc's, close enough if needed but not so close as to be caught in the same killing zone if we were ambushed. After we sat for a minute, a lieutenant came from the front of the convoy and said something to Phuc, who jumped out of his jeep and hurried in that direction. Before I followed, I made a precautionary radio check with the district advisory team in Cai Lay. As I came abreast of the convoy's lead vehicle, I grasped the problem and saw Phuc trying to solve it. A large bus traveling in the opposite direction had broken down. Some vehicles in the long line behind the bus had tried to pass it and now were in our lane, nose to nose with the front of our convoy. With traffic still piling up in both directions, Phuc talked rapidly to the bus driver, who was under the raised hood of the bus. From the motioning and the shouting, I grasped that Phuc was telling the driver to have the truck behind the bus push it to the side of the road, and the driver was protesting that he had to get to the safety of the My Thuan ferry before dark.

Without warning, Colonel Phuc exploded and grabbed the driver. Phuc removed his pistol from his holster and put it to the driver's head

As Phuc shouted at the top of his lungs, the driver went limp and covered his face with his hands. When Phuc released him, the driver scurried to the bus and ordered the passengers out. By this time, the sun was a large, red disk settling quickly behind the palm trees to the rear of the convoy. Since Phuc seemed to have regained his composure, I walked up to him, displayed my map, and pointed to the location of a battery of U.S. artillery in position a little southeast of Cai Lay. He agreed to my recommendation that I radio and arrange for them to fire a check round near us. He also approved for me to adjust their fire onto any target from that check round if we needed it. The passengers now were streaming from the bus, and Phuc started toward them. I caught his arm and asked where the area was that he was most worried about, so that I could fire the check round there. Phuc pointed to a thick line of palm trees about eight hundred meters across the rice paddies on the north side of the road. After he assured me that there were no civilians at that location, I turned and jogged back to my jeep.

The artillery battery near Cai Lay was placed there, as were others in different locations, to protect the large U.S. 9th Infantry Division base at Dong Tam on the Cuu Long River west of My Tho. I'd seen the unit as we passed in the morning, with its self-propelled 8-inch howitzers, potent weapons. After I called in the fire mission and was informed that it was ready to be fired at my command, I ran to tell Phuc.

He was still at the bus and had the passengers and driver pushing the side of the bus to try to rock it off the road. He called for me to go ahead and shoot, and I raced back to the jeep and gave the order to fire. Almost immediately, the muffled sound of howitzer firing reached us, followed by the familiar whine of the shell cutting through the air overhead. The airburst was right on target and at perfect height. A mammoth orange explosion erupted about twenty meters above the paddy, splashing steel fragments into the water for about eighty meters on either side. It looked awesome and surely impressed any VC in the vicinity.

Back at the bus, a number of soldiers had joined the passengers rocking it, as darkness was deepening. Phuc, grinning, gave me an animated thumbs-up sign and pointed to the black smoke dissipating from the burst. With a *squoosh* sound, the wheels on the far side of the bus finally bounced off the road and onto the slippery mud shoulder. Then, under continued pressure from the pushing mob, it started a slow, steady slide until it bumped and settled into the paddy. Phuc immediately dispatched some soldiers to move the traffic facing us back into their correct lane. It was completely dark when we got moving again, and even small, battle-scarred Cai Lay looked good as we rolled through to its safer east side.

Thereafter, Phuc often told the story of the artillery round with great relish, referring to me as his excellent province senior artillery advisor.

Later, he assured me he never would have pulled the trigger on the bus driver, but I wouldn't have bet on that.

As operations continued, morale of the territorial force units improved as a result of the training and support they received from the advisors who went along. Moreover, when advisors accompanied them, unit commanders were able to exercise more control over the actions of their troops toward civilians. Although mistreatment of the population by division soldiers was a much greater problem, it remained a concern that territorial force troops stole chickens and indulged in abusive behavior in the contested zones and fringe areas of pacified regions. Phuc reported that improved troop behavior had brought expressions of personal appreciation from several hamlet chiefs and village elders.

Only a few operations resulted in contact with the enemy and losses to their side. While several military triumphs undoubtedly would have helped pacification, the increased level of operations nonetheless did help to relieve enemy pressures on the population. People began to travel more, and rural markets began to flourish, giving a needed boost to local economies. Teachers started returning to open previously abandoned schools, and medical teams began venturing out to dispensaries constructed by village self-help programs. That, after all, was the whole point.

Chapter 5

Poll Tax

As the first national elections drew near in September 1967, Colonel Phuc became more and more involved in efforts to conduct them fairly and safely. Although security of the population remained a primary election concern, he had to stop going out on operations and devote attention to administrative matters. I stopped going out, too. There was enough to keep busy with in My Tho and the districts, including security against terrorist acts in polling places located in areas heretofore considered secure.

Phuc looked gaunt and talked slowly. I'd never seen him so tired. He repeatedly reminded me to remain alert to prevent the enemy from interfering with this historic event. I assured him that all my advisors would do everything possible to help his people. As we shook hands, he put his left arm around my shoulder, a sincere and unexpected gesture that totally surprised me.

Before our involvement in election preparations became nonstop, Phuc and I had a needed opportunity to relax together. The Go Cong Province senior advisor and his counterpart challenged us to a doubles tennis match. Thinking that flawlessly proper Phuc wouldn't consider it, he proved me wrong, and the experience turned out to be a memorable one.

The match was played one Sunday on a private court inside the Go Cong border and progressed on equal terms—only because the talent of both province chiefs was offset equally by the bungling of their advisors. When we got to the final and deciding game, the monsoon rains came upon us in full fury. Against all rational thinking,

Phuc and the Go Cong province chief insisted on finishing the game, pretending province honor was at stake. The bodyguards hunched in the cold rain, disbelievingly looking on as their superiors and the U.S. government representatives skidded, tumbled, and clowned through the downpour in disregard of decorum, rank, and station. Although Phuc and I lost, our opponents declared the match a draw.

A group of some thirty U.S. senators and congressmen arrived in Saigon to observe the election. Our team was notified that Sen. Edmund Muskie of Maine would be coming to My Tho to observe at our location. Phuc, Mr. Hoi, and I met immediately to outline a plan for the visit. I suggested that, after appropriate greetings, Phuc turn the senator over to Mr. Hoi. That would properly place the civilian administrative aspects of the elections in the forefront and keep associated military actions in the correct perspective, as a security shield behind which the elections could proceed. While the military probably was being pressured to support General Thieu, I was convinced that most officers also were committed to preventing the VC from disrupting the election and letting the civilians have a chance to choose for themselves. I was convinced, too, that Hoi would carry off escorting the senator well. Hoi spoke perfect English, had an engaging personality, and was a polished diplomat. I would accompany them only to assure the senator's safety and to be available for whatever he needed. Otherwise, his visit was to be an all-Vietnamese show.

Everything went well, and Muskie left satisfied that the election would proceed as well as could be expected. At one point in his tour, I pointed out to the senator that the election was an amazing undertaking for a country that, after only four years of independence from the autocratic Diem regime, was having democracy shoved down its throat by a country that was still developing the process after two hundred years of trial and error. He appeared to take my taunt in good humor and thanked me for the thought. There were no repercussions.

Election day, September 3, 1967, dawned bright and clear after a night of heavy showers, a spate of VC propaganda, and some violence. During an early morning meeting with the team, I cautioned all to stay well in the background and to keep abreast of reports from the central operations center and results from election return headquarters in the province administrative office. Team members were to stay out of the way of their counterparts but be available to assist if requested. Starting around noon, I drove past a number of polling places and stopped in at the election tallying office several times throughout the day. I had wished Phuc good luck the evening before and said I'd see him after sundown, when the polling stations around the province were closed. He recently had conducted the elections for village councils and hamlet chiefs, which on the surface appeared to have gone well, and he faced the elections for the House of Representatives in October. When we shook hands and parted, Phuc wearily joked that installing democracy was many times more difficult than fighting the enemy to permit its birth.

The VC tried to disrupt the election, but they succeeded only in turning back some people going to the polls after sunup in several remote areas. People throughout the province were determined to exercise their new privilege, and late afternoon figures forecast a turnout in excess of 80 percent of those eligible! The most serious VC incidents occurred in Vinh Kim, a village whose people I had come to respect and admire. The VC mortared the village as the polling place opened, following up with a ground attack that wounded about fifteen people in line at the polling station. When the machine-gun and rifle fire ended, those who were in line when it began returned from cover and resumed voting. Other than that incident, all was going well.

My plan was to go to the election tally office around 7:30 or 8:00 P.M., but Phuc phoned about six o'clock and asked me to join him. Exhausted but elated at the successful proceedings and the expected final results, Phuc had tea brought in and asked me to join him at a wooden bench opposite a large blackboard resting on two chairs against the office wall. If there was no dramatic change, Nguyen Van Thieu would be president, and Vice Air Marshall Nguyen Cao Ky would be vice president. It was going to be interesting to see how the rivals worked together in office. Senatorial results, to which I paid little attention, filled the bottom half of the blackboard. Phuc never stopped jumping up and moving about, as he continued to answer the phones, post the board, and direct the few province military officers still in the office.

Around 9 P.M., we heard a commotion in the street outside, and a bloodsplattered sergeant hurried into the office and blurted out something to Phuc. I couldn't understand a word he said, as he was speaking in heaving gasps and obviously was in pain. As Phuc raced out the door, I hurried to follow him. As the six ancient French armored cars of the Headquarters Security Platoon, commonly called the "Armored Car Platoon," rolled to a stop, a horrific sight greeted us. One of the almost comical tanklike antiques, which often were the butt of jokes by U.S. advisors, had a gaping hole in its side. Soldiers from the other vehicles were carrying or assisting crew members of the damaged car and others it had been transporting to a grassy spot illuminated by light from the office windows. Groans still came from inside the armored relic.

I grabbed the flashlight hanging from my belt and ran to the open rear hatch. As I peered inside, with Phuc behind looking over my shoulder, the flashlight's beam illuminated a grisly scene. Amid motionless torsos completely severed from legs, other forms writhed and moaned. I leaned into the gore and gently lifted the nearest moving body out, then carried him to my jeep. Phuc carried another soldier to his jeep, shouting for all the wounded to be taken to other vehicles. Evidently we had had the same idea, as we raced to the province hospital two blocks away. Once there, I hoisted the more seriously wounded of the two and carefully rushed him into the hospital corridor. Running back to get the second man from my jeep, I passed a gaunt and bloody Phuc carrying in one of the soldiers from his jeep. Having carried the remaining man on my back, I laid him on the emergency room floor next to the other wounded now being brought in by their comrades.

Phuc was already gone when I returned outside the hospital, so I drove back to the tally office. He was sitting next to the teapot on the bare bench, hunched forward with his head in his hands. I quietly sat next to him. He didn't seem to notice. After a few minutes, his shoulders began to shake, as he sobbed gently into his hands. In a reflex action, I put my hand on his shoulder, and he reached back with one hand to pat mine as he turned his head away so I wouldn't see his tears. Some of his officers were sitting silently near the tally board, but Phuc continued to cry despite their presence. I just felt numb.

The Armored Car Platoon functioned almost like Phuc's personal bodyguard, and he knew most of the men individually. Because of their responsibility for his safety, they all were selected for their loyalty and trustworthiness. The loss had to be a deep personal blow for Phuc. When he finally wiped his eyes and stood up, I just stayed seated on the bench. He mustered a weak, wordless smile, reached out and touched my shoulder, then turned and walked slowly in the direction of his house.

After Phuc had gone, I learned how the incident had happened. The Armored Car Platoon had been assigned to protect the polling place and the road at the Trung Luong intersection where Highway 4 branched, going west toward Cai Lay and south into My Tho. When the poll closed, the platoon remained long after dark until other security forces passed the intersection and were relatively safe on the way to their home locations. Then the platoon turned and headed for My Tho. In an area just north of town, where no VC attack was expected, the third vehicle in line was hit broadside by a B-40 rocket. Without stopping, the other vehicles pushed and pulled the disabled armored car to their assigned posts for the evening, protecting the province headquarters. As I wearily drove past the hospital, still busy and brightly lit, on my way to the team house, artillery and mortar fire continued to rumble from all directions out in the distant darkness. I wondered how many more wounded would litter the emergency room floor before the night was over.

When I entered the team house, some of the team members, alarmed at the blood soaking my uniform, jumped up and ran to me. I looked in the mirror and was jolted by my own appearance. Bits of coagulated blood and small white pieces of cartilage stuck to my face, hands, and shirt. After cleaning up, I rejoined the team, downed the drink someone handed me, and related the sad close of that historic day. While I was still talking, the phone rang. The first sergeant told us that 83 percent of the people had voted and that Thieu was the new president. I corrected him. He was not the *new* president; he was the *first* president.

In the weeks that followed, filled with enough somber activity to keep us fully occupied, Phuc found ways to make some time available to relax. We never could plan far ahead, so I became accustomed to spontaneous evening phone calls asking if I could come to his house. Most of the time, we sat quietly and listened to his large selection of mostly Vietnamese music tapes. No one disturbed us, and we said nothing to each other. On one beautiful October evening with a full moon, Phuc thoughtfully sent his driver to bring me to the veranda of his house to watch the Children's Moon Festival holiday parade with his family. Hundreds of small, beautiful children filed by, singing and buzzing with excitement, their candle-lit lanterns swaying in the gentle evening breeze. The scene filled my heart with both gladness and sadness, and I thought how wonderful this land would be when all the violence and sorrow ended. The excitement of Phuc's own children added to the marvelous setting, as they bounded around the veranda in their pajamas and called their parents' attention to particularly beautiful or intricate lanterns. From the poorest farmers in the hamlets to the wealthy families in Saigon, all wanted things to be better—for the children's sake. I too looked up at the bright moon and said a silent prayer for all the children. The uncertainty of their safety and their future weighed heavily on my heart.

The phone rang in my room as I lay in bed reading, tired from a long day walking the rice paddies with Phuc in Cai Lay. I jumped up to answer, since a call at that late hour usually was from the province operations center, relaying bad news of some incident. The voice of Major Binh, the 7th Division's intelligence officer, surprised me. He apologized for phoning so late, but he was calling a special meeting at his house to discuss something important that just came up. Could I come? Whatever it was must be unusually urgent, I thought, as I had little direct contact with the division and none at all with Binh. I replied that I'd be there as soon as I could dress. Binh gave me directions to his house, admonishing me to be sure to come alone and not to tell anybody I was going. When I hung up, I looked at my watch. It was a quarter past midnight.

While driving through the deserted streets, I suddenly wondered if it really was Binh who had called. I thought I recognized his voice, but now I couldn't be sure. Why the caution to come alone? Why the secrecy? Was

I getting sucked into something? As I found the darkened house, I wondered if it was even Binh's. Parking the jeep a safe distance away, I drew and cocked my pistol and tried to approach noiselessly.

As I climbed the front steps, the door opened a crack and Binh poked his head out to make sure it was me. As I fumbled quickly to put away my pistol, he ushered me inside, where several dark forms were dancing in soft, muted lights. I followed him past the dancing couples to a low table covered with food and drinks. Colonel Phuc and several pretty young ladies were sitting on the floor, laughing at the joke that had brought me there. Phuc explained that Binh, a longtime close friend, had arranged the surprise party to help Phuc escape the pressures of the job and relax. Because of Phuc's position, the get-together had to be kept secret. Phuc wanted me there with him so I could relax, too. He gave an impish smile as I crossed my legs and sat on the floor beside him.

Having pretty girls to dance with at a party was an innocent, accepted practice, akin to having Geishas entertain in Japan. When Phuc left around 2 A.M., I did, too. In the heavy press of business that followed, neither of us ever mentioned the party. It was as if it had never happened.

The pace of economic and social programs had accelerated over the preceding two months of 1967, leaving little time for Colonel Phuc and me to be together as before. That more time was required for economic improvements and less for operations I interpreted as a good sign, and I hoped that progress out in the villages and hamlets was construed by the people in the same way. Phuc and I seemed always to be rushing from one project to another. Ten new hamlets were constructed to take care of the influx of people leaving VC-controlled areas. Councils were elected in twenty-nine villages, and elections for hamlet chief and assistant hamlet chief were held successfully. Where marginal security didn't permit elections, village administrative committees and hamlet chiefs were temporarily installed. Throughout the province, twenty-eight new school rooms were completed, and thirty-two others were being built. Because teachers were a prime target of VC terrorism, it was a special mark of confidence in the improved security situation that new teachers coming out of national training were accepting positions in the rural areas to reopen many closed schools. Rice production was up to a new high of 203 tons, as a result of the government's distribution of fertilizer at cost. Farmers everywhere were beginning to emerge as the new prosperous class, as pigs, chickens, and pond fish were given to them to promote diversification. The Agro-Development Bank broke loan records. Irrigation canals, roads, and bridges were being repaired or rebuilt, and medical services were reaching the hamlets as trained nurses became available.

Phuc's speech on National Day, November 1, 1967, was directed more at the people of the province than at his Saigon superiors, and the tone was more optimistic than cautious. He seemed infused with new strength and vitality. When I submitted my required reports on the progress of the province's programs, I included several stories of families who moved to government-controlled areas because life was much better there and they wanted that for their children's future. As an afterthought, I added the comment that perhaps the way to win the war was not to try to outshoot the enemy, but rather to "out-economy" him.

Not long after the elections were over, a gradual change began to be felt in the province. Each hard-won bit of progress in the war and each positive accomplishment in the pacification effort was counterbalanced by some reversal or sorrow. After a territorial force operation captured a large array of enemy weapons and ammunition north of Cai Lay, VC mortar rounds hit the grade school in the town, killing or maiming thirty children. Later I was invited to attend a festive lunch in Vinh Kim, given by the village council in appreciation for receiving donated building material for construction of their small maternity hospital. Two of the elders who hosted the luncheon subsequently were assassinated by the VC. When the local VC squad of a village on the outskirts of the province capital voluntarily surrendered, widespread psywar coverage emphasized that they brought their weapons and important documents in with them. Within a week, the city began to be mortared for the first time. The mortaring of such an important provincial capital forecast a more ominous turn of events, but we failed to grasp its true significance at the time.

I attended memorial services for two crewmen of a U.S. Navy river patrol boat who were killed when another boat from their squadron accidentally discharged a deck machine gun. The boat the two dead crew members belonged to was the one that had taken me along on a routine patrol down the Cuu Long River a week before. During the services, I remembered how the crew had stopped at an isolated outpost and shared their food, cigarettes, and ammunition with the grubby little outpost's occupants.

Finally, after we proudly reported steady increases in the percentage of the province's population that was under government control, reaching over 60 percent in October, we discovered that our own friendly artillery and air strikes had caused a disproportionate share of the seventeen thousand recently dislocated people to move to the secure areas. Subsequent inspection of the refugee camps disclosed that the Refugee and Social Welfare Service was hard pressed to care for the influx. Moreover, misappropriation of funds and supplies contributed to the squalid living conditions prevalent in the camps.

Toward mid-November, I started to feel ill. My sickness came and went and had all the symptoms of a lingering flu, so I disregarded it. There was just too much to do to slow down. Recurring cold sweats, fever, and chills eventually made me visit the 7th Division advisory team's dispensary. The diagnosis was possible malaria or dengue fever. Because the symptoms never stayed for long and I bounced back, feeling well each time, I was given antibiotics, and little more thought was given to it.

After worsening and lengthening weakness, requiring two more visits to the dispensary for more tests, a symptom emerged which allowed positive diagnosis of my problem. My urine was the color of Coca-Cola. I had hepatitis. Ordered to report immediately to the U.S. evacuation hospital at Dong Tam, I returned to the team house to pack a small bag. I didn't know which made me feel worse, leaving or the hepatitis. After packing my toilet articles and a change of clothes, I telephoned my deputy, Pete Brownback. Saying I'd be back as soon as possible, I urged him to visit Colonel Phuc, explain the situation to him, and volunteer to take my place in all business with Phuc and not wait to be invited.

The hot mid-November sun made little difference on the slow, bumpy, dusty ride to Dong Tam. I'd been sweat-soaked constantly for the previous week and was so now. When I entered the evacuation hospital, the unexpectedly, icy air-conditioned cold put me into an almost convulsive chill that didn't leave until the helicopter took me to the Third Surgical Hospital in Saigon the next evening.

Chapter 6

Out of the Frying Pan

On my second day at the Third Surgical Hospital, I was processed to be flown to Japan that evening. It dawned on me that I might not return to Dinh Tuong. Then, with a jolt, I realized I might not even return to Vietnam. One of the medical corpsmen had mentioned that most cases sent to Japan eventually were evacuated to the States. Cases expected to be returned to duty after hospitalization were kept in Vietnam and treated at a convalescent hospital in Cam Ranh Bay, about 180 miles north of Saigon. In a state of mixed despair and panic, I lay back thinking rapidly what could be done to see that I was sent to Cam Ranh Bay instead of Japan. How damned ironic! Ninety-nine out of every one hundred servicemen in Vietnam at this very moment would instantly have traded places with me. But here I was, scheming to stay in Vietnam. The magnitude of the contributions still to be made only now became clear.

In desperation, I devised a plan. I would phone the ambassador and ask him to intercede. When I couldn't contact the ambassador or his deputy, my voice must have reflected despair, for the person on the other end of the phone asked what the problem was. When I blurted out my predicament, he sympathetically recommended a call to Brigadier General Knowlton, the deputy assistant chief of staff for CORDS. General Knowlton was the man who had gotten me out of Pleiku and into My Tho. After hearing my story and plea, which came out in short gasps due to nervousness and weakness, the general laughed back his response. Telling me to go back to bed, he promised he'd take care of things.

Around eight that evening, a group came in and began preparing a dozen or so patients for movement. As the litters were being taken out, a corpsman responded hastily over his shoulder to my nervous question about what was happening. It was the shipment to Japan. I was not included, so I settled into a peaceful sleep.

The next morning I was strapped to a litter and flown by C-130 to Cam Ranh Bay. The next four weeks of convalescence were quiet and relaxed. When the date of my release was confirmed, I phoned Saigon to schedule my return to duty and sadly learned that I would not be returning to My Tho. Enemy activity had increased alarmingly for the past two weeks, and CORDS had decided that Dinh Tuong needed a military senior advisor. Over Pete Brownback's protest, another lieutenant colonel had been assigned in my place. I was scheduled to go to Chuong Thien Province as the senior advisor there. The man I was replacing already had departed, and someone with experience was needed quickly to take his place. I recalled Chuong Thien only vaguely but quickly agreed. Although it wasn't going to be My Tho, it was a field assignment and infinitely better than being stuck in some staff assignment in Saigon.

The hospital library had an embassy pamphlet with statistics and information about all the provinces; I checked it out and took it back to my bed. Pillow behind my head, I read about my new home:

> Chuong Thien: Province capital is Vi Thanh. Location: 150 miles southwest of Saigon at the head of the Ca Mau Peninsula.
>
> The area has long been a safe haven for the VC. In an attempt to establish control in the area, President Diem created the province several years ago out of the bordering four Mekong Delta provinces of Kien Giang, Ba Xuyen, Bac Lieu, and Phong Dinh. The latest countywide security rating placed Chuong Thien last (44th) out of the 44 provinces of Vietnam.

Two days earlier, my Combat Infantryman Badge had been delivered in the mail. Although I had qualified for the award by getting shot at in Dinh Tuong, as things turned out, I would earn the badge several times over in Chuong Thien.

During the first week of December 1967, the sights, sounds, and smells of Saigon made me grateful to be free of the hospital. Briefings on Chuong Thien at MACV headquarters confirmed in detail the shaky situation in the province. Nonetheless, I was anxious to get there and get to work. I wasn't so anxious, however, that I couldn't relax and enjoy my scheduled two days in Saigon before going. Once outside the gate of Tan Son Nhut Air Base, I took a taxi to the heart of the city, where Det, his wife, and I had arranged by phone to meet.

As the taxi dodged down Cong Ly Boulevard, I remembered that Colonel Lien's house was on the boulevard and looked in my notebook for the address

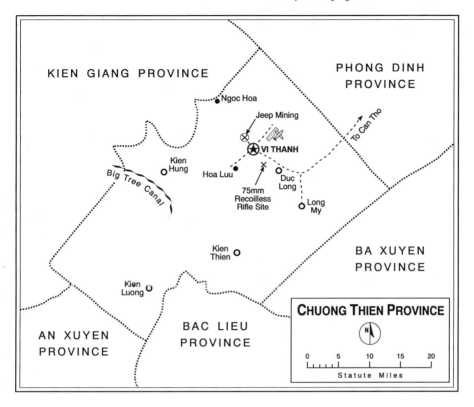

he had given me in Pleiku: 384/51 Cong Ly. Even if Lien wasn't there, somebody would be, and I could leave word of my new assignment and let him know I'd stopped by. The taxi driver missed Lien's house at first, because it was small and almost hidden between two large new villas. A small, neglected garden and a high wrought-iron fence were all that separated it from the crowded sidewalk and noisy road thronged with traffic. After I rang the bell for the third time, an old woman cautiously looked out the front door, then shuffled to unlock the gate. Introducing myself, I said that I was a friend of Colonel Lien and hoped that he or his wife was at home. The old woman blinked and answered almost too quickly for me to grasp. Colonel Lien was dead. Madame Lien was in the house; did I want to see her? I asked her to repeat herself, this time more slowly, but I had heard correctly. Lien had been killed over a month ago in Kontum. I thanked her, said not to bother Madame Lien, and returned to the waiting taxi. I wanted to go back to MACV at Tan Son Nhut and find out the details of Lien's death.

Leafing through reports for November, 1967, an intelligence officer found what he sought, read for a moment, then replaced the report in the file cabinet and told me what had happened. Colonel Lien, his advisor, and the entire crew of their helicopter all had been killed when the ship was hit by a B-40 rocket near the Cambodian border in western Kontum. A rare and lucky shot for the B-40 gunner. When I stopped at the Saigon cathedral on my way back downtown, I prayed for Lien, the others on the helicopter, and their families, as well as giving thanks being alive myself and able to remain in the country.

Meeting Det in Saigon shed some light on the extraordinary enemy activity throughout the country as 1967 came to an end. Also confirmed was my initial impression that Chuong Thien Province wasn't going to be the best place to sit and ponder what it all meant. The taxi delivered Det, his wife, and me to An Hong Restaurant, the eatery most renowned in Saigon for "beef fixed seven ways." The large crowd lined up outside dissuaded us from even leaving the vehicle. People were staying up late, shopping, and eating out because Tet, the Lunar New Year of 1968, wasn't far off. I had forgotten about Tet until Det mentioned that he and his wife were taking advantage of their pre-Tet visit with his family to shop and also to meet with me. Det was determined to feed me the seven beef dishes, so we headed to Cholon to another restaurant.

As time to part neared, Det became very serious. Reaching across the table to grasp my arm, he narrowed his eyes, lowered his voice, and warned that the situation in Dinh Tuong had deteriorated. The VC were very active, creating much trouble. My Tho was being mortared often; if the situation was that bad for him, he worried about what it would be like for me in Chuong Thien. On the street outside the restaurant, large, happy crowds ambled along, in no hurry to end the evening. Trying to make parting less painful, we promised to try to arrange a Tet visit in My Tho. More fundamental concerns would occupy us both when the time came.

My schedule permitted an overnight stay in My Tho, with pickup early the next morning for the flight to Vi Thanh in Chuong Thien. Lt. Col. Ed Schowalter had been moved over from Vinh Binh Province as my replacement. The first sergeant informed me that Schowalter was a tough and difficult man, had won the Congressional Medal of Honor in Korea, and already had made a lot of changes. Knowing Phuc's sensitivities, I hoped that the changes would not be for the worse.

After visiting the CORDS staff offices to say good-bye, I went to Colonel Phuc's office. He was out but was due to return around 3 P.M. I went over to the 7th Division for a few quick farewells. Colonel Tue, Major Binh, and several others were there, and we talked briefly. While chatting with Binh, I couldn't help noticing that the intelligence map on his wall had more than the usual number of red marks showing enemy locations and activity. Both Binh and Tue smiled when they heard that I was going to Chuong Thien and wished me luck.

I returned to the CORDS offices to say good-bye to Pete Brownback. I asked him how the new province senior advisor and Phuc were getting along, and Pete replied that Phuc considered Schowalter heavy-handed— too direct and blunt.

When I met Phuc, he insisted that I spend my last night with him and his family. He was sitting in his living room when I returned just after dark from dinner at my driver's house, and we talked over coffee and cognac late into the night. Though he showed no emotion other than being a little quieter than usual, he said outright that he was sorry I was no longer his advisor. He regretted that he felt he could never confide in Schowalter. I assured him that his new advisor was a good soldier, probably a better one than I was. Emphasizing that in Korea he had received our nation's highest medal, I added he had been an excellent advisor in Vinh Binh and brought valuable experience with him. Phuc was smiling, but not his impish smile. After a little silent reflection, Phuc stood, put his hand on my shoulder, and said that, although it would be difficult, he would try. He quickly added that Schowalter must remember whose country he was in and who was the province chief. Because we were the only ones still up, Phuc went and got more coffee. He returned with a gift for me which couldn't have been more thoughtful. He had recorded both popular and traditional Vietnamese songs on a large tape, making certain that those which had come to be my favorites were included. The box was inscribed simply in his handwriting: "To Colonel Metzner, from Colonel Phuc, 1967—— [signed] Phuc." When the coffee cups were empty, he quietly escorted me to one of the second-floor guest rooms and said good-night. At 5 A.M., a knock on the door awakened me. After a quick breakfast together, Phuc and I shook hands and parted, never to see each other again.

The airfield at the province capital of Vi Thanh was much larger than I had expected and was neatly paved with blacktop. Much larger My Tho City had only a small dirt strip which could handle nothing but light planes. I was puzzled until I remembered the isolation of Chuong Thien and the fact that the province could be reached dependably only by air. When the helicopter put down in front of the small terminal building, I jotted the date and time in my notebook, 9:10 A.M., December 12, 1967. Several attempts to use the military phone sitting on one of the concrete wall benches were futile, so I sat outside on my baggage and waited.

Twenty minutes later, a jeep came churning up the road at high speed and skidded to a screeching stop in front of me, dust boiling up all the way. A gangling, grinning, awkward Vietnamese bumpkin bounced out, saluted, and introduced himself as Mai, my driver. After we loaded my things in the back of the jeep, we speeded off for town, careening in the same manner in which Mai had arrived.

Even though I had been prepared for the remoteness of the province capital Vi Thanh, its poor, ramshackle appearance came as a shock. Mai guided the jeep through the dusty streets, past the fish market on the canal, and left along a side street (actually more of an alleyway) crowded with small shops and houses. A short distance further, he jolted to a stop in front of a sign that read: "Welcome to Advisory Team 58." The team compound, wedged in between neighboring civilian houses, was a greater shock than the town. The gate, made of welded engineer stakes and hog wire, stood wide open. A province soldier on guard waved us in and, as we passed, waved at us again. Mai pointed me in the direction of the administrative office just beyond the crowded parking area inside the gate, then started hauling my belongings toward a row of connected wooden rooms. When I introduced myself to the team clerk, he jumped up and ran to get Major Kennedy from the motor pool at the rear of the compound.

Moments later, Ed Kennedy hurried in, wiping grease from his hand for the handshake after the salute. Ed was short and overweight but moved lightly and quickly on his feet. He apologized for not being available to greet me, but he had not known that I was arriving. I accepted his offer of a cup of coffee and a short initial briefing while I unwound.

The mess hall was constructed in much the same manner as all the other buildings, with a concrete floor, a two-by-four beam frame, wooden slats covering the bottom half of the outside walls, and wire screening completing the upper half. The roofs were a hard, corrugated material like asbestos. Kennedy, the deputy senior advisor for territorial forces, gave me an introduction to the small team, its civilian members, and the current situation in the province.

Official reports optimistically put the VC in control of about 60 percent of the province, but a more realistic figure was 70 percent. Except for the residents of Vi Thanh and two of the nearer of the five district towns, the population was not committed to either the government or the VC. The rest were waiting for the outcome of the war, wanting to be left alone and responding only in the direction opposite to the constant violence. Six and again four weeks before I arrived, the ARVN 21st Division and some attached Ranger battalions had caught large enemy forces within six and twenty miles of Vi Thanh and come out the winner both times. Total enemy casualties, most of them confirmed by advisors, were 690 killed and 4 captured, the prisoners ranging in age from thirteen to sixteen. Despite these heavy losses, the VC were increasing the pressure, particularly around Vi Thanh, and had overrun two outposts close to town last week, causing their abandonment. The 3rd Regiment of the 21st Division was stationed at a compound in the southwestern corner of the town. In the entire province, only twenty-five kilometers (about sixteen miles) of road were usable, due to lack of security or because the roads had been dug up by the VC. Even on the usable portions, it was not safe to travel without adequate security.

I interrupted Kennedy to ask if he could continue his rundown as he showed me around the compound. He gulped his remaining coffee and replied that the tour wouldn't take long, because there wasn't very much to see. He was right. The entire compound was about eighty meters by sixty meters. Squeezed into that space were two rows of living quarters, mess hall, motor pool, parking area, administrative office, a single communal latrine and shower, water tower and pumping shed, command bunker, four fighting bunkers, and, in the center of it all, a newly built club with outdoor concrete patio. A flimsy fence, six feet high, with three strands of barbed-wire baffle extending from its outer base, surrounded the crammed facilities.

Outside the fence, a road and a canal bordered both the front and the back sides, running generally east and west. Civilian houses were flush against the south side, and the town's only tennis court, a swamp, and a radio relay tower 120 feet high lay just outside the northern boundary. As we walked around, I started making mental notes of our obvious vulnerabilities, but stopped. The whole setup invited disaster. To complicate our problems, the small number of civilian advisors on the team lived in a totally unprotected, newly built cinder-block cottage outside the east fence. Other than the sandbagged bunkers in the compound and a concrete bunker inside the civilian cottage, the only form of protection was two layers of sand-filled fifty-five-gallon drums that shielded the walkways in front of the wood-framed living quarters. The province chief provided Vietnamese guards for twenty-four-hour security inside the compound, and, to date, not one shot ever had been fired in our direction. That last fact gave me little comfort; I wondered why we'd been so lucky.

We had stopped in front of my room, which was in the center of the row of living quarters nearest the center of the compound—a signal that the tour was over. When I asked when I could expect to meet the province chief, Kennedy replied that Major Dao usually had an afternoon staff meeting at his house. He'd phone Dao and let him know that I would go there for a visit near 5 P.M. I thanked Kennedy and pushed open the screen door to my room. Mai and a plump, middle-aged woman were finishing hanging up and putting away my clothes. He introduced Ba Hoa, my housemaid. Like Mai, she spoke no English and was delighted that I spoke understandable Vietnamese.

The province chief's house was a very small villa, similar to the others on the same street and not very far from the compound. From what I'd already seen of the town, my impression was that nothing in it was very far from the compound. Maj. Le Minh Dao leaped up from his meeting to greet me. About average height for a Vietnamese (a head or so shorter than I),

Dao was skeleton-thin, with large, round eyes bulging from a taut face. Despite his broad smile and disarming, friendly enthusiasm, his eyes remained piercing. After briefly introducing me to his staff, he dismissed them and invited me to sit with him for iced tea. Dao's English was flawless. He knew of my previous assignments and grinned at my surprise when he explained that Colonel Phuc had told him about me when they were together at a meeting in Can Tho last week. He seemed genuinely pleased to have me there, and I found myself liking this strange, tightly-wound coil of energy vibrating in the chair in front of me. After apologizing for the fact that he couldn't spend much time with me that evening, he bounded out of the room to get and introduce his wife and children. He ushered in an attractive woman and five well-groomed children who all looked exactly like him. Madame Dao also spoke English, and two of the children introduced themselves in labored English, as they were pushed forward to shake hands and welcome me. I thought of Major Kennedy's remark that Dao's wife was nicknamed "the dragon lady," after a newspaper cartoon character. The nickname was meant as a compliment, because Madame Dao was aggressively active in province social welfare programs. Since I felt sure there was need for a lot of social welfare in Chuong Thien, I was glad we had a "dragon lady" to exert influence on the programs.

During supper, I met most of the team. It was a small group, about one-third the size of the team in Dinh Tuong. Kennedy sensed my surprise and explained that about half the team consisted of enlisted men and half of officers. The province pacification program was modest; there just wasn't much to pacify, with the VC controlling as much as they did and the people sitting on the fence. Security was the big problem and got most of the group's attention. The three civilian team members involved in development and pacification easily handled all such requirements. The fourth civilian was a CIA representative.

After dinner, as I started to write some letters, Kennedy dropped by the room to tell me that the movie was starting at the patio in five minutes. When I arrived, the whole team appeared to have congregated, and Kennedy motioned me to a seat he had saved for me up front. Again he sensed my question and volunteered that, for security reasons, the town was off-limits after dark. The movies and the club supplied the only available recreation. I left halfway through the film, wrote some notes for the morning meeting I had called, and went to bed. Machine guns rattled across the large canal by the front gate, and isolated shots rang out to the rear of the compound as I fell asleep.

We were about twenty minutes into the 7 A.M. team briefings when a Vietnamese soldier came in looking for me. True to stated intention of continuing our talk, Dao had sent his driver for me. Dao was in the province administration headquarters a short way beyond the team compound and just off the road to the airfield. With only him and me in his office, Dao gave me a thorough, detailed briefing which covered all friendly and enemy activity in the province. As Kennedy had noted, security was Dao's main concern and improving the training and efficiency of the province territorial forces his first priority. The entire time we were together, he never sat still, preferring to pace up and down before the large wall map to which he frequently pointed.

I decided that if Phuc had talked to him, Dao must know what kind of a person I was, so I decided to gamble. Putting polite and diplomatic maneuvering aside, I asked honest, straightforward questions right from the start. Major Dao's reaction was to narrow his intense eyes, smile, and give me honest answers. Before I left, he introduced me to some of his small civilian staff. For the rest of the day, I drove around the town, visited the regimental compound and introduced myself to the senior regimental advisor, inspected the airfield, and took a slower, harder look at the team compound.

The team briefings continued in the mess hall after the Vietnamese help had left for the night. Kennedy originally had arranged for the briefings to be given in the club, but I didn't want to tie up the only entertainment the team had. The club was a self-help project, built by the team in their spare time from scrounged material. It was the only air-conditioned enclosure in the entire compound—or the entire province, for that matter. Nobody ever asked where the air-conditioner had come from; it was simply enjoyed.

Except for the CIA man, a few senior non-commissioned officers (NCOs), and the agriculture advisor we shared with adjacent Phong Dinh Province, the team was very young. But, to judge by my initial impression, they seemed to make up in spirit what they lacked in experience. By the end of the briefings, several had impressed me particularly. One was Will Pryor, a clean-cut, personable, athletic Ivy League product who was our novice AID representative. The others were Kennedy; Capt. Len Silvers, our supply officer and logistics advisor; and Staff Sergeant Sumner, the airfield coordinator. One key problem became apparent during the briefing. With an admittedly modest province pacification program and counterparts who were reluctant to travel outside the province capital because of poor security, the team's eagerness and frustration led its members to try to do the job by themselves. This had prompted the Vietnamese officials to do less, adding to the team's frustration.

When the briefings were over, I told the group that I understood what was happening and why, but that I wanted no more "American only" activity. I repeated Major Dao's statement that security was his first concern for the immediate future and added that we should concentrate on helping the territorial forces become better soldiers and units. As I also felt that some selected pacification projects could be pushed forward, I applied my old tactic of asking for a plan. To get the team more involved with their counterparts, I required a one-month plan of action and a three-month projection of following actions that gradually would involve their counterparts in joint U.S.-Vietnamese actions. I wasn't interested so much in results as in doing things together with counterparts, no matter how ineffective.

Faced with a completely new situation, I departed from my previous insistence that any U.S. effort should be kept completely in the background. I was willing, I said, to let team members go with their counterparts and show the people both flags. I made sure to stress the word *jointly*. In view of the long history of instability in the province, I had determined the night before that it might be a good idea to let the people and the enemy alike see evidence of American presence and of our support for the government. I also was prepared to recommend to Dao that our team begin to invite counterparts to go along on inspections and fact-finding visits, supposedly instigated by me. Everyone had to make *me* appear the villain. "Inviting" counterparts to accompany actually would mean diplomatically coercing them—without embarrassment, if possible—to come along.

In answer to Will Pryor's question about how they would get to all the isolated government centers, I told the group that I'd do my best to get more helicopter support for the team. I closed my instructions and pep talk with a quotation from Lawrence of Arabia: "Better they do it imperfectly than you do it perfectly, for it is their country, their war, and your time is limited."

Dao agreed immediately to my suggestion that I provide the helicopter transportation and he prod his administrators to go out jointly with my advisors. Fixing his unblinking eyes on me, he spit out his words in machine-gun fashion. The people did need more evidence of the government and of what it was trying to do for them. As the last remark hit directly on my favorite theme, I launched into a philosophical discourse on the insurgency and what I thought it would take to defeat it. During our talk, I mentioned the paper Lien had given me in Pleiku, "Would There Be Another Dien Bien Phu?" Dao was surprised to hear that I knew and had served with Lien, and, speaking more slowly than usual, he said that he had known Nguyen Ba Lien very well. Sadly he added that, for all his faults and revolutionary thoughts, Lien had been a patriot and a good man.

Deciding to change the subject, I walked over to Dao's office window, which looked out on the canal and the insecure rice paddy area across it. I recalled his remarks the day before about security being his first priority and about the need to make province forces more effective. When I asked what his plan was, I was shocked to find that he had none, other than to motivate unit leaders to greater dedication through his own charismatic leadership. In response, I put forward an idea I had for enhancing the effectiveness of province forces.

During my stopover briefings in Saigon, I had learned about the new Mobile Assistance Teams (MATs). Each team was made up of three advisors—an officer, a senior NCO, and a radio operator. Teams could be requested expressly for the purpose of living with and training province companies and hamlet platoons in the necessary fundamentals of operating and surviving. The MATs sounded like just what we needed. The teams would be provided completely equipped to be self-sufficient. They could be kept as long as needed and were to be supported and controlled by the province senior advisor. Only an interpreter needed to be added from the province team. I explained how I thought the teams could help us and asked if the idea appealed to him. Dao bounced up again, having sat for only minutes in the hour we had been talking, and said he thought it was a fine idea. Could I request eight? I had been thinking of only one or two teams to start, but I answered that I certainly would try. On the way back to the compound, I thought about Dao's positive attitude and about the fact that he didn't hesitate or procrastinate but made up his mind on the spot. I hoped that it was because we thought alike and not because he was patronizing and trying to please me. I felt that we thought alike, however.

When I radioed IV Corps from the command bunker, I was promised priority to receive three MAT teams, the first predicted to arrive in two weeks. But there was a catch. I was going to be given a searchlight section as well. What in hell would I do with a searchlight section? I had no need for one, and I didn't want one. Regardless of the total absence of any rational use for the section, the two jeeps with mounted lights and three men for each would be flown to us in a matter of days. As I left the bunker, I looked around the crowded compound, trying to think how the added people and vehicles could be squeezed in. The MATs would have an important purpose and, after a short stay with us, would move out to live with the territorial force companies. But the searchlight teams were going to be dead weight. Sadly, that description of the unneeded searchlight crews would turn out to be all too accurate.

Vi Thanh was mortared that night, with four rounds falling in the vicinity of the 3rd Regiment compound. All missed the compound, but one hit civilian houses nearby. I visited the site with Dao in the morning. Three civilians had been killed and four severely wounded, including children and an old lady. Before we left, Dao made cash indemnification payments on the spot and had social welfare people on the scene to help. The payment of money so soon after the death of loved ones appeared crude and unfeeling to me when I first saw Phuc do it in Dinh Tuong, but I had learned that such a gesture was appropriate, appreciated, and needed. Once we were outside the house, Dao replaced his quiet, sympathetic concern for the families with an explosive, vehement tirade against the VC. I sensed a deep concern for his people mixed with hatred of the enemy.

I followed Dao from the scene of the mortaring to the regimental compound, where he introduced me to his old friend Lieutenant Colonel Hung, the regimental commander. When Hung regretted that, due to other commitments, he couldn't conduct operations where Dao suspected the mortars had fired from, Dao coldly replied that the regimental compound and the vicinity probably could expect more shelling. Two nights later, the mortar rounds fell again. This time six were fired, and two hit the regimental compound, damaging two trucks and causing some slight casualties. Another round maimed more civilians.

Dao sent for me and asked if I would accompany him the next morning on a province operation where he thought the mortar sites were located. Of course, I would go; that's what I was there to do. I wondered what the previous advisor did or didn't do, that Dao should ask "if" I'd go.

The road from the airfield into town continued through town and on south for another five kilometers, where it ended at Hoa Luu village. Hoa Luu was the suspected location of the mortaring, with security, as well as the road, terminating there. Dao's plan was to truck two territorial force companies down the road to join with local units for a sweep of the jungle surrounding the small, sleepy village. By mid-afternoon, the operation had concluded without a shot being fired, but no mortar positions had been found. Dao unexpectedly spent most of the day directing the sweep from a hammock strung between his parked jeep and a store's front gate. While reclining, he continually barked directions and questions at the province deputy for security and his radio operator. After a late, simple soldier's lunch of boiled rice, fish, and green vegetables, we convoyed back to Vi Thanh without incident. Whether as a result of the operation or not, the VC shelling ceased for three days. When it began again, the team compound became a target.

Shortly after midnight, an explosion jarred me awake. I rolled to the concrete floor, scrambled under the bed, and helplessly lay there as four more explosions rocked the room. Each impact was preceded by an oddly familiar buzzing sound. When all was quiet again, I pulled on my pants, strapped on my pistol, and went to see what had happened. One round had fallen in the motor pool, flattening some tires and putting a few small holes in several jeeps. That was the only damage. As best we could determine in the dark, the other rounds had fallen outside the fence near the tennis court and the radio tower. I couldn't get back to sleep, so I sat and reflected on the compound's vulnerabilities. If any of the rounds had hit the sleeping quarters, it easily would have penetrated the thin roof and caused a disaster. The only places that offered any protection from a shelling attack were the sandbagged command bunker and the four fighting bunkers at each corner of the fence. All were too far from where we slept; it would be foolhardy to try to reach them after the shelling started. We needed protection nearer our beds. Surviving any more shelling became the top priority. Getting to the fighting bunkers after shellings, so as to defend against a ground attack, was next in importance.

At breakfast, I directed Kennedy to get all the sandbags we had out of supply and to send Len Silvers to get as many more as he could lay his hands on. Also, the entire team was to be organized in shifts, from sunrise to sundown, to fill the bags. That chore would be our only job until it was finished. When Kennedy replied that the only place to get sand was a pit near the airfield, I pushed him on his way. My plan was to build a set of large, low bunkers between the two rows of sleeping quarters. Those living in the row of rooms behind my quarters would have their doors facing the bunkers and could crawl two steps through holes we would cut in the fifty-five-gallon drums to reach protection.

As for the rooms in my row, we would have to cut small swinging doors in each rear wall, through which we could dive into the same bunkers. Work went on for four days, and I took my turn at the pit shoveling sand into the bags. Another round fell in the compound and more outside near the radio tower before we completed the task, spurring us on in spite of sore muscles and blistered hands.

The rushing roar that preceded each impact still bothered me, so I gathered up some of the shell fragments and sent them to IV Corps for analysis. The answer identified the weapon as a Chinese 75-millimeter recoilless rifle. As I should have guessed, only a high-velocity weapon, and not a mortar, would make the pre-impact sound I had heard. Crater analysis of the shell holes in the compound further showed that the shells came from the paddies southeast of the compound and not from Hoa Luu.

Although Dao was interested in the information, he was more concerned about other developments. He showed me a note sent to him by the VC, asserting that they would eat Tet dinner in his house. Civilians from the outlying areas also told of uncharacteristically open VC boasts that they would soon attack and overrun Vi Thanh. Increasing enemy activity on every side of town—in fact, throughout the province—was adding substance to the boasts. Dao said that he was convinced the attack was coming and devoted himself almost exclusively to plans for defense of the town. Tet was to begin on January 29, only nine days away.

I knew that Tet, the Lunar New Year, was a significant holiday; I had joined in the 1965 celebration in My Tho. But I wanted to understand more about it. By reading pamphlets written for advisors and asking questions of interpreters and province officials, I pieced together its real significance. Tet was the most important and longest holiday of the year. It corresponds to the American Christmas, New Year, Easter, All Souls' Day, and 4th of July combined. It's a family reunion, a spring festival, a national holiday, and everybody's birthday, because everyone is considered one year older on this day. It's a three-day holiday which signifies the beginning of spring as well as a new year. For all Vietnamese, it is a time of solemnity, happiness, and hope. It's a time to pay homage to ancestors, visit family and friends, observe religious strictures and good-luck superstitions, and, of course, celebrate. On the Lunar New Year's eve, every street grows quiet, as families remain at home to participate in required religious ceremonies.

No one imagined that during this Tet, 1968, the enemy would do the unbelievable and violate the agreed-upon annual truce to attempt a countrywide knockout blow. Taking advantage of the deserted streets, the VC counted on the noise of firecrackers—set off at midnight to herald the new year and chase away evil spirits—to mask the initial gunfire of the sneak attack. This year, candlelit ceremonies to honor good spirits and ancestors would be replaced by terror, destruction, and death.

Only one person on our team was exempt from sandbag-filling duties in our wild rush to complete the new bunkers—Capt. Len Silvers, our supply officer. One of the things I'd done soon after arriving was to instruct Len to stay in the air flying to Long Binh supply depot north of Saigon, attempting to requisition, purloin, scrounge, borrow, or steal anything he thought the team might be able to use. Soon he had a daily stream of Air Force cargo planes unloading everything imaginable at the airfield, including mounds of sandbags, stakes and wire, beds, jeep parts, radios, PX supplies, alcohol, stoves, refrigerators, generators, and all manner of other items. I never knew how he did it and didn't ask.

One of his scrounged articles had immediate application in our preparations for the expected Tet attack: a large and very loud Navy electric siren. We hooked it up on the patio roof as our attack alert signal. The siren produced a fierce wail that I'm sure could be heard clearly far out into the rice paddy surrounding Vi Thanh. I often wondered what pandemonium it caused in the civilian families living next to the compound.

As the days ticked by to Tet, the tempo of enemy activity increased, prompting a rise in regimental operations, some in conjunction with province forces around Hoa Luu. On the first such joint operation near Hoa Luu, province units had significant contact with a VC force at a time when I had wandered away from the command post and was looking at the large selection of boa constrictors for sale at a small market beside a canal. When I heard the firing, I started back to where Dao was and met his driver coming to get me. Thinking that the firing meant some trouble which might require me to radio for helicopter gunship support, I double-timed ahead of the driver to the command post, which was set up in a deserted shop on the village street. Nothing was happening there, and the deputy for security casually motioned with his thumb to Dao's location across the street.

When I walked into the open-front building, Dao was playing pool on an old, dusty pool table he'd found. He had sent for me to challenge me to a game. As I leaned against the wall sweaty and panting, shaking my head, he laughed and handed me a cue stick. If Dao sometimes surprised me, he also never failed to do the expected—taking time to mingle and talk with the village and hamlet people wherever we went. He got them to do the talking, and he did the listening. After each conversation, he'd immediately instruct his staff to take whatever action was needed to remedy all legitimate complaints or problems. When operations were over, too, he always waited until all his troops were safely on their way before he'd leave the area. The more I saw of this man, the more I liked him.

When the Hoa Luu operation was finished, our advance security went first down the road, followed by the trucks of province troops, then Dao, myself, and the rear security. About a kilometer out of Hoa Luu, we were ambushed from the banks of a small canal, as the troop trucks crossed the narrow wood and iron bridge over the canal. The VC had let the regular army battalion go by before hitting us. When the shooting began, Mai screeched to a stop just short of the bridge, and I dove from the jeep into the bushes beside the road. Intense pain immediately wracked my right chest and shoulder. I had hit a stack of steel girders that had been placed beside the road for emergency bridge repair and had been obscured by the rapidly growing foliage. As I tried to clear the stars from my head, I heard Dao's voice over the rising crescendo of fire.

Running at a crouch, I arrived at the bridge and saw Dao standing upright on the wall of the bridge security outpost, firing an M-79 grenade launcher and shouting obscenities at the VC. As he reached back for another round from his bodyguard, he was shaking the launcher in the direction of the VC and shouting more epithets. Because the volume of fire from his own troops wasn't great enough to suit him, he turned and directed his anger at them until they responded, then turned it back at the enemy. I couldn't see a thing to shoot at but knew that somebody was out there because the bullets kept zinging overhead, thudding into the mud outpost walls, and ricocheting off the bridge girders. When the firing from Dao's troops began to shred the coconut trees down the canal where the VC shooting was originating, the enemy fire trailed off and stopped. As the troops were loading up on the trucks, a voice from the canal shouted something in our direction which I couldn't understand. Dao turned back, shouted a terse reply, and spat in the direction of the tormentor. Walking back to our jeeps, I reached inside my jacket to rub my aching shoulder, and my hand came out slightly bloody. Dao noticed and asked what had happened. When I told him, he grinned at me with those fishlike eyes, then started to chuckle through pursed lips. I sarcastically thanked him for his sympathy and mustered a forced smile. As his jeep took off, he waved me along, his shoulders now rocking with laughter.

Back at the compound's first-aid shack, I had the medic clean and dress the cuts and bruises. After he finished, he started to ask questions about where and when the ambush had happened and began filling out a pre-printed form. When I found out that he was applying for me to get the Purple Heart, I exploded that he'd better not pull such a trick for me or anyone else. I added that I hoped we never had anybody get wounded, but if we did, he could get them the Purple Heart. I calmed down when I saw that the medic was offended and shaken and tried to put him at ease with a smile and a pat on the shoulder. I found that I couldn't raise my right arm because of the pain and finished the gesture with my left.

Near one o'clock the following morning, the duty radio operator awakened me to tell me that Kien Long District town was under attack and the VC had penetrated to near the advisor's house. I confirmed on the radio that the team was all right, but the district senior advisor gave me a confused and rambling account of what was happening. He ended by requesting immediate helicopter gunship support. Current rules of engagement required that the district chief also concur in the request, so I phoned the Tactical Operations Center for confirmation. Dao came on the phone and answered that the district chief did indeed concur. After I passed the request to corps, I dressed and drove to the operations center to get a clearer picture of what was going on. Dao was leaving just as I drove up, and he assured me that everything was under control. He asked if I could get a helicopter to take us down there first thing in the morning. Did I know that we could no longer use the road to drive? No, I didn't know. I had not realized that the district town was now isolated.

Major Kennedy met me back at the compound when Dao and I returned from Kien Long and visits to two other district towns no longer accessible by road. Can Tho had radioed that Don Oberdorfer, a newsman, was on the way down to visit us. I hadn't heard of Oberdorfer and didn't need his visit at this time, but it was too late to try to stop it. I still had unpleasant memories of reporters who came to Dinh Tuong with their minds already made up about what they wanted to report. They just continued to ask questions of the Vietnamese until they got the one answer they were looking for and then quoted it, disregarding many replies to the contrary.

Oberdorfer arrived on schedule. From the beginning he seemed to be different. He said little as Dao briefed him, and he continually jotted down notes. When he and I were alone later, he squatted on the floor of my room as I spread my map out and continued to write much and say little as I covered what was happening in the province. While declining my invitation to stay and have dinner with the team, he did accept a drink. While I poured it, he alluded to the tense situation depicted on the map, suggesting that I didn't need an uninvited guest to care for. Although I hadn't requested it, Oberdorfer was thoughtful enough to mail me a copy of the story he sent home. I appreciated his gesture and, more important, was gratified to read the factual account he submitted:

Vi Thanh/Oberdorfer

The Vietnam war began in the rice-rich, people-rich Mekong Delta region, and some say that is where it will end. On his third tour of the Vietnam countryside, correspondent Don Oberdorfer reports how far the allies still have to go in an embattled province capital in the Delta.

By Don Oberdorfer

Vi Thanh, South Vietnam—The Viet Cong are spreading the word that they'll eat Tet dinner late this month in the Province Chief's house of this embattled province capital. Major Dao, the plucky Vietnamese Province Chief, says to that—"They'll do it over my dead body."

Lt. Col. Edward Metzner of New York City, the chief U.S. advisor at province headquarters, believes it is possible that the VC will fulfill their boast—but they will have to gulp their New Year's dinner pretty fast if they try.

"If they want to gamble and take the losses, the chances are they can come in and hit us," says Metzner, displaying a map of large areas where four main force VC units roam pretty much at will. "They can't stay long, though," he adds. "A raid here will be only for the propaganda value—and most of that for outside consumption." Vi Thanh (pronounced VEE TAN) is not typical of all Vietnam, but for several reasons it is not a bad place to begin a return journey to the wartorn Vietnamese countryside.

This is the toughest of the tough, hard-core Viet-Cong region, the Mekong Delta. It is also an area where the government troops, the Army of the Republic of Vietnam (ARVN), have at least begun to fight.

Just about a month ago, the ARVN 21st division met two dug-in Viet Cong battalions along a canal in enemy territory six miles north of town. All day and all night, government soldiers hemmed in the enemy, while air strike after air strike rained bombs, napalm, and bullets down on them. More than 400 VC were reported killed, along with 60 ARVN. The action was wildly hailed as the biggest Vietnamese Army victory of the war in the Delta. The headlines were a rarity. Because few American troops are fighting here, the Delta war lacks its share of world publicity. Yet in many ways it is the fundamental theatre. Nearly half of South Vietnam's people and most of her rice are located in the flat and fertile paddy lands stretching from Saigon south along the narrowing Indochina Peninsula to the South China Sea.

This abundant rice bowl of Vietnam is the prize for which men have fought for years. It is often said that the war began in the Delta, and it will end in the Delta.

Judging from the case of Vi Thanh, some progress is being made in this important area—yet there is a very long way to go. Barring a change of heart by North Vietnam or the Viet Cong, final success could take many years.

Vi Thanh itself, a cluster of tin- and thatch-roofed houses and government buildings around a muddy canal, is a former French fortified hamlet, about 150 miles southwest of Saigon. In the first Indochina war, most of this area was controlled by the communist Vietminh, with government influence limited to a few scattered towns. That remains true of the situation today. Officials estimate that the Viet Cong now control 56 percent of the people and area, the government about 30 percent. The rest is contested.

In this situation, the ARVN victory of December 8 was considered particularly significant and important. According to government claims, the enemy in the province was literally decimated: of some 4,000 Viet Cong under arms, about 400 were reported killed.

But only one month later, measurable consequences of this are difficult to find. "For six days the enemy was quiet as a mouse," says one close military observer. "Since then the mice have started getting bigger."

Certainly the enemy hasn't given up on Vi Thanh. Since the big battle VC have overrun three outposts on the edge of town, forcing the government to abandon them and consolidate its guards in fewer and sturdier strong points. During the same period, the VC have shelled Vi Thanh eight times. On five of those occasions, enemy shells fell within the perimeter of the small, heavily guarded U.S. military advisory compound. Miraculously, no Americans were killed.

A week ago, two enemy platoons invaded Kien Long District town, one of the lesser capitals of the province. They ran up two National Liberation Front flags, propagandized the people and marched off the local hamlet chief, another government official and two young men. They have not been heard from since.

All this has minimized the propaganda impact of the ARVN victory among the people around Vi Thanh. Few of them have time to gloat, being too busy building shelters near their beds against the shelling.

Almost every night, the Vietnamese living near the U.S. compound and the government buildings leave their houses at dusk to sleep elsewhere, hoping to escape incoming barrages. Security in the town itself is considered so poor that a U.S. civilian advisor [who has been] in Vi Thanh a month has never ventured across the canal which bisects the town.

"I believe the VC have a definite commitment to hit us," says Lt. Col. Metzner, the Senior Province Advisor. "If they don't do it after all this talk, they may even have trouble collecting rice and taxes."

Metzner sleeps with his steel helmet near his bed, and a path cleared to the shelter outside. "We're not sitting on our duffs," he assures visitors. "We're filling sandbags. We are getting ready."

End Vi Thanh . . .

As I was relaxing one evening before making final checks of the guards, I was called to the bunker radio. The message from corps headquarters was simple and direct: I would be picked up by an Air America plane at the airfield at 2 A.M. I was to be in complete uniform, including steel helmet and web gear. The Can Tho operator said that was all he could tell me, but the message was by order of the corps senior advisor. Further attempts to find out more failed. It was already after 11 P.M., and frustration compounded my weariness. I informed Kennedy of the radio message and asked him to get someone to drive me to the airfield, then arranged with the operations center to provide a security escort.

While waiting in the cool darkness of the runway, I tried to imagine reasons for such a strange requirement. Just then the sky in the direction of Long My lit up with flashes reflecting against low and swift-moving clouds. Distant explosions followed. I switched on the jeep's radio and called the operations center as the flashes intensified. Long My was under a determined attack from a large VC force. The attack was backed up by mortars and recoilless rifles, indicating its seriousness. Since this was no time to be leaving the province, I decided that I was staying; to hell with the trip! Under the circumstances, I'd take the consequences of disobeying the order and live with them.

Just then, the Air America plane's engine roared, as the pilot reversed propeller pitch and rolled to a stop nearby. I hadn't heard his approach while I was busy on the radio. As the pilot leaned over to unlatch and open the door, he shouted for me to hurry; he was running late now and had two more stops to make. After some hesitation, which elicited more urging from the pilot, I jumped in, and we immediately sped off. Once off the ground, the plane banked in a right turn, and I could clearly see the flashes of the battle around Long My. I kicked myself for impulsively jumping in the plane, but it was too late.

Hours later, after changing planes in Can Tho and Saigon, we arrived at our destination, Cam Ranh Bay Air Base. The skies over Cam Ranh were clear, as the central coast was in the middle of its dry season—the opposite of the Delta's monsoons. The mid-morning sun radiated heat off the blacktop runway where we unloaded, and perspiration immediately started to prickle my back. U.S. troops were sprawled everywhere, and more were arriving all the time. Rumors were exchanged as to why we all were there. A group of officers from one of the U.S. divisions had heard that a special V.I.P was coming to see us.

After three hours of waiting, sweating, and eating another paper sack meal, someone finally shouted and pointed out over the bay at a large, sleek jet banking for its landing approach. When the plane got closer, I could see that it was an Air Force passenger jet. After it taxied to a point near the center of the troops and stopped, President Lyndon B. Johnson emerged.

He joined General Westmoreland aboard a jeep for a drive-by review of the formations. That quickly completed, he climbed a low platform and addressed us, to resounding cheers and applause from the other thousands present. I was too far away to see or hear anything and had little real appreciation for the whole affair. All I wanted to do was to get back to Vi Thanh as quickly as possible and see if we still owned Long My. I felt indignant that I had been taken away from the province at a critical time in order to listen to a presidential pep talk.

After a long journey back to Vi Thanh, I listened as Kennedy gave me a complete rundown on the Long My attack, noting Dao's confusion as to why I had disappeared. The attack had been driven off just before daylight, but civilian and military casualties were high. Thankful that we at least retained control of Long My, I went to Dao to explain my abrupt vanishing act. Instead of sharing my frustration and irritation over the whole inane affair, he, in the Vietnamese spirit of respect for power and for authority figures, congratulated me on the honor and the splendid experience.

Chapter 7

Projectile Drift and the Grace of God

Shelling of the town and the team compound continued, and Tet was now only three days away. More civilians were killed and maimed, but our luck at the compound continued to hold. Most of the shells fired at us still luckily continued to fall outside the fence, near the radio relay tower and tennis court, but from one to three hit the compound during each attack. The command bunker and the club were hit, the bunker while it was occupied and the club while empty. Replacement of shredded sandbags was all that needed to be done to repair the bunker, but the round that tore into the club destroyed the only air-conditioner in all of Chuong Thien. I kept my steel helmet, flak jacket, and weapon next to the swinging-door entrance to the protective bunker we had just finished and recommended that the others do the same. Two steps and a dive from the bed let me scoop up my gear and tumble through into the bunker. As soon as it was deemed safe, we would all move out to our defensive positions around the compound. A Team would go to each of the four corner fighting bunkers and a machine-gun crew to a bunkered position I had had built inside our flimsy front gate.

My place was in the command bunker with the radios and the telephone lines to each of the other compound positions. After I arrived, the first order of business was a roll call. A small reserve reaction force was kept in the command bunker, ready to be sent to reinforce where and when needed.

Try as I might, I couldn't get Dao to make a sweep where I was convinced the 75-millimeter recoilless rifle hitting the compound was firing from. He had his hands too full with other security requirements. But the repeated mortaring of the town did move him to conduct another operation at Hoa Luu. As we arrived to set up operations in a farmyard outside the town, the persistent VC opened fire on us with small arms and machine guns from a thick coconut grove about eighty meters away. As the bullets zinged overhead, I dove into a depression a few steps to my right. Unfortunately it was a hog wallow, but at least it got me below ground level.

When the troops moved to flank the treeline and the VC fire stopped, I crawled out of the hole a stinking mess. Since the hot sun was rapidly baking the rank mixture into my uniform, I excused myself to go to the canal to wash off. Dao dispatched someone to follow me and keep watch while I bathed and got rid of most of the foul odor. The search for evidence of the mortar positions proved as futile as our previous attempts, but the local Hoa Luu VC village squad was caught and five were killed.

When the shelling of the compound began, I suspended the movies until after Tet. I didn't want the team bunched up in one small location. As a result, there was little to do except read and try to relax, and these I did until near 10 P.M. Removing only my boots and socks, I lay down on the bed, set the alarm for 11 P.M., and turned out the light. I would do the same for 1 and 3 A.M. Since the VC threat to attack, I had walked around each night at approximately those times to check the Vietnamese guards personally. Decent sleep had become difficult, if not impossible. All was well on my 11 P.M. rounds. A little after 1 A.M., I was with the gate guard and had just offered him one of the cigarettes I carried for that purpose. As he puffed away at it and assured me that he was awake and that everything was normal, I gave him a few parting words of encouragement and started for the guard post at the rear of the compound.

I was only one step onto the concrete walkway in front of the latrine when the frightful roar of an incoming round engulfed me. The explosion of impact caught me in mid-air, as I dove headlong onto the walkway, trying to get behind the sand-filled fifty-five-gallon drums. An instant before I bounced on the concrete, something slammed into my back. I couldn't breathe, I felt numb all over, and I fought to keep from blacking out. Oh God, I thought, I've been hit.

As another round crashed into the mess hall nearby, I forced myself up onto my knees, shot a quick glance back at the gate guard, and reached around to my back to feel the extent of the damage. The guard was okay, having just squatted in place where I left him. The first round hit between us in the parking area; miraculously, he was untouched. As I ran in a painful, limping crouch to the command bunker, pieces of blacktop from the parking area and mud flaked off my back. That was what had hit me. Thank God that was all. Before I reached the bunker, another round crunched to my left, and I dove to the concrete one more time, splinters of wood raining down around me. Finally inside the bunker, I told the radio operator to report the attack to corps, then I turned to the first sergeant and asked for a telephone head count from the other bunkers. Another round crashed nearby, and I knew it had hit the club next to us. Two rounds in rapid succession slammed into the roof of the bunker, raining sand and dust down on us and causing my ears to ring as if someone had clapped them with cupped hands. More shells fell, and I could tell by the different sounds of impact that most were finding their mark inside the compound.

Reports from the bunkers kept coming in. The civilians were all inside the cottage bunker and would head for the compound whenever the shelling let up. One man in the compound was still unaccounted for—a sergeant first class who had joined the team only days before. My watch showed ten minutes since the shelling began. Although a round would whine in and crack every now and then, I wanted to find out about the missing sergeant. If he were hurt, he could be bleeding to death. There was instant and unanimous response to my request for two volunteers to go and look for him. I chose the medic and one of the missing sergeant's roommates. As they prepared to leave, I instructed them to start looking at the man's room and then proceed to bunker number three, where he should have been heading; and to crawl low all the way. They instinctively cringed for a split second at the bunker exit as a shell exploded nearby, then they disappeared. During the long wait for them to return, I concentrated on trying to keep the mosquitoes off my bare ankles. Wearing rubber shower sandals when I went to check the guards was a dumb error that I swore I wouldn't repeat.

When the two searchers returned, the missing man's roommate slumped in a corner. Doc came close enough to whisper that the sergeant was dead. A fragment had hit on the left side of his head above the ear, and they found him on the walkway near his room. Damn, I thought; he must have been running upright instead of in a crouch, or his head would have been below the oil drums. The shelling appeared to have stopped, but small-arms fire still crackled from the direction of the outposts near our edge of town. I called to the first sergeant to have someone go and bring the body to the bunker.

Within minutes, they gently laid the man on a stretcher taken from the wall, and only the buzz of the mosquitoes and static from the radio broke the bunker's gloomy silence. Even though the body was now covered by a blanket, the thick, unmistakable smell of death was strong. The dim emergency lamp, still swaying slightly, cast an eerie, dancing shadow on the dark form on the stretcher. One by one, the reserve reaction squad got up and moved to the opposite wall, as far away from the stretcher as the confines of the bunker would allow.

It was near 2 A.M. by the time that all was quiet enough to call off the alert. As the men drifted back to their rooms, Kennedy, the first sergeant, and I surveyed the damage. One jeep was burning in the motor pool, and several other flames were sputtering nearby. The first sergeant called some people back to shovel dirt on the fires, and we continued our inspection. The mess hall had been hit and also the water tower, pumping house, and club. Considering the number of rounds that had fallen inside the fence this time, the total amount of damage was not too bad. While we were walking beside the demolished pumping house and I was thinking that the round that hit it probably killed the sergeant, a sharp pain stabbed my right foot. I jerked the foot up, and a piece of splintered, wooden planking came up with it. A large nail protruded from the top of my foot behind the middle toe. I had stepped on scattered wreckage from the pump house, and an exposed nail had pierced the shower sandal and my foot clean through. As I cursed and danced around to shake off the plank, the first sergeant pinned it down with his boot, and I jerked free. Limping over to the first-aid shack, I muttered that this was a hell of a way to end a rotten night.

Doc was sitting in his shorts drinking a beer when I walked in. I was so drained of energy and emotion that I hardly felt the antiseptic he poured into the nail hole or the tetanus booster shot he stuck in my arm. Wanting very much to be alone, I hobbled back to my room. When I finally started to relax, my chest, back, elbows, and knees began to throb and ache from my dive onto the concrete and from the tar and mud blown on me by the first explosion near the gate. Returning to Doc's shack to have the scrapes and bruises cleaned, I caught him filling out another Purple Heart form. My name was on it, so I slowly and without a word leaned over and crumpled the sheet from his pad and stuck it in my pocket. As he started to argue the legitimacy of his case that my foot wound was the direct result of enemy action, I admonished him not to demean the medal that some people were getting for being shipped home in a box, no matter how honest his intentions were. The minute the words were out of my mouth, I was sorry I had said them. With our first casualty still lying in the bunker, the timing of that remark couldn't have been worse. As Doc sat slumped on his stool with his sweaty bald spot illuminated by the single ceiling bulb, I wanted to bite my tongue off. I apologized, emphasizing how much I appreciated everything he'd done, especially tonight. When I suggested that we both try to get a little sleep, a weak smile was his only reply.

Sleep eluded me for the rest of the night, and, judging from the muffled conversation, sounds of opening beer cans, and the radio music coming from the other rooms, I wasn't alone. The Medevac helicopter came to retrieve the body long before dawn, landing near the bridge on the road to the airfield and quickly spinning away. I heard Kennedy taking care of things, so I stayed in my room.

Dao was not surprised to see me sitting in my jeep waiting for him outside his house, even though I usually met him each morning either at the operations center or at his office. Before I could say a word, he said that we were going to clear out the area where I suspected the 75-millimeter was firing from. He knew that I would be insisting on some kind of action because of my dead sergeant.

Dao hadn't put together a very large operation, just some police and about half a company of territorials. I felt reassured, however, when we drove past the two artillery howitzers he characteristically had positioned southeast of town to support us. A couple of kilometers beyond the howitzers, we parked and transferred to motorized sampans and began a water and land sweep of the suspected firing area, hectare by hectare. After noon, Dao's radio operator handed him the handset. When he finished talking, he called to me that the searchers had found what they thought was the firing site. The sampan surged ahead, followed the small canal a short way, and pulled up beside a group of police and soldiers waiting on the bank.

A lieutenant led us into the rice field where two low, crude bamboo cradles stood. The bamboo was lashed together and raised at a fixed elevation. Each tripod arrangement still had straps hanging from the cradle where the recoilless rifle quickly could be attached for firing and just as quickly taken away. Empty fiberboard ammunition containers were strewn on each side, and the rice shoots to the rear were black and burned from the backblast of the weapon. Dao took my arm, led me aside, and told me that the police had received word from an informer two days earlier that the VC were operating from here. He was sorry that nothing could be done before my sergeant was killed last night. The informer told him early this morning that a VC squad with a cadre advisor from the North brought the weapon and ammunition to this place by motor sampan each night. They quickly took it away the same way after firing. I thanked him and went back to look at the crude but effective firing cradles. Because recoilless rifles are high-velocity, flat-trajectory weapons and are not made to be shot over long distances, somebody had had to calculate a rough set of range and elevation tables in order to use it in this manner. Most likely it was the North Vietnamese advisor. As an artilleryman myself, I grudgingly gave him credit for his cleverness.

When I leaned down to look along the line of sight of one of the cradles, our radio relay tower loomed exactly in dead center. It was the same for the second cradle, too. What a convenient and unmistakable aiming point for them! It then struck me why most of the rounds fell outside the compound fence. While the enemy gunners certainly were smart, they apparently had overlooked or didn't know about projectile drift.

The right-hand twist of a barrel's rifled grooves causes a projectile to spin in flight to achieve greater stability and accuracy. The spin is to the right and causes the projectile to "drift" in that direction off the original line of aim. Unless you compensate for the expected drift to the right by correcting aim an equal distance to the left of target, the projectile will impact off line to the right. Since the enemy gunners fixed their aim directly at the radio tower, which was on the right side of the compound as they looked at it, most of the rounds drifted a little to the right of the tower and fell outside the fence. The smaller number of rounds that did fall inside the compound were due to either normal dispersion or unintended mistakes at the gun. In either case, the miscalculations had saved us untold grief.

A visitor from Corps was waiting for me when I got back to the compound. It was Col. John Hill, the corps deputy senior advisor. If somebody from corps had to come to see us at the time, I was glad it was him. He'd already seen the results of the night's shelling, so I gave him a detailed account of the events. After I added the findings of the morning's operation, he fell grimly silent. Although I was tired and exhausted, anger pushed me to demand that the radio tower be moved as quickly as possible. While he understood and agreed, he cautioned that the tower's removal might be difficult to accomplish. As he left, he promised that he'd do his best to get approval and action to move it as soon as he returned to Can Tho.

By early evening, Colonel Hill personally radioed back that he'd been unsuccessful in his attempt. A Signal Corps general in Saigon had sole authority over the tower, and the general refused to move it. The tower was a vital link in maintaining constant communications throughout the Delta, he said. Because I didn't want to discuss the details of my concern in the clear over the radio, I answered that the tower's importance made it a priority target and suggested that we shouldn't be surprised if enemy saboteurs got to it and blew it away soon. Hill knew what I meant and sternly, though with a tinge of sympathy in his voice, warned me not to do anything rash while he continued to press for the tower's removal. I felt certain he knew that I intended for the tower to come down, one way or the other, and didn't care that I'd be in a great deal of trouble if I had to do it my way and was found out.

Tet was the day after tomorrow, and tensions were rising visibly with each hour of its approach. Both Dao and I continued to do whatever we could to make sure we were ready for the announced attack. When he had an idea, he'd call me to come and discuss it, and when I had one I'd go to him with it. During one such talk, he asked how long it would take to get the nighttime standby gunships to us. I honestly didn't know but guessed forty-five minutes to an hour, if there were no higher priority missions. I'd just finished adding that we'd probably have to live with that kind of delay and plan around it, when another idea popped into my mind. Desperate situations take desperate solutions, and the more I thought about the idea, the more I was convinced it would be worth a try. I excused myself to go obtain some information, adding I'd return shortly.

We had an exceptional young army pilot, Capt. Bob Langevin, flying a light observation airplane for the province. The unit Bob came from had the radio call sign *Shotgun.* All Shotguns were proud of their missions and loyal to the teams they were assigned to support. Although their primary missions were observation, artillery adjustment and coordination, and direction of helicopter gunship and Air Force attack sorties, they willingly undertook any other necessary job. Armed with only small marking rockets which produced a low-order burst, Bob had made his light and slow-moving plane vulnerable several times by swooping in to shoot his rockets at VC targets when time was of the essence and no other help was available. I'd flown in the back seat with him half a dozen times and respected his skill and dedication.

My idea was to see if Bob would be willing to stop flying during the day and fly instead at night. VC returnees in Dinh Tuong Province had reported that the sound of an airplane or helicopter overhead at night often made enemy units slow down, hesitate, or change tactics. Perhaps the sound of a Shotgun at night might induce the same caution. Even if Bob's being in the air didn't deter night attacks, he would be in position to help us react by providing rapid and accurate situation reports and then adjusting our artillery counterfire against observed enemy gun flashes.

When I proposed my idea to him, Bob answered enthusiastically that he worked for me and if I thought he should fly at night instead of during the day, he'd do it and the heck with what his unit would think. He'd start tonight. Dao also was delighted and agreed to my stipulation that he had to increase security at the airfield after dark and provide armed escort to take Bob out there and back. While Bob was on the ground, his safety was my responsibility. Once he was in the air, he was in somebody else's hands.

Mortars hit the town again after midnight, this time near its congested center next to the market. Only two 75-millimeter recoilless rifle rounds were shot at the compound, and both landed short, near the civilian team cottage. A fragment hit the entrance of the civilian bunker after they were in it, causing a chip of concrete to strike the right eye of our new civilian police advisor. A Dustoff Medevac helicopter took him to Can Tho, and we heard in the morning that he had lost the eye and soon would be en route home. Long after the shells had stopped falling, the thud and clatter of firing from the outposts on the perimeter of town continued. I knew Dao would be at the operations center, so I drove there. He was standing beside the table of radios, thumbs in pants pockets as usual, wearing a headset and monitoring the incessant chatter of messages. After five minutes or so, he saw me and said that the VC were testing us with probing attacks north and east. While I waited for him to finish listening, I phoned back to the compound to get an update from the district teams. Some were suffering through an eerie quiet, while others had had activity similar to ours on their perimeters. Dao was through with the radio when I hung up, so I asked about the civilian casualties from the mortaring. Twelve were dead, and the hospital was filled with the wounded. I excused myself and phoned the compound again and instructed that Doc wake up an interpreter and both go to the hospital to help out. Dao overheard and motioned a thumbs-up sign.

Almost as an afterthought, he mentioned that Mr. Son, the province council chairman, was one of those wounded at the hospital. Dao knew that I liked Mr. Son, a small, white-haired, energetic man who had to be in his seventies. Dao respected the old man, too, because he led just about every activity in town and was fiercely anti-Communist. Whenever Mr. Son and I met, he always came to me to shake my hand. Many times he would speak a rapid string of sentences too fast for me to understand, except that the few words I did grasp let me know that he was reproving somebody, probably either someone on the council or the VC. When Dao left to go home, I went to the hospital.

The scene there was grim. The small staff was busy working on the more serious cases, and Doc was equally busy tending those he could help. All were using flashlights, as the few dim yellow lightbulbs hanging from the ceiling served only to attract some of the hundreds of mosquitos buzzing everywhere. I asked after Mr. Son and was directed to where he lay on the floor. He was suffering in silence, as were all the others. Except for an occasional low groan of pain that couldn't be repressed, the wounded always remained ghostly silent and still.

A young girl comforting Mr. Son, probably his granddaughter, quietly answered my question about his wound. When the shelling started, the old man herded the family into its small mud and wood bunker. He had been hit in the left leg by a fragment before he could get entirely into the bunker. The wound was between the ankle and the knee, and, although it didn't look serious as I knelt and touched his arm, I saw that his face was the ashen grey pallor I had come to associate with death. Speaking softly, I told him that I was sorry he was hurt and to rest. He opened his eyes momentarily, closed them again, and whispered something that I couldn't hear. I patted his arm once more, then wandered through the rows of other injured, wishing there was something I could do to help before returning to the compound.

On the way back, I heard the familiar sound of Shotgun's engine throbbing above the town and hoped that Langevin had spotted the mortar flashes and directed artillery on them. I said a prayer for luck and for his protection.

Chapter 8

Eve of Destruction

The day before Tet January 29, 1968, dawned quiet and surprised us by remaining that way throughout the day. Dao had scheduled a rare morning briefing so that his staff could have the evening free to spend time with their families, circumstances permitting. He concluded his briefing by urging everyone to stay ready and fight courageously if required. Because I was certain that, between official and family requirements, he would be tied up on Tet, I said I wouldn't see him again before late Tet, adding that the team and I would be as ready as he and all his soldiers on an evening that should have been the happiest and most relaxed of the year. As I started to leave, Dao hurried out to the gate and held up his hand to stop me, reminding me that I must come to the Tet party for his staff at one o'clock this afternoon. Trying to sound relaxed, I thanked him and asked if he had heard how Mr. Son was doing. Without any change in expression, Dao replied that Mr. Son had died just before morning from loss of blood. Straining hard to match Dao's unemotional manner, I said that I was very sorry and asked him to express my regret to the family.

Just before time to go to the party, I met with Major Kennedy, the first sergeant, and Will Pryor to check our plans for the last time. Other than staying on increased alert, we planned a quiet day. The team needed an opportunity to unwind and rest up a little before the night ahead. They had measured up well during the weeks when I'd pushed them so hard.

Dao's party was under way when I arrived; everyone looked genuinely relaxed and in good humor. As host,

Dao moved about seeing that all were properly taken care of. Although by other province standards his staff was small, all its members respected and liked Dao. Taking my drink to a wooden bench in the shade of a tree blooming with beautiful purple flowers, I sat alone until I was joined by the province deputy for security.

A large, single explosion boomed somewhere in the distance. I instinctively looked at my watch; the time was exactly 1:43 P.M. Later, when I read the activity log at the operations center, I would note any entry for this time or ask questions if nothing was entered. Five or ten minutes later, Dao motioned to the deputy for security, who leaned over to listen and then went into the house, presumably to call the operations center about the explosion. He returned a few minutes later and talked to Dao; when nothing more was made of it, I remained relaxed. But when a black column of smoke became visible rising over the canal to the west of town, I caught Dao's eye and pointed to it. He glanced at it and looked back at me with an "I don't know" shrug of his shoulders. Soon a soldier tapped my arm and said I was wanted outside the gate. It was the team operations center duty sergeant, who said that the compound had called and wanted me back there right away. I interrupted Dao's conversation with some of his civilian staff and town council members, apologized, and said I'd be back as soon as I could. Mai had the day off to be with his family, and I was content to drive myself and exercise a measure of control over that aspect of my destiny.

The first sergeant met me at the gate and took me to the first-aid shack, where Doc was attending to one of the searchlight crew members. Another crew member was slowly pacing about outside. The man receiving Doc's attention was in a state of dazed shock, but looked all right physically. The first sergeant then quickly told me what had happened.

Without permission, five members of the searchlight team had decided to get in some target practice at the province rifle range after lunch. The range was over the canal in the rice paddies just outside the least secure part of town. Major Kennedy pieced together the story from the almost incoherent survivor in Doc's shack. The jeep passed the range. When the driver realized what he'd done, he started a wide turn and hit a mine. The man who had made it back was blown clear, got up dazed but unhurt, and ran the two miles back to the compound. Kennedy then grabbed an interpreter, jumped in his jeep, and dashed to the scene.

As I ran to my jeep, I cursed Kennedy's impulsive stupidity and uttered a prayer that he would be okay. The VC often waited in ambush around a mining site to fire on those responding or had other mines emplaced to cause additional damage. The first sergeant jumped into the jeep beside me, and we drove over the bridge to the territorial force outpost halfway up the road to the rifle range.

The gate guard summoned the lieutenant commanding the outpost. He understood the situation and immediately provided some of his soldiers to accompany me on foot to the site of the mining. About ten or fifteen soldiers hurried out in various states of undress, strapping on ammunition belts and plopping on helmets as they hustled onto the road. As we moved out at a fast but cautious pace, they fanned out properly on both sides of the road. The lieutenant caught up with us after about thirty meters and, as we cleared the edge of town, I could see the still-burning jeep ahead, upside down. Kennedy's jeep was parked at the firing range entrance, and he was slowly walking to meet us, his head down, staring at the ground. He saluted, which was absurd under the circumstances, then ambled beside me for the remaining twenty or thirty meters to the wreckage. Almost apologetically, he told me that it looked like three bodies were still in the jeep. I sent him with his interpreter to ask the soldiers who were moving out in a circle around us to search and investigate carefully. When he asked what they should look for, I barked to look for trip wires, electrical wires, bodies, parts of bodies, anything.

The crater made by the explosion was very large, and the jeep had been thrown about ten meters to the side, landing just short of a small canal. Flames still licked its burning tires, masking any odor of burned flesh. Still, I instinctively moved around to the windward side of the jeep as I counted two charred skulls and part of a torso through the tangle. As large as the mine must have been, it was a miracle that the man who ran back to the compound had emerged unscathed. When Kennedy arrived back with the truck I'd sent him after, we used its fire extinguisher to douse and cool the twisted snarl of metal before attaching a rope and pulling the jeep wreckage upright. As the jeep rolled over, so did the charred remains, revealing four bodies instead of three. I told Kennedy to take the first sergeant back to the compound and request a helicopter to evacuate the bodies, then to get plastic body bags and meet me at the bridge. Next I turned my attention to getting what was left of the bodies into the back of the truck.

When we were finished, I jumped up onto the truck's running board on the driver's side for the trip back. Although we traveled slowly along the rutted trail, each bump produced a jolt which jarred the charred bodies into new and grotesque positions. The sweet, sickening stench of burned flesh saturated the heavy, still air. I felt nauseous and jumped off the truck and walked far behind it to find a breath of fresh air.

The helicopter was waiting at the clearing near the road to the airfield as we transferred the remains to the body bags. Doc went with the bodies, and I returned to the compound to see if corps had been given all the information needed. When I went to check on the survivor and was told he had been put aboard the evacuation helicopter for Can Tho, I flew into a frustrated rage. How inconceivably thoughtless to make the man ride beside the bags containing the remains of his friends, right after such a nightmarish experience! Banging my fist against the wall, I shouted that the manner of the survivor's evacuation must be clearly stated in the report, so any psychiatrist in the future could know about the circumstances.

After I washed up, I returned to Dao's house, where the party was still going on, although only about half the original number of people remained. Dao immediately came over and asked what happened. When I told him, he grimaced the word *stupid*. When I asked if any cognac was left, Dao slapped my arm and poured one for each of us. By the time we finished our drinks, most of the remaining guests had gone, and I remembered that I hadn't stopped to thank the outpost lieutenant. I asked Dao to make sure that the lieutenant knew of my appreciation, and he assured me that he would see to it personally. As late afternoon shadows darkened the yard, he nodded and waved as he gathered up his children and walked up the front steps into the house.

The eve of Tet came and went without the all-out attack we had anticipated. Nevertheless, tensions remained high, and I rotated reduced crews to occupy the bunkers continuously. Each unfamiliar noise brought a rigid pause, as each man tried to anticipate what might follow. Although I was bone weary, the adrenalin kept flowing, enabling me to keep moving, inspecting, and encouraging. Conditions in the bunkers were wretched, particularly in the machine-gun bunker facing the front gate. Mosquitoes were bad everywhere, but the machine-gun bunker had a foot of water in it, and this seemed to draw triple the normal number of the oppressive insects. All I could do was to visit often, reinforce the necessity of staying alert, make sure the men had enough mosquito repellent, and sit for awhile with them, sharing the futile swatting and the stinging bites.

If Vi Thanh was fortunate enough to be experiencing a relatively quiet night, in the outlying district towns and most of the rest of the country the night was bloody and tragic. I spent the evening and early hours of Tet morning rotating between the compound and the operations center, where reports of probing attacks, shelling, and infiltration attempts continued to arrive each hour. Between my travels, I tried to relax over a beer in the patched club, where small groups came and went throughout the night. Will Pryor, Sergeant Sumner, and I engaged in a game we had started soon after I had canceled the evening movies a week before. The game was a quiz concerning old movie trivia. Our nightly quiz grew into a relaxing and enjoyable diversion. We often carried some particularly vexing challenge to bed when the club closed, hoping triumphantly to return the next evening with the correct answer.

Will Pryor quickly had developed into a dedicated, supportive pillar of strength for the team. Eager to learn and do, he now capably handled three jobs—his own, that of the skittish departed AID advisor, and that of the wounded police advisor. He also was a polished tennis player and used that talent to make friends with Dao's civilian staff. This night, Will, our CIA representative, and the agricultural advisor from Phong Dinh Province would be staying inside the compound with the rest of the team, because I felt it prudent to insist on that precaution. On my last round of visits to the Vietnamese guards in the compound, I gave each two packs of Salem cigarettes and wished them health and prosperity for the dawning Year of the Monkey.

I made my courtesy Tet visit to Dao and his family near noon. I didn't go earlier because I wanted to make sure that visitors of the correct status and prescribed qualities had time to precede me. The Vietnamese believed that the family's fortunes throughout the coming year would be greatly influenced by the importance, stature, and wealth of the first visitor to the house on the first day of Tet. The more important, prosperous, and successful the first visitor was, the more promising the year would be for the entire family. Bad luck was sure to follow if the first to enter the house was unimportant or of low status. Our conversation stayed light and carefree; any other tone would have been in bad taste on the holiday. When it was appropriate for me to leave, I gave each of the children a traditional red envelope with new money in it for good luck and offered Dao and his wife the correct New Year's wish in Vietnamese.

While the notorious 1968 Tet Offensive started with enemy attacks in all but three of the forty-four province capitals, Vi Thanh went unscathed. Ed Schowalter, my replacement in My Tho, was badly wounded in the fierce fighting there and later was evacuated. From Saigon on down, cities that had been secure became battlegrounds. Why then did Vi Thanh remain relatively quiet? After numerous discussions, Dao and I came to several conclusions. First, the town was not much of a capital to begin with. Second, it housed a regular army regiment, and Dao had a reputation as a tiger. Finally, the province was more important to the enemy as a staging area and logistics base for attacks on other provinces in the Delta that were more significant politically. The enemy probably was content to bottle us up so that we wouldn't interfere with their movements. In any case, Dao didn't stay bottled up for long. He went on the offensive.

Although the attack on Vi Thanh didn't materialize, problems abounded throughout the rest of the province. For ten days after the first day of Tet, Dao put together operations to relieve the pressure on the districts. He combined provincial units from Vi Thanh with those of the districts and moved artillery from the capital to augment district guns. At first, the limited security of the road network restricted where we could go. By traveling east for ten kilometers, we could reach Duc Long. From there, another five kilometers to the southeast and we could get to Long My. The other districts could be reached only by air. Kien Long, thirty-five kilometers southwest, could be reached by helicopter or fixed-wing aircraft. Kien Thien and Kien Hung, thirty-five kilometers south and twenty-five west, respectively, could be gotten to only by helicopter. Long My and Kien Long towns were being shelled and were under nightly attack, but they were holding their own. Kien Thien and Kien Hung were surrounded and shelled around the clock, in an attempt to starve them out or force evacuation. Because of their total isolation, there was almost nothing we could do to help other than request air support. All except Kien Hung were small towns. Kien Hung was no more than a fortified outpost with two dozen mud huts clustered around it.

During our ten days of constant operations, we motored six times to Long My to sweep known VC strong points. The Long My district chief, Major Hy, was a fiery and competent battler. The VC respected Hy and many nights tried to eliminate him by pinning down outposts near his house and firing directly on it from jungle tree lines nearby. Hy just kept going after the VC with a vengeance the next morning, patching up his house, and moving his wife and children to the end of the house away from the firing when it began. Dao liked Hy, and, although he never told me much about him, I got the impression that they had been good friends for a long time.

Our helicopter visits to Kien Thien and Kien Hung during this time were hazardous gambles which could be attempted only if the pilot agreed to take the risk. The only way to get into Kien Thien was to descend abruptly and follow a tree-lined canal until abreast of the town, then make an immediate hard turn to the right and fly at top speed just above open paddies into the town's center. The final approach across the paddies ran a gauntlet of VC fire from a tree line paralleling our direction of flight.

I sat in the seat facing out the door, looking into the muzzle flashes of the enemy guns firing directly broadside at us. Dao never wore the flak jacket Len Silvers had scrounged for him, because his troops didn't have any. In deference to his decision, I would sit on mine in the helicopter instead of wearing it, trying to derive some small comfort from the fact that at least my rear end was protected. On these flights I never failed to experience a chilling, profuse sweat, despite the wind rushing through the cabin.

We only could move about in Kien Thien in a low crouch, or the encircling VC would open up with everything they had. The pilots restricted our visits to ten minutes, and they lifted off leaving us behind when the enemy fire came too close. Our first visit was made solely to deliver the payroll to the troops—something I decided not to tell the pilot. Without it, the soldiers and their families couldn't have eaten. Other trips were made to deliver ammunition, radio batteries, and encouragement.

Little Kien Hung was a different story. It sat on a rise completely in the open. When I first saw Kien Hung, I thought of isolated frontier stockades in the Old West under siege by encircling Indians and of the Alamo. Although the oversized outpost technically was a district capital, I couldn't help wondering why either side would shed blood to possess it. Since there wasn't any cover to use in our helicopter approach, we could only be deposited in the center of the cluster of buildings if the pilot imitated a wounded duck and spiraled straight down from a safe altitude. Once on the ground, the pilot would urge us out quickly and spiral up to orbit at a safe altitude again, so as to escape the indiscriminately falling mortar rounds and machine-gun fire until we radioed for pickup. Our visits here served the same three purposes as at Kien Thien—pay the troops, deliver urgently needed supplies, and boost morale a little just by being in that God-forsaken place with them. My greatest concern for the Kien Thien and Kien Hung advisors was that they had become so inured to the danger that discretion was being replaced with bravado. Each time we returned to Vi Thanh, it didn't look as bad as it had when we left.

During the post-Tet period, Vi Thanh continued to be mortared, but less frequently than before. The compound never was shelled again, and I forgot about my intention to blow up the radio tower. We did engage in a twenty-minute firefight one night with a VC platoon that infiltrated to the field between the compound and province administrative headquarters. When the enemy opened fire, the team manned the bunkers in force and released all its pent-up tension and anxiety by therapeutically firing back ten times the amount necessary.

Each day we found it easier to get out and operate farther from Vi Thanh, and we pushed out in directions not attempted before. After being on the defensive for so long, Dao was in his glory. Each operation revealed a new facet of his personality. He was relaxed, happy, and sometimes even mischievous but always the professional commander of his troops and, to the population, a considerate province chief. In late February, Dao was promoted to lieutenant colonel—small enough reward for the extensive contributions to security he was making.

Almost daily operations continued into mid-March, always pressing farther from Vi Thanh. Intermittent early rain showers slowed the movement of troops through the rice paddies but not the tempo of action. As we sat relaxing over a pot of thick, black tea in a mud-and-thatch farmhouse on the banks of the O Mon Canal in an area we wouldn't have dared to enter before Tet, Dao was discussing the intelligence that had brought us to operate there. The recent ambush of a VC courier had revealed the hiding places of the Vi Duc village local VC committee and the time and place of a scheduled meeting. Dao's operation caught the gathering in progress, and a short fire fight ended with four VC killed; blood trails through the thickets indicated that some of those who had escaped were wounded. In

Vietnamese 7th Infantry Division Psychological Warfare Section.

Ban Me Thuot, Central Highlands, April, 1967.
Lt. Col. Nguyen Ba Lien, II Corps deputy for pacification, inspecting rural development projects. Dick
Kriegle, AID representative, is in the center; I am
on the right. Lieutenant Colonel Lien later was killed
when his helicopter was shot down by ground fire.

My Tho City, Dinh Tuong Province, September, 1967. Visit of President Nguyen Van Thieu. To the left rear are Lt. Col. Tran Van Phuc, province chief; myself; and Peter Brownback, deputy province senior advisor.

My Tho City, Dinh Tuong Province, September, 1967. Visit of U.S. Sen. Edmund Muskie to inspect preparations for the first presidential election. Briefing the senator are myself and Mr. Hoi, province deputy for administration.

Chuong Thien Province, March, 1968. Province Chief Maj. Le Minh Dao in a province operation command post.

Da Dung Mountain (Nui Da Dung), April, 1970. This Viet Cong fortress, honeycombed with caves, was located inside Cambodia near Ha Tien, Vietnam. The province chief of Kien Giang was ordered by the ARVN to capture it with his province militia.

Hon Soc Mountain, U.S. radar site, May, 1970.
Major Canh, site defense commander, and his son,
shortly before the Viet Cong attacked.

Tieu Can District, Vinh Binh Province, December, 1970. Left to right: Captain Gam, Tieu
Can district chief (later killed in an ambush); Lt. Col. Nguyen Van Tai, province chief;
myself; and a local hamlet chief.

Vinh Binh Province, February, 1971. Col. Chung Van Bong (second from right) arrives to replace Lieutenant Colonel Tai as province chief.

Kien Giang Province, 1972. I am surrounded by children of Hieu Le village in the U-Minh Forest, after its reoccupation by Captain Trinh.

Kien Giang Province, September, 1972. Col. Huynh Van Chinh, province chief (front left, in fatigue uniform) inspects a Revolutionary Development Cadre youth program. I am following.

Continental Palace Hotel, Saigon, May, 1973. Major General and Madame Dao, far left and right, attend my wedding to Pham Thi Cam Nhung, national women's tennis champion of the Republic of Vietnam (center, right).

a matter-of-fact tone, Dao related that he had forgotten to tell me they also captured a document indicating that the VC had put a price on my head. Thinking he was kidding, I asked what I was worth. Dao turned to the province intelligence officer, who took out his notebook and answered 25,000 piasters (approximately $200 U.S.). I should be honored, Dao said, because that was a lot of money for a mid-level foreigner and showed that I had impressed the VC spies on the province staff. I replied as jauntily as I could that I was indeed honored; but inside I was suppressing a queasy feeling. The thought that informers in Vi Thanh were paying attention to me made me wonder what added precautions I should be taking.

My preoccupation with security and the amount of time spent on operations made me all but forget the other side of pacification. Like so many others, I was beginning to equate winning the war with killing the enemy. Reviewing and editing the team's "Quarterly Review of Pacification" report after Tet, I received a pleasant surprise that helped me place things in perspective. While I was making mental excuses for concentrating on the shooting side of the war, the team members and their counterparts who were responsible for development programs were moving ahead quietly on their own.

In order to get children back into hamlet schools with no teachers, Rural Development Cadre teams were rotated into Vi Thanh and trained to teach. The same was done with medical training, so that rural dispensaries could be reopened. Several hamlets in marginally secure areas even bought material and built their own schools, to entice the cadre to come to them. Joint U.S.-Vietnamese teams were conducting public administration courses out in the districts and were making unannounced follow-up visits to check on the conduct of civil programs. A similar joint effort had brought about improvements in the squalid province prison, with a variety of courses offered to both police and prisoners.

In addition to overseeing the completion of the new AID-funded province hospital, team members bought cement with their own money and built a helipad next to the hospital in order to speed both local treatment and evacuation. Although I had seen the medical civic action teams that accompanied province operations and accomplished so much good with the rural population, similar teams now were going with district troops and were working alongside civilian medical cadres in district and village dispensaries. In a surprising move, the national police headquarters in Vi Thanh had formed a cultural drama group that was giving performances for hospital patients and townspeople. Voluntary social welfare projects were springing up everywhere under the guidance of Madame Dao.

While the list of accomplishments perhaps was modest compared to what was being done in other provinces, our progress was being made against tremendous odds, given the long-standing VC control and influence, and

I recognized the unwritten courage and dedication required to achieve it. A handwritten note from Will Pryor was clipped to the bottom of the report, telling me that all the advisor teams were giving English language classes to various groups throughout the province. The Vi Thanh team also had started its own "Clothes for the Needy" program. Friends and families at home were being urged to donate money, old clothes, toys— anything—for the poor and the refugees.

But the single most important, and the most gratifying, accomplishment of all was the institution in Chuong Thien of the country's first land reform program. Selecting a province rated as the most insecure in the country for such a politically and psychologically charged pilot program initially might have seemed .unwise, except for two things. The attitude of the province chief and his staff toward land reform was positive, and they pledged wholehearted support and cooperation. Second, Chuong Thien contained within its borders thirty thousand hectares of former French land—the largest amount in any of the provinces. (A metric system hectare equaled approximately 2.47 U.S. acres.) Some of the land, ten thousand hectares, had been expropriated from the French government after the fall of Dien Bien Phu in 1954. The remaining twenty thousand hectares had been purchased from French landowners by the government in 1960. Prior to 1962, the expropriated lands had been given to 9,331 farmers, but until now only 309 titles had been distributed. Under Dao's supervision, his newly arrived land chief was forging ahead with title distribution, astonishing the Saigon bureaucrats by clearing 185 additional titles in the few weeks he'd been in the province.

In spite of the obvious popularity of the program with the farmers, there were problems implementing it. Some Saigon officials harbored hopes of getting large tracts for themselves, and many village officials persisted in the old practice of collecting rent for land already owned by the farmers. In addition to processing and distributing remaining ownership titles, the program called for selling outright the twenty thousand government-purchased hectares to farmers who presently were cultivating the land. Because only one-fifth of that land was located in areas under government control, its distribution would send a deep and long-lasting message throughout the VC-controlled areas.

One of the initial goals of officials of the province Land Affairs Office was to make eight hundred farmers in marginally secure Vi Duc village the owners of the eighteen hundred hectares they were currently cultivating. After only twenty-eight hours of registration, half of those eligible responded, including families of VC soldiers out in the jungle. Anyone presently working the land was eligible to own it, a five-hectare limit being the only restriction. Depending on the land's productive capacity, the price ranged from 2,500 to 8,500 piasters per hectare, or $20 to $68 U.S. Payments were to be spread over a twelve-year period, with no yearly payment to exceed the current annual rent.

When the Vi Duc village administrative committee opposed and tried to sabotage the program because they were collecting the rent for the government and were allowed to keep up to 20 percent, Dao personally went to the village and quickly remedied the situation. Word of his anger rapidly spread to other village committees, and few were as open in their dissent. One seventy-year old farmer in Vi Duc lifted our spirits when he told Dao he hoped the government would win over the Communists because this government finally had recognized his ownership of the land he had tilled as a tenant for over thirty years. I remembered an old saying: the guerrilla wins if he does not lose, and the conventional army loses if it does not win. Maybe the land-reform program and the concern it was causing the VC would mark the start of our winning.

Since the pendulum of violence never stopped swinging, sad events kept me from becoming complacent about security. The province chief of neighboring Phong Dinh Province was killed in an ambush that just missed catching his advisor, too. They had become just a little too predicable in their movements. An electrically detonated mine made the province chief and his jeep unrecognizable. His advisor, following behind, was just far enough away to escape injury. Not long after, the civilian province senior advisor of Go Cong Province east of Dinh Tuong, Rudy Kaiser, was killed while accompanying province forces on a sweep through an area I had visited many times. An otherwise routine operation became a tragedy when a larger-than-expected VC force was encountered and Rudy went to help. Since I would have acted similarly, a CORDS message cautioning all province senior advisors to stick to our advisory roles and exercise prudence struck me as ludicrous as well as tardy.

The familiar voice of Bob Langevin on the radio at night was always a comforting reminder that Shotgun was overhead and ready to help where needed. Bob already had saved one outpost from being overrun, by firing his marking rockets at a VC mortar position and at enemy troops closing in on the outpost's perimeter wire. The turning point came when Bob scored a direct hit on one mortar. When responding helicopter gunships arrived, Bob then accurately guided their fire to help rout the attack. A few nights after that episode, the VC attempted to ambush Bob at the airfield. It was a simple task for the enemy to get a few men with automatic weapons through the thinly spread perimeter guards, who undoubtedly had become complacent during weeks of uneventful night takeoffs and landings. The VC hid beside the runway and opened fire as Bob was accelerating past. Luckily, when he saw the tracers converging on him, he was able to jerk back on the stick and lift above them. After he radioed the position of the VC fire to the operations center, Bob continued his flight over the province. We both interpreted the attack as affirmation of his effectiveness.

Kennedy was promoted to lieutenant colonel, finished his tour, and went home at the end of May, 1968, happy on all counts. Before he left, Dao put together a ceremony between rain showers in front of the muddy fish market. He presented Kennedy with a medal. Medals were the only available way to express thanks, and most advisors got one before leaving for home. The citations accompanying all advisors' medals included a glowing description of accomplishments which either were grossly exaggerated or never had occurred. Supposedly, such hyperbole was necessary to assure that the medals would be approved by corps headquarters. While the citations added a rare note of humor to an otherwise fairly grim existence, the situation was sad, too, because the Vietnamese soldiers bearing the brunt of the violence had to accomplish the truly heroic to be given even small recognition.

Only the award given to faithful and reliable Shotgun accurately recorded his quiet bravery and calm courage, because appreciative district chiefs contributed parts to Langevin's citation. Bob hurriedly left when his tour was over, eager to join his family in Rhode Island, and I had to forward his medal for presentation at his next assignment. I hoped that when his new boss read about Bob's deeds, he would appreciate what type of man Bob was.

Sad events continued each week. The persistent and shrewd enemy floated an unexploded thousand-pound U.S. Air Force bomb down the canal. It was wired to blow up the main bridge connecting the east and west sides of town. Luckily, one of the wires snagged on some submerged roots, and we escaped the destruction that would have engulfed the homes crowded near the bridge.

Several Lambretta minibuses fell victim to mines outside of town, and all aboard were killed or maimed. With the same disregard of human life, the VC murdered outright or abducted village and hamlet officials, teachers, respected elders, police, territorial force soldiers, and their families. Most of those abducted never were seen again. Major Hy's luck ran out in Long My, too. He was killed while doing what the VC feared and respected him for most—leading an attack against them. While Dao showed no outward sign of emotion at each sad turn of events, he pushed operations with new intensity after each setback.

Some good things occurred, too, and human nature helped us to focus on the positive. Len Silvers succeeded in surpassing all his previous performances by "expropriating" vast amounts of the correct medical supplies at the time they were most needed at the hospital. And a bus company in Can Tho began to schedule daily trips to and from Vi Thanh, an unprecedented acknowledgement of new security on the road. On a personal note,

Dao called me to the police station to present me with a Vietnamese national identification card. The ID card was authentic in every respect. I was fingerprinted, photographed, made an honorary citizen, and given card number 0000001, with the name Nguyen Van Metzner. As Dao presented the forged card with the assistance of a nervous police chief, he announced that he had chosen the family name of the country's president for me. Shaking my hand, he said that I was more Vietnamese than I knew. It occurred to me that if an American could be given a forged controlled document, the VC surely have all they need, too. The realization didn't diminish the honor I was accorded, however, and I humbly thanked Dao.

Chapter 9

Battle for a Church Steeple

Dao surpassed all his previous exploits one evening in mid-June. A telephone call summoned me to his house around 9 P.M. Seated at his dining room table, he was poring over a map with the deputy for security and the commander of province units northwest of Vi Thanh. Dao cautioned me that we must take every measure to keep this operation secret, particularly since VC informants had penetrated the province headquarters. As the plan unfolded, I couldn't believe what I was hearing.

Probably every province chief and military commander in the country was being coaxed, flattered, coerced, and even threatened by advisors to operate at night. Yet Dao, on his own, had decided to go against a VC target at night in an area I wouldn't have recommended. Until the attack began, only the three of us in the room, plus several trusted troop commanders and the advisors to accompany them, were to know the objective and the details of execution. When Dao finished explaining, the time was 9:40. I was to gather and brief advisor teams for four territorial force companies and the command group and return to Dao's house with them at 1 A.M., ready to go. Not only were we going this very night, but, led by Dao himself, the entire force would *walk* to the objective!

Leaving our jeeps at Dao's house, we walked with him to the marketplace in the town's center, where two of the four companies had assembled. Advisors joined their units, and the column filed silently toward the bridge leading to the western half of town. Only the muffled clanking of equipment and weapons hinted at anything out of the ordinary in the still, moonless night.

Once over the bridge, we made brief stops at two outposts to pick up the remaining companies. After each pause, during which a chorus of barking dogs and honking geese sounded disturbingly louder than usual, the line continued through the rest of town and into the flooded paddies to the northwest.

Our objective was the village of Ngoc Hoa, exactly ten kilometers away. An informer had identified the village as a frequent resting place for one of the local VC companies, and the unit was reported to be there now. In addition, Ngoc Hoa was the hiding place for a large number of government army deserters. I'd seen the village many times from the air, and it had the deceptively peaceful, sleepy look of a rural town. The village center was dominated by a surprisingly large Catholic church, its tall spire visible far above the surrounding palm trees. As we began our march through the rice fields, it occurred to me that anyone in the church steeple could see out for a great distance.

Although small canals paralleled our route through the flooded rice paddies, Dao chose to walk rather than risk giving the operation away by collecting the large number of sampans required to transport the troops. We had four hours and forty minutes before dawn to travel the ten-kilometer distance, gather sampans in the vicinity of Ngoc Hoa while detaining their farmer owners, cross the canal that formed the village's southeast border, move all units into final position, and execute the surprise attack. Flank security fanned out once we reached the open fields, then the long line clanked, sloshed, and gurgled slowly forward. Radios had to be turned off, so, when information had to be passed, word was whispered forward or backward. Occasionally a light flickered momentarily in the far, flanking tree line, and several distant flares from some remote outpost caused progress to clank to a halt. Movement resumed again when all seemed to be well.

About half way to Ngoc Hoa, a bright, yellow glare lit up the column ahead of the place where Dao and I were positioned. Dao uttered a curse— one of the few I ever heard from him—and we both sped ahead to see what happened. A circle of soldiers surrounded a frantic advisor who was stomping a still-sizzling smoke grenade into the mud beneath the paddy water. It was my turn to curse when I saw that an advisor was at fault. The captain had hung several of the grenades on his backpack by their pin rings, and a stumble in the mud had torn one loose and activated it. I knew that Dao had two concerns: a possible ambush, or that the VC force in Ngoc Hoa would be alerted and steal away. After he conferred with his deputy for security, they decided to risk continuing on, since runners from peripheral security squads persuaded them that our location and intentions weren't compromised.

When we reached the canal before Ngoc Hoa, it was light enough to distinguish forms, and the wind surged, bringing brief showers. All the troops ferried across in the appropriated sampans and secured the far bank. The command group followed over the canal, which was wider and flowed much more swiftly than I had expected. As I balanced precariously in the narrow, bobbing sampan, we reached the other side safely. My relief was short-lived, as I saw that two log bridges remained, over a turbulent feeder canal. Such rural bridges were called "monkey bridges" by the Americans, because it took the agility and balance of a monkey to keep from ending up in the canal. I wasn't that agile and even in good weather had extreme difficulty navigating this kind of obstacle. Now rain and slick mud from the feet of those who had preceded me made the logs as slippery as grease. I made one foolish attempt to cross the logs upright and sprawled forward, straddling the main log with my arms and legs. Then I flipped over on my back and squirmed in that manner to the other side. The second bridge was traversed in a similar manner. As soon as I was across, shots rang out, signaling that the attack was under way.

Dao was nowhere in sight, but the deputy for security waved for me to follow as he ran by. The command post was settling into a storage-like concrete structure at the edge of the village market place, and the advisors and Vietnamese radio operators were struggling to erect their long antennas outside the entrance in the worsening wind and rain. Wiping the rain from my face and pausing to catch my breath, I radioed back to the compound to have the new Shotgun replacement standing by at the airfield, ready to come up over the operation if the weather cleared. Langevin's replacement was a first lieutenant who, because of his youth and inexperience, caused me more than a little concern.

By mid-morning, the rain and sporadic, lingering gunfire both ended. The results had not been all that we had hoped for, but they were not bad: no friendly casualties, eight VC killed, two weapons recovered, and sixteen VC suspects and army deserters captured. Dao called for me to go with him to the church, where more VC and deserters were hiding up in the steeple. An attempt to climb the single ladder to the highest part of the steeple elicited shots, all luckily missing the climbers. When we reached the church courtyard, Shotgun appeared overhead, and his arrival gave me an idea. Dao agreed. With Shotgun and the compound command bunker both on the operation radio frequency, I instructed the compound to get twelve gas masks and six tear and vomiting gas canisters from the supply that we had stored for compound defense and to package them securely and watertight for a drop at our location. The parachute was to be a bed sheet from the laundry. I had to talk around the identification of the actual items, because I didn't want to identify the masks and the gas in the clear on the radio. The compound got the message and agreed.

The plan was to have Shotgun drop the package in the large front courtyard of the church next to a landmark he couldn't miss, the steeple. After being instructed in the use of the masks and the gas, soldiers selected by Dao would try to force out those still in the steeple loft. I knew that there were those back home who had protested the use of riot-control agents for purposes other than defense, even when it meant saving lives, but I didn't care if word of my use of it leaked out.

When Shotgun radioed that he had the package and was returning to the operation, I went to the church courtyard with a backpack radio to direct him on the drop. When he was overhead, I told him to circle the church. As he did, I asked if he could see the large courtyard in front, next to the steeple. He asked which side of the steeple. I growled that there was only one courtyard and that I was standing in the middle of it, waving my arms. After telling him that he was too high and should descend more and look for a square, open place near the steeple with red flowers around it, I switched off the microphone and shouted in the air that he must be blind not to see it. How I wished Bob Langevin were still with us! The pilot said that there were people all around the church and asked if I could give him a compass bearing from the steeple. Just as I was about to lose my temper and let fly a string of obscenities I'd be sorry for later, the lieutenant broke in and added that he thought he saw the courtyard now. Yes, he had it, and the package was away. Not wanting to believe what I saw, I watched the bedsheet balloon away from the plane on the opposite side of the church, then disappear into the mangrove beyond. Despite forty minutes of close searching by twenty or thirty soldiers, the package was lost.

As we left Ngoc Hoa, I had the uneasy feeling that we'd see the masks and gas again. The VC were extremely skillful at using our side's mistakes against us, as with the thousand-pound bomb floated under the bridge in town. As for the VC and army deserters in the steeple, surprisingly they were allowed to stay where they were, after the church's rector interceded to dissuade Dao from burning down the steeple.

For most of the long walk home through the steaming rice fields, the sun stayed out, baking the mud that was splattered up to our hats. A little over halfway back, four large motorized sampans came up the canal parallel to us. From the edge of the canal, Dao shouted to ask if I wanted a ride back. As much as I wanted to accept, I asked if he was riding back. As I had suspected, he said he was walking back with his soldiers. I replied with a forced smile that I also was walking back. Some of the lame and those with heavy loads climbed into the sampans, including half of the radio-toting operators, and the boats putted off. Our slow, plodding trudge continued past the edge of the paddies, through the western side of the town, over the bridge, and into the marketplace. We arrived at 4:30 P.M., fifteen and a half hours after we started.

Back at the compound as the first gulps of a cold beer washed away my parched hoarseness, I could hear the story of the experience being told and embellished upon in the adjoining rooms. Immediately after my shower, I sat down to write the after-action report of the operation, while details were still fresh in my mind. I needed no embellishment to impress Can Tho and Saigon with Dao's daring and only omitted one thing, our abortive air drop. The whole operation, from beginning to end, had been unmatched as a display of initiative and courage, and subsequently it was cited as an example many times, the limited results notwithstanding.

My shortening temper signaled that it was time for me to get a change of scene. I applied for rest and recuperation (R and R) leave in Bangkok and eagerly awaited my orders to go.

The seven days of leave went quickly. I ate well, drank well, saw Thai boxing, visited all the temples and the floating market, and closed the nightclubs in the wee hours of the morning. Early-afternoon soaking baths and massages rejuvenated me. Although I felt relaxed and was having fun, my dreams and nightmares took place in some rice paddy. If I awoke during the night, it took a moment of adjustment to realize that I was in a hotel room and not in my room at the compound. Whenever that happened, I'd get dressed and go for a long walk, something I could not do in Vietnam, then I returned to a restless and uneasy sleep. It was early July, 1968, and my tour of duty in Chuong Thien would be finished on August 22. I tried to push the thought out of my mind.

Back in Vi Thanh a big problem greeted me. Two battalions from the U.S. 9th Division at Dong Tam had been moved into the province and were camped around the airfield and beside the road. As Mai sped from the airfield to town, we passed troops sitting on open, unshielded wooden-box latrines, waving at passing sampans on the canal and passenger-loaded Lambretta minibuses traveling the road. Other soldiers with only towels were going to and from a shower set up on the canal bank. The towels were draped over their shoulders. Given the natural modesty of the Vietnamese and the pains they took to hide the naked body, I knew things had to be in an uproar in town.

On each of the last three days, Dao had checked two or three times to see if I was back. When I walked into his office, he brought the problem up right away, describing the steady stream of town councilmen and elders who had filed in to complain, imitating their irate words and gestures for my benefit.

In a stroke of good luck, Lt. Col. Ish Pack was the commander of the U.S. task force at the airfield. Ish and I had been together three years earlier with the 7th Division advisory detachment in My Tho, he as an operations advisor and I as the psywar advisor. Now Ish was second in command of the parent regiment of the two battalions and was commanding the units on the mission in the province. When I explained the problem and told him of the concerns of the townspeople and the province chief, he at first gave me the old line that, since we were in the middle of nowhere, it wasn't that big a problem. I strongly asserted that it definitely was a big problem and that he had to put up latrine and shower screens. Ish knew that if Dao complained, he'd be ordered to comply, and he promised to do what was necessary to set things right.

Eager to find out why U.S. units had been sent to the Delta south of Dinh Tuong Province for the first time, into an area heretofore the exclusive responsibility of the Vietnamese, I asked for a rundown of the plan that had brought him here. Ish took me to the map and outlined his mission in general terms. It was a simple plan, dumb and straightforward. Staging out of the airfield, the battalions were to conduct heliborne assaults into VC bases located in the most impenetrable and difficult areas of the province. The VC were there, all right, and the base areas were accurately defined and pinpointed by Corps in Can Tho and by headquarters in Saigon. Dao and I had known all that for quite awhile. But we had stayed out of places into which it would have been disastrous to venture. The enemy had prepared positions and could easily evade, hide, ambush, attack, or hit and run at will. He never could be surprised in his own territory. Not only were Dao and I not consulted prior to or during the U.S. move into the province, but also none of the details of subsequent operations were confided to Dao for fear of compromise. I was excluded as not having a "need to know." Dao just shrugged it all off as one more example of foreign prejudice.

Ish's operations went on for several weeks, with unnecessary casualties and minimal results. Had the decision makers at Corps and Saigon conferred with Dao and me beforehand, we might have saved them the trouble and the losses. After the battalions left, Vi Thanh returned to normal—no better and no worse.

The initial nudity problem, while small and unimportant in itself, was symbolic of a larger problem. The U.S. military was out of touch with Vietnamese realities in general and with the goals and objectives of the political conflict in particular. The episode reinforced my early realization that the farther removed one was from the roots of the struggle, the more distorted and bewildering the play of events seemed.

The remaining weeks sped by too quickly. My orders arrived, assigning me to command an 8-inch self-propelled howitzer battalion at Fort Carson, Colorado. Getting an artillery command pleased me very much, temporarily softening my sadness at leaving. During the final week, Dao, his staff, and the team took time to express their appreciation and even said that they were sorry I was leaving.

Dao's staff hosted a dinner for me at the home of the deputy for security, at which the deputy presented me with a 9-millimeter French pistol captured at Ngoc Hoa. Dao followed with a garden party at his house in my honor. Guests included his civilian staff, the town council, and some of the more prominent town elders. A number of the staff from the province hospital even dropped by the compound to wish me well. And the day before I was scheduled to leave, the team invited Dao to the club to participate in my farewell party. I felt privileged to have had the good fortune to serve with such uniformly fine, considerate, dedicated, and courageous people. I found it difficult to put my feelings into words when they gave me a plaque and a framed citation. Will Pryor read the citation:

> The Officers and Enlisted Men of Advisory Team 58 unanimously select Lieutenant Colonel Edward P. Metzner, Province Senior Advisor, as a Lifetime Member in appreciation for his outstanding leadership and personal interest in the health and welfare of each and every one under his command.

I didn't sleep after the party. In the morning I'd be gone, and I wanted to stay awake and remember. I dressed and walked slowly around the dark, quiet compound. I gave my remaining Salems to the guards, talked about families and small things, and stopped to dig my toe in the pitted blacktop where the VC recoilless rifle round had fallen between me and the gate guard. Looking back, that incident seemed very long ago. A flurry of small-arms fire clattered somewhere out along the road to Duc Long, and I imagined that the firers were telling me that nothing would change when I left. On impulse, I got into my jeep and drove out the front gate, past the befuddled guard who opened it. Occasional showers cleared the pre-dawn mist as I circled the deserted marketplace, went by the hospital where lights still burned, and drove past the partially reconstructed civilian houses hit by the last VC mortar attack. When I returned to the compound, the sky to the east of town was beginning to turn from black to a morose grey.

Dao had asked that I drop by his house before leaving, and I hurried loading the jeep with Mai so I wouldn't be late for the helicopter, which was due in shortly. After his whole family bid me farewell, Dao presented me with his gift, a large and beautiful picture. Against the black lacquer background, an ancient battle scene was inset in etched mother of pearl. The dominant figure was a leader on horseback, charging forward with a sword outstretched in his right hand. A brass plate at the bottom was inscribed to me as province senior advisor, "Presented by Lieutenant Colonel Le Minh Dao, Chuong Thien Province Chief, Republic of Vietnam." As Dao handed it to me, his intense eyes softened as he explained he chose this because it reminded him of me, always charging hard ahead.

I broke our prolonged handshake to say that it was time for me to go. Dao, his wife, and all five children waved from the gate as Mai careened off toward the airfield. Three vehicles of advisors joined in behind us as we passed the road to the compound.

A crowd of other advisors, Vietnamese staff officers, civilian officials, Ba Hoa, and some of the kitchen help were waiting for me in front of the airfield terminal building. Fighting back tears and forcing a wide smile, I moved quickly through the group shaking hands, as Mai loaded my belongings into the helicopter. Will Pryor was the last in line and thrust an envelope into my free hand. I felt an urgent need to get to the helicopter, and when I did, Mai was grinning and weaving his nervous shuffle while saluting and extending his other hand at the same time. I ruffled his hair and shouted above the whir of the rapidly turning rotors for him to take care of himself and to slow down for the next senior advisor. Turning to a crewman, I asked where the black lacquer plaque was and, when he pointed to it, I cautioned him to be careful with it and jumped in.

As we lifted off, I put the headset on and asked the pilot to take one last turn around the town for me. We made a wide, lazy circle, which, because of the town's small size, didn't take long. My gaze moved from the high church steeple in distant Ngoc Hoa to the still unfilled mine crater on the road near the rifle range, then to the radio relay tower and southwest toward the VC recoilless position. The helicopter suddenly climbed rapidly, then went into a steep dive and bore down on the airfield at top speed. As we ran the length of the runway at a height of about fifty feet, the crowd was still there waving. Then they sprang their final farewell surprise. Flares and colored smoke grenades were fired and tossed high. Shotgun came flying by in the opposite direction, throwing out more smoke grenades which streamed down and bounced off the runway. The helicopter pilot and copilot turned around and gave me a thumbs-up sign, teeth grinning under their helmet visors. I smiled and threw a thumbs-up back, to show appreciation for their part in the last-minute gesture. I also appreciated that they didn't make any comment over the intercom. At that moment, I couldn't have answered. I was reading the note Will Pryor had handed me.

August 22, 1968
LTC Edward P. Metzner, PSA, Chuong Thien Province
Dear LTC,
It isn't very often that someone comes along in your life that affects and inspires you to be a better person and to think more deeply into your job, your life, your goals and sensitivity to others. You are one of those people, and serving with you has enriched my life and ideas, and I am grateful to have been an associate.

As you have often said, "We in Chuong Thien with Team 58 have a special bond." I will always remember these days with great affection and appreciation.

Every best possible wish for your success in the future, and I know we'll meet again some time . . . maybe at an old movie.

Regards,
Will

Chapter 10

"The Ambassador Requests Your Return"

When I arrived at Fort Carson, Colorado, in September, 1968, the weather was beautiful, with the awesome majesty of the Rocky Mountains and Pike's Peak framing the fort. The battalion worked hard and well through a cold, snowy winter. As spring approached, I began thinking of the new assignment due soon and decided to make an early call to Washington to influence the outcome. This time, I didn't volunteer just for Vietnam but boldly specified a third return in the job of province senior advisor (PSA). A letter from the army chief of staff arrived in June, 1969, inviting me back into a guaranteed PSA assignment. One statement in the letter revealed the reason my Washington phone call had received such a quick and positive response. Prior to leaving Saigon, Ambassador Robert Komer had requested my return in the PSA program. En route, I attended a specially arranged four-month Vietnamese language course, something I could more profitably have used four years earlier. When the course was over, I was elated to hear that, because of my experience in the Delta, my assignment was as PSA in Kien Giang Province there.

During my ten days of leave before departure, I enjoyed quail hunting with an old friend in the beautiful Virginia tidelands. On our first hunt, as a covey rose in front of us, I almost couldn't bring myself to pull the shotgun trigger. I wanted to let the birds fly away and live. For that brief instant, I had the power of choice between life and death—a choice I would lose when I returned to the war. I shot.

After enjoying the first Christmas at home with my

family in fifteen years, I was ready and eager to return to Vietnam. Travis Air Force Base hadn't changed since my earlier trips through it, but now I found that I had changed. I had a new respect for the young officers partying at the club, for the courage and self-sacrifice concealed beneath their prankish behavior. As I sat in the plush club, I felt like the old hand, the seasoned soldier, deeply aware of the responsibility I had toward others like them in the job ahead.

When I arrived in Saigon, it hadn't changed much, either, except that more free-spending Americans milled about. Even though South Vietnam was increasing its role in the war (a process called Vietnamization), U.S. forces still stood at 479,000 at the end of 1969—the lowest number in two years. In spite of the reduction of 64,000 U.S. troops, U.S. combat deaths that year totaled 9,414 Since I had previously served in country and was on a directed assignment, I was able to avoid most of the basic in-processing requirements and concentrate on getting information relevant to Kien Giang.

Kien Giang was the largest province in the Delta, stretching from the notorious U-Minh Forest in the south to the Cambodian border in the north. Chuong Thien and three other provinces formed its eastern border and the Gulf of Thailand its western side. Phu Quoc Island was one of the province's eight districts. Of the provinces in the country, Kien Giang was one that had highest priority and was considered very difficult. Because of its importance, I would be commanding one of the largest teams. Mine consisted of 63 officers, 103 enlisted men, and 15 officer-level civilians, spread throughout 22 locations. The VC presence, both stationary and moving through from Cambodia and the U-Minh, was huge. The population of the province was 432,000, a quarter of it in the autonomous city capital of Rach Gia. Province forces totaled over 9,000, in 122 territorial force units.

My head was spinning when I left the initial briefing, but one point stood out in my mind. The province chief, Lt. Col. Nguyen Van Tai, was notoriously slow to accept new advisors. The Corps senior advisor considered him one of the less capable province chiefs in the Delta.

I was able to fly directly from Saigon to Rach Gia. The fifteen-minute drive from Rach Soi Airfield to the triple arches marking the entrance to Rach Gia held some pleasant surprises. Starting with a large ice plant directly across from the airfield, we passed numerous commercial plants I never would have imagined existed outside Saigon. The broad, tree-bordered main avenue into the town was neat, clean, and lined with thriving shops of every description. Tong, my new driver, gave me a tour en route; since he spoke no English, I had good practice for my enlarged language-course vocabulary.

A six-story building sat directly opposite my living quarters in a mid-town villa. In the final stages of construction, it was destined to house all

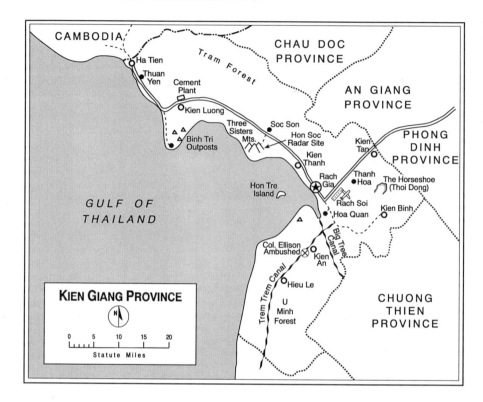

the military team members, presently spread in four locations throughout the city. As I helped Tong unload the jeep, a huge man ambled out to welcome me. He introduced himself as Billy Stansberry, the man I was replacing. Billy helped me get moved into the large, windowless room he had vacated and told me about a joint farewell and welcoming party at the province chief's house later in the evening. Billy apologized for the fact that he was due to leave the next day. We would not have the opportunity to sit down together and go over his assessment of the situation in detail. Because of my previous tours, he felt I'd have no problems getting started. I began the job of unpacking, wondering why in hell things couldn't be better arranged to give me some time with the man I was replacing and allow me to benefit from his experience.

The party at the province chief's house was an elaborate affair on the private tennis court, with colored overhead lights illuminating the large gathering. The spacious grounds were on the banks of an estuary that flowed past a large fish market near the center of town and then connected with the sea a short distance farther. The opposite side of the estuary was lined with impressive villas and business establishments, beneath which a solid line of trim fishing boats floated, moored against the quay. The entire scene picturesquely blended ancient Vietnamese, old French, and present-day commercial adaptations. In the distance, the last rays of the sun cast faint pink streaks in the sky above the grey-green forms of Hon Tre and Hon Minh Hoa islands, rising above the gently rolling Gulf of Thailand. The entire setting was so captivatingly peaceful and beautiful that I had to remind myself throughout the evening that this province was part of a country engaged in a ruthless war.

Mr. Hoi, previously the province deputy for administration in My Tho, was waiting for me at the front gate. After I recovered from my surprise, he told me that he had been sent to be the mayor of Rach Gia seven months earlier. As he escorted me to the tennis court, he continued to give me news about Dinh Tuong Province. Dao was in My Tho now as province chief and was a full colonel. They had talked about me often before Hoi left, as did Colonel Phuc before he was transferred to the staff of the National Military Academy in Thu Duc, north of Saigon. Seeing Hoi strengthened my feeling of being at home.

When Hoi introduced me to the province chief, Colonel Tai's appearance was not at all what I had expected. Tai was very short, very fat, and very dark; his short arms and bowed legs looked much too small for the rest of his body. His hair was wavy, not straight like that of all the other Vietnamese, and he half-slyly grinned at me through thick, protruding lips. He finished his quick, limp handshake gesture while I was still in the act of extending my hand. Tai spoke fluent English but gave it a jocular, theatrical flair that made me uncomfortable. He briefly mentioned that Colonel Stansberry had told him about me and said he was sure we'd work very well together. While we were exchanging pleasantries, he interrupted to motion a waiter to bring me a drink. When I had it, he excused himself to go and talk with some important guests. As Tai waddled off, Hoi led me to some other guests. I saw Billy towering over a group of civilians to whom he was talking animatedly, and we waved at each other. I didn't see Tai again until about forty minutes later, when we sat down for dinner at the same table.

When dinner was finished, a microphone was set up at one end of the tennis court. Tai used it to get the attention of the guests. Speaking first in Vietnamese and then in English, he explained the dual reason for the party. When Billy was introduced and strode to the microphone to address the crowd, I almost choked on dessert. He spoke fluent Vietnamese in the northern accent. He had the gathering laughing at times, looking sad at other times, nodding their heads in agreement, and giving long, resounding applause when he finished. Later Billy would be a principal interpreter for the My Lai massacre investigation.

I only understood small parts of Billy's rapid-fire speech but heard him introduce me as an advisor of long and dedicated experience. As he stepped back from the microphone, motioned me forward, and joined the polite clapping of the guests, I feverishly tried to make up my mind whether to speak Vietnamese or not. Earlier I had thought I'd make a good first impression by doing so, but now, after hearing Billy, I had lost all my composure and confidence. I forged ahead anyway, cutting short what I originally had intended to say. When I returned to the table, Mr. Hoi smiled knowingly and handed me a drink, which I finished in two gulps.

Tai never got back to me that evening. I didn't mind, since Mr. Hoi stayed with me, either because he felt obligated to or because it had been pre-arranged that way. In any case, we had an informative talk about the province, and he introduced me to some of the military staff and a few civilians who came over to welcome me.

One thing happened later in the evening which gave me a bad initial impression of Tai. Followed around by a waiter carrying two bottles of cognac, he coaxed and pushed others into the bottoms-up toasting game with him. The supposed joke was that, to the amusement of onlookers, Tai filled his victim's glasses with real cognac while he was drinking iced tea camouflaged to look like cognac. When Tai got to his deputy for security, a large man already obviously on the verge of being drunk, Tai concentrated on him until the man was almost incoherent. Although others in the group laughed along with Tai, I sensed that they were uncomfortable and a little embarrassed, but Tai pressed on, having great fun.

Back at the team house, Billy told me that he had been turning over to Tai the monthly imprest fund allocation of 100,000 piasters, which was authorized for outpost improvement. Although he knew Tai was using most of the money for intelligence and not to fix the outposts, he let it go because we needed good intelligence and he trusted Tai. Billy had told Tai that he would tell me this and recommend I do the same with Tai. I answered that I'd have to think about it and asked what assurance Billy had that Tai actually was using the money for intelligence. None, Billy replied, but he trusted Tai. The added imprest money for the outposts was a new authorization, and, while it was left up to the province senior advisor to account for it, that responsibility was inherent in the authorization. As I went to bed, I wished I hadn't been confronted with such a touchy problem at the outset of my tour.

It was several days before I heard from Colonel Tai. I didn't think about it, however, as I was busy getting acquainted with the large team and being briefed by them. A divided picture of the province emerged. Thriving economic development, progress, and strong support for the government characterized the controlled population centers, but indifference and a wait-and-see attitude reigned in the rural areas. In that sense, despite regional variations, it was not much different from other provinces. The big problem was the enemy's control and use of the vast areas of the province for training bases, staging areas, medical sanctuaries, ammunition factories, and supply bases. Since most of these were in the U-Minh Forest, they were untouchable except by air strikes, which depended for locations on our sparse and unreliable intelligence reports. Sea and land infiltration into the bases was another problem. Tai had been little involved personally in military operations to counter VC initiatives. He was not much of a military leader and left most of the operational planning and execution to his deputy for security.

My civilian deputy, Chuck Rheingans, gave a good account of himself during the briefings, and the team seemed to know what they were doing with the many pacification and development programs. I planned to spend as much time as it would take to make early visits to all the outlying teams in order to get their assessments of the situation and acquaint myself with the province.

For the next ten days, I traveled most of the time. I had known that the province was large, but I was unprepared for the great distances involved and the vast differences in the land. I went by jeep and boat to Kien An District town, located on the banks of the Trem Trem Canal in the southern part of the province. The Trem Trem Canal, called the "Anti-American Canal" by the VC, flows south from the Big Tree Canal past the district town and into the depths of the U-Minh Forest. When the boat docked at Kien An, I was met on the small wooden dock by the fiery district chief, Captain Trinh.

Beyond the heavily fortified town, government control extended in patches along the canal for one kilometer on both sides. Between the patches and beyond the two kilometers bordering the canal, government influence was non-existent. The important point stressed many times during the Kien An briefing was that the people lived on the canal, which—apart from some wood gathering in the vast wasteland beyond—held the key to their livelihood. So, in claiming control of only 5 percent of the land, the government was claiming control of 95 percent of the population. Captain Trinh was a tall, gaunt fighter who was outspokenly proud of his Cambodian ancestry. He had been the chief of Hieu Le District, south of Kien An, until the VC had pushed the government out four years earlier. Hieu Le lay totally within the deep, water-saturated U-Minh.

After Trinh's briefing, I was given a fast, nervous boat ride to visit a MAT team at the last outpost down the canal. This outpost marked the border of government control. I spent the night in the team's mud hut, both because it was getting late and because it wasn't wise to travel back up the canal so soon after the trip down had made my presence known. My replacement later disregarded such caution and paid for it with his life.

I next drove to Kien Thanh and Kien Tan districts and visited MAT team locations in the countryside. On each visit to the MATs, I was appalled by the team's isolation and precarious security but impressed by the members' courageous determination. One MAT team was living with and training a village platoon in the village of Soc Son north of Rach Gia. The village was only a wide spot on the road to Kien Luong District, and the team was training fifty village members of the People's Self-Defense Force (PSDF), in addition to a province security platoon. The PSDF were volunteer civilians armed with M-1 carbines. The guns had become available after the Tet Offensive of 1968, when territorial force units had been supplied with more efficient M-16 rifles. As the name indicated, the mission of the PSDF was to help secure and protect their own hamlets and villages, mostly at night. Ambassador Komer had persuaded the Vietnamese government to agree to the concept of arming civilians, though the government initially had worried about which side the civilians would back. But the PSDF did support the government and did the best they could under the circumstances.

The aim in arming the villagers and some city dwellers was not so much to add to the defense of their homes and families as to get the people off the political fence and committed to the government. The idea was working, with one drawback. Most PSDF tended to bunch up at night. As stationary targets for the VC, they often suffered casualties, whose weapons and ammunition then went to the VC. Numerous PSDF units, though, acquitted themselves well when the VC attacked their villages.

Remaining districts had to be visited by helicopter: Kien Binh, in the thick jungles bordering Chuong Thien Province, not far from the high-steepled church in Ngoc Hoa; Kien Luong on the road to the Cambodian border, where a mammoth, French-built concrete plant dominated the small town; and finally Ha Tien, along the border itself.

Variations in the topography were exceeded only by those in the socioeconomic and security conditions of the province locations. In the southwest lay the vast, flooded U-Minh Forest. To the north, the center of the province contained most of the agriculturally rich rice land. The center's northern fringes gradually became parched and infertile, with sparse arable portions only bordering the many canals. Near the sea northwest of Rach Gia, vast swamps surrounded the Three Sisters Mountains. Farther north and east, the land was desolate with high, razorlike shards of dark granite abruptly rising out of a broad, low tangle of reeds, brush, and mangrove swamps. Eastward to Chau Doc Province and turning northwest to the Cambodian border, the low, scraggily trees of the Tram Forest were surrounded by murky, waist-high water. In the middle of this forlorn region, where the province bordered Cambodia on the Gulf of Thailand, stood the placid, sleepy, and picturesque district capital, Ha Tien. At that part of the border, isolated granite peaks rose from the rice fields and were honey-combed with natural caves. Considered holy, these contained ancient shrines and Buddhist temples.

Dedicated teams of district and MAT advisors were at each location helping to fight the relentless enemy, build the nation, and help the people. The only group of Americans tasked exclusively with fighting the war was a section of twenty soldiers atop Hon Soc Mountain in the Three Sisters Mountains cluster thirty kilometers northwest of the province capital of Rach Gia. The team operated a radar site and monitored the readout consoles of hundreds of electronic sensing devices, planted by air around the heavily used enemy infiltration routes passing the base of the mountains. When targets in the area were indicated, the team passed the locations to a Vietnamese artillery battery of four 155-millimeter howitzers, also stationed on the mountain. The battery then would fire on the area of enemy movement.

During the ten days it took to complete my visits to all the teams, I saw Tai only once. On that occasion, he invited me to breakfast at his house before we stood together for the Monday morning flag-raising ceremony in front of the province administrative headquarters. Both the breakfast and the following ceremony became a weekly ritual. I wanted to discuss with Tai the impressions I had gotten from all the team briefings, but he restricted the breakfast conversation to small talk and quickly excused himself after the ceremony, retiring to his balconied office on the second floor of the province office building.

A week later, Tai invited me to accompany him to several village council meetings at district headquarters and to a province council meeting to develop civil programs funded in the annual budget. At each, he acted the amiable leader until some official argued too long or too effectively for some item of local interest. Then he became arrogant and sullen. At first, I was surprised that Tai called the village councils to the districts instead of going to the villages to meet with them, but I soon understood that he rarely risked his own safety. On the rare occasions when he ventured away from his office, he was under the constant protection of two bodyguards who traveled in the back of his jeep.

All districts were conducting three and four operations each week, but Tai showed no inclination to initiate any operations at province level. Four weeks after my arrival, the VC blew up the rubber helicopter refueling bladders at Rach Soi airfield. The bladders and some rocket storage lockers had been placed at the airfield by the U.S. helicopter units based in Can Tho, to save replenishing time during operations in support of Kien Giang and adjacent provinces. Tai sent his deputy for security with me to Rach Soi to inspect the extent of damage, and I reported to Tai that it was evident that night security was too lax. When he said he had no more men to add to the airfield security, I asked that he at least order the province operations center to send an officer to Rach Soi to make periodic, unannounced night checks at the airfield. Although he agreed, the checks never happened. After that, I drove alone to make the airfield check by myself one or two nights each week, hoping the effort would help retain our helicopter support.

The IV Corps deputy senior advisor for CORDS was now John Paul Vann. He previously had been an army lieutenant colonel and had been the senior advisor to the 7th Division in My Tho in 1963. Vann resigned his commission when his superiors in Saigon covered up pessimistic reports arguing that the war in the Delta was being lost to large VC units who had abandoned small guerrilla tactics and had moved into large-scale unit attacks. Vann was a tough man who was grudgingly admired by the Vietnamese because he usually was right. He now held the civilian rank equivalent to brigadier general and was a tireless worker, continually traveling throughout the Delta in his personal army light helicopter to get first-hand reports. Although he was assigned a pilot, Vann did most of the flying himself. His boss, the corps senior advisor, Maj. Gen. Hal McCown, was another tough professional, and they made a team I was happy to have in command.

Vann visited during my second week and was interested in how I was getting along with Tai. He didn't think much of Tai and was considering pressing for his removal. After communicating my uncomplimentary impressions, I requested more time to work on Tai before making up my mind.

Chapter 11

Disaster in the Horseshoe

Late in February, 1970, more than a month after my assignment to the province, Tai started asking me to arrange visits to the districts via the helicopter (called the sector ship), now assigned to the province team for daily administrative use. Our first trip was to Ha Tien and, on the return trip, to Kien Luong. Other than personal visits with each district chief and a discussion with the manager of the Kien Luong cement plant, we did little at each location. Because cross-border smuggling was a thriving business from which district chiefs extracted a percentage of the profits, and since the district chiefs relied on the province chief for their jobs, I suspected that Tai might be collecting his share of the take during the visit. My impression seemed to be confirmed by the bulging satchel zealously clutched by Tai's bodyguard during the return trip.

Protection similarly might have been paid for at the cement plant, but with corps taking a share of the payoff. The plant was an important national asset, requiring two territorial force companies under Corps control for its continued operation. Large barges filled with bags of the plant's finished product safely traveled the canals of the province on their way to Can Tho and Saigon, always avoiding the mishaps that befell other types of cargo. Surely this was due to more than luck or timing. Either province special security was being bought, or the VC were being paid directly for safe passage—probably some of both. Although there was much circumstantial evidence of Tai's illicit operations, getting solid proof was going to be difficult, since almost everyone from top to bottom, except soldiers at the lowest ranks, must be getting a piece of the protection payments.

On our way back to Rach Gia in the helicopter, Tai leaned over and asked about this month's money for intelligence and if Colonel Stansberry had talked to me about their arrangement. I had hoped that Tai had forgotten about it and answered that I could agree with letting him use half the monthly allocation for intelligence as before. However, the outposts I'd seen were much in need of improvements, and we must use the other half of the money for its intended purpose. He raised his hands and gave a forced smile, but it turned to a frown when I added that I would require receipts for the outpost improvement material for my records. He became silent and withdrawn for the rest of the trip, now knowing that I didn't trust him.

Tai finally began province-level operations after I complained to John Vann about his inaction and about his leaving aggressive security tasks to the district chiefs. I imagined that Vann had mentioned it to the corps commander, who then nudged Tai. More U.S. helicopter support had become available, and I had been pushing Tai to use it for surprise assaults, remarking that surely he must be getting some intelligence to exploit from the outpost improvement money.

Our first operation was in the Thoi Dong area, on the boundary of Kien Tan and Kien Bien districts. The area was difficult and isolated, sitting astride one of the main infiltration routes that crossed from Cambodia in the Tram Forest east of Ha Tien and continued southeastward through Kien Tan and Kien Binh into the base areas of Chuong Thien. Our target area was nicknamed "the Horseshoe" because it was a large patch of jungle in that approximate shape, surrounded by rice fields and canals. Tai had received reports that the Horseshoe was a major resting, regrouping, and resupply stopover for infiltrating groups bringing men and supplies to the U-Minh. If that were true, local VC units also would be there to guide, take care of, and protect the infiltrators.

Tai and I were in the command and control ship over the selected landing zone as the gunships escorted in the troop-carrying ships. Three lifts were required to get the three territorial companies into the open paddies a kilometer short of the Horseshoe, during which time Tai was continually talking over his radio with his units and I over mine with the accompanying advisor teams. When all units were on the ground and the lift ships were out, the gunships emptied their rockets into the treeline edge of the Horseshoe, then made several machine-gun runs in the same area before departing to refuel and rearm. As they disappeared toward Rach Soi and the troops got up and moved on the treeline, all hell broke loose.

One of the advisors panted into his microphone that they were receiving heavy fire, including machine guns and B-40 rockets. I answered a quick "Roger," then switched to the intercom and told the pilot to get the gunships back as soon as possible. Switching back to the advisor net, I called Shotgun, who was orbiting above us, to see if there were any air strikes en route to nearby targets that could be diverted to us. I also reminded him to tell Can Tho that we had troops in contact. His toneless reply indicated that he was aware of the ground unit's problems and would get right on it. Tai was shouting into his microphone and pointing out the helicopter door, as if that might make his instructions clearer. Another advisor came up on the radio, reporting that they were pinned down and couldn't move. Fire was still heavy. After a pause, he reported that the VC were attacking and the troops were running back in disorder. I could hear the firing in the background, then large explosions. The advisor, panting in gasps, called that they were pulling back, as a louder explosion interrupted him. With his microphone transmit button still depressed, I heard him shout for Thanh to hurry, faster, and to drop that goddamn pack. Another close explosion erupted, and he moaned that his interpreter had been blown away, as had many others. Shotgun broke in that four sorties were on the way from Phong Dinh, about ten to fifteen minutes away. I called for each team to report their situation and the estimated location of the VC. One was slowing down, with firing breaking off. Another was okay, but the unit had casualties, and his counterpart had lost his radio. The door gunner tapped me and motioned for me to switch to the intercom. I nodded and waved, then continued telling the advisors on the radio to try to get counterparts to regain control and secure their areas, because air strikes were about ten minutes away. When I switched to the intercom, the pilot let me know that the gunships were lifting off from Rach Soi and would be here in eight minutes.

I turned to Tai, who was doing most of the talking in the conversation with his commanders, and told him that the gunships and air strikes were minutes away. He nodded and kept on talking into the microphone. I tapped him again and told him about the unit that had lost its radio. I told him to ask his unit commanders where the heaviest fire came from, so we could put the air strike in there. When he waved in the general direction of the Horseshoe, I yelled again for him to ask his commanders and shoved my map at him. When he finished talking on the radio, he took a grease-pencil from his jacket and circled a section of the Horseshoe's fringe. I too thought the fire was coming from there. I gave the coordinates to Shotgun and switched to the frequency he used to talk to the planes in order to listen and make sure he got the coordinates right and gave them to the pilots correctly. The troops were close to the target, and we didn't need another disaster.

As Tai and I watched the jets roll in and hit the area, I told the command and control pilot to pass on to the gunships now orbiting south of us to wait three or four minutes after the jets departed, then have them plaster the same area. I hoped that would catch some of the VC coming up out of their holes. He nodded, and I continued that he should have the troop carriers come back when the gunships had finished some runs on the treeline and could cover the extraction of troops. There were wounded on the ground, so the lift out would have to be where the troops were now.

After I radioed the teams to have their counterparts ready to load up and lift out, I turned to Tai and told him to tell them the same thing. He shouted back that he already had told them to attack again. Shaking my head violently, I roared that I didn't recommend that. It looked like we had caught a large unit in the target area, and I didn't know how long it would take to get the gunships back after they rearmed. I couldn't believe Tai was going to send the troops across the open area back into the treeline where the VC obviously were dug in. If he persisted in the dumb decision in spite of my protests, I was stuck. Even if I told the advisors to stay in place, I was sure they would go with their units. After a long pause and a scowl, he agreed and radioed the change of order.

When the last lift was up and out, we returned to the airfield, where Tai gave me the report of casualties. Twelve were killed, half of them still lying out in the paddies; and eight were wounded, four seriously. One of my interpreters, Thanh, was dead, hit in the back by a B-40 round.

It was a disaster of a first operation, and I could only hope for two things. First, I hoped that the air strikes and gunship assaults had more than evened the casualty score. Second, I hoped that Tai wouldn't be reluctant to try again, though with better intelligence next time. Intelligence for today's operation had not been bad; indeed, it had been too good.

On the drive from the airfield to my office, I thought about Thanh the interpreter and made a note to visit his wife and give her indemnification money from the imprest fund. Thanh was one of the interpreters we could trust. The best and most trusted ones were always the ones we selected to go out on operations with the advisors, and he had paid for his honesty and dependability with his life. Our heavy reliance on interpreters put the team and the whole advisory effort at a distinct disadvantage, and we knew it. The interpreters were paid and controlled by the division and province authorities who provided them to us, and, regarding sensitive matters, we were told what the authorities wanted us to hear. Most advisors tried to develop close relationships with their interpreters and to establish mutual trust. Sometimes it worked, especially when hazardous circumstances pushed them toward an interdependence for mutual safety and survival. Most times it didn't work.

As we remained busy with budget reviews, planning meetings, visits to agricultural and fishery projects, and village administrative cadre training class graduations, military operations slowly increased. Two operations conducted just inland from the mangrove swamps of the seacoast south of Rach Gia, on the fringes of the U-Minh Forest, in fact were raids. Because of the need for surprise, the troop-carrying helicopters and gunships traveled as if preparing to go into an area different from the selected landing zone. Tai and I in the command and control ship made a wide pass of the target area until the exact map location was identified on the ground. Then we swooped in low and at top speed, to throw out a smoke grenade and mark the landing zone. The gunships immediately followed, circling the designated landing zone until the troop carriers had discharged their loads. All helicopters except the command and control ship then withdrew to be on call. Vibrating in the uncomfortable seats and leaning out the open helicopter doors for four to six hours made me ache long after we landed. Nevertheless, it was better though than being on the ground with the daring troop units, walking into the eerie, tense stillness. Although Tai seemed to appreciate my help and tolerate my advice during each operation, in between he reverted to an occasional, usually trivial call.

I kept busy traveling to visit my teams at every opportunity and induced Tai to come along occasionally when it happened to suit his purposes and we would be traveling by helicopter. It was obvious that Colonel Tai was coasting in the job. He left most of the planning and execution of the civil programs in the hands of his administrative staff and much of the military side of things to his deputy for security. He shrewdly presided over meetings and committees and impressed visiting dignitaries by hosting sumptuous seafood luncheons and personally conducting showy briefings from notes prepared by his staff.

As months went by, the American presence in the province kept growing. A detachment of Navy Seals was assigned to conduct covert intelligence operations along VC infiltration routes. Shortly thereafter, two teams of Navy Construction Battalion personnel (Seabees) temporarily were attached to work on village self-help projects and road repair. As the senior American in the province, I was responsible for the safety and security of all these individuals. That was difficult to arrange for the Seals, who were tough, dedicated, and superbly trained for their dangerous missions of covert incursions into enemy territory. At times, it was also difficult to protect the hardworking Seabees, as they accomplished their helpful, constructive tasks with the assistance and great appreciation of remote villagers. They were contributing to what the VC didn't want to see—progress.

In March, 1970, the long-awaited national land reform program, which had been tested in Chuong Thien, was enacted into law. Named Land to the Tiller (LTTT), the program was begun with great fanfare. Tai inaugurated LTTT with a large rally and a long speech in Rach Gia, followed with similar appearances in three of the more secure districts. While, probably on specific direction from Saigon, he put on a good show at the start, he characteristically soon disengaged himself from the promotion and execution of the vital program and turned it over entirely to his land affairs chief. Always the master showman in front of his superiors, Tai delivered impressive briefings on the program's progress at the monthly province chiefs meetings in Can Tho. The corps commander was content to sit back and absorb the suspect statistics on the elaborate charts, asking no questions. While there wasn't a lot of arable land available for the program in the province, for that which did exist, the political and psychological potential of the historic program never was properly realized.

On Monday of the third week of March, 1970, I was shaving in my room at 6:15 A.M., preparing to go to the weekly flag-raising ceremony with Tai. Suddenly a loud explosion shook my shaving mirror. Noticing the time of the incident as always, I decided to drop by the operations center after the ceremony to find out what was recorded at that time. The phone rang as I finished dressing, and one of Tai's servants said that there would be no breakfast with the province chief this morning.

When Tong turned the jeep into the broad, cobblestone driveway of the province administrative building, instead of the quiet, orderly groups casually waiting and talking in formation and the band tuning up to play the national anthem, things were in a turmoil. Tai was already there and was glowering at a group of officers he was addressing. After he finished, they scurried away to join the soldiers, bandsmen, and civilians who were searching the grounds. When Major Holland, my deputy for territorial forces, saw me, he left the small group of key advisors who stood in ranks along with the Vietnamese for the ceremony, walked over, and explained what had happened.

A claymore-type directional mine accidentally had been detonated by the old cleaning man while he swept the front entrance and walkway to the office building. His broom had hit the electrical connecting wires. The camouflaged mine was attached at the top of one of the entrance columns, where the column supported the ceiling of the lobby veranda. Fragments from the mine that pockmarked the concrete entrance and cobblestones showed that the mine had been aimed at the exact spot where Tai and I always stood during the weekly ceremony. The movement of the wires obviously had caused some kind of short-circuit, which prematurely set off the mine. The old man was shaken but unhurt.

Tai seemed satisfied that there were no other explosives around and took his place for the ceremony. As the soldiers, civilians, and band scurried into formation, I moved and took my place beside him. When the large flag ballooned to the top of the tall flagpole and the last notes of the anthem floated across the quay and estuary, Tai, without a word, gave me a quick, dead-fish handshake and rapidly strode into the building. Customarily he chatted for a few minutes and told me about his plans for the day.

That evening, a series of attacks started on the isolated outposts along the outer fringes of Kien An District near the sea. Three of four outposts were overrun, obviously with help from inside. Although the VC penetrated the outpost that held out, the defenders put up a fierce and determined resistance and forced the enemy to withdraw. Friendly casualties were heavy, though. As usual, they included families.

Next morning Tai phoned me in my office. He asked if we could go to Thu Sau outpost by the sector helicopter. It was the Kien An outpost that had survived, and he wanted to visit quickly to congratulate and support it. Even though the area was insecure, I knew the pilot no doubt would agree, so I assented. He told me in a flat tone not to call, just to come to his office.

Several things about this call were out of the ordinary. First, he never called me in person, having his secretary or a duty officer do it instead. Second, he was never that polite. Third, the visit sounded like it was to show compassion and concern for the troops. Fourth, he didn't divulge ahead, over the insecure telephone, the exact time and route of our travels, as he normally did. No matter how hard I tried to convince him that it wasn't healthy to say when, where, and how we were going to do something, he never quite understood why. Maybe the VC assassination attempt had shaken Tai. Then the thought came to me that possibly it wasn't the VC at all who had planted the mine, but some of his own people. Perhaps Tai had considered that possibility, too.

The pilot tried to put the odds against drawing VC fire in our favor by a daring approach to Thu Sau outpost. We whistled down to wave-top level off the coast, then zigzagged at top speed over the mangroves and flooded brush until the pilot abruptly flared up and spiraled down onto the narrow mud trail above the swamps leading to the outpost. Tai just had time to gain his composure before he tumbled out to meet the outpost commander and review the tired, disheveled honor guard lined up along the trail. I followed, and the pilot lifted off as prearranged to circle and await our smoke grenade signal for his return.

As I followed Tai's ducklike waddle, the loud hum of buzzing flies called my attention to the row of dead VC beside the pathway, neatly placed as if for inspection, too. I counted nine as we strode by. Inside the surprisingly large mud-walled outpost, the commander gave us a tour and a detailed account of the fight. Expended VC AK-47 automatic rifle shells and some unexploded homemade grenades still littered the ground around the command bunker and inside the family sleeping huts lining the walls. Unfortunately, many blood-soaked beds, family clothes, fighting positions, and bunkers throughout the outpost showed the price of the victory. After Tai spoke to the soldiers, he pulled some medals from the leather briefcase he always carried and ceremoniously pinned them on a dozen or so tired and dirty but proudly standing men. I walked out the gate and threw the smoke grenade for the helicopter to return.

On the flight back to Rach Gia, I wondered why the VC had made a coordinated attack on the four outposts situated along the coast, when previously they had ignored them. That night I sat down with Lt. Frank C. Howard III, an excellent young officer who was the team intelligence advisor. As we sat late into the night, Frank and I pieced together what we knew about the latest series of attacks and what might have prompted them. The reason for the attacks on the Kien An seaward outposts slowly became obvious. After half a year of making no contacts during their patrols and ambushes, all the Kien An outposts had reported enemy activity and small contacts within the last month. Other seemingly unrelated incidents and unit action reports from around the province pointed to an increase of enemy infiltration and resupply by sea.

The more we went over the reports, the more a pattern began to emerge. The number of successful ambushes to stop infiltration along land routes from the Tram Forest down through the province and across the Kien Tan road into the Horseshoe area was steadily decreasing. Informant reports substantiated that fewer groups of infiltrators were passing previously used guide points. Sensor and radar readings in the area of the Three Sisters Mountains indicated more enemy activity, but additional nightly ambushes placed along the coast northwest of Rach Gia to catch the movers came up empty-handed. Just recently, coastal sampan traffic and fishing boats were complaining about having to pay Vietnamese Navy patrol boats to work in, or pass through, the restricted coastal zone. But with payment, prior arrangements could be made to travel, even at night, without stop and search.

Now we had the attacks on the outposts inland from the Kien An coast which were given the mission of interdicting or preventing movement through the area. Just inland and south of those outposts were the large, protected, known VC bases in the U-Minh. Together, everything pointed to a change from the enemy's almost total reliance on inland infiltration to increased use of the sea. First-time night contacts by the U.S. Navy off the coast of Ha Tien completed the theory and picture that Frank and I had been drawing on the map.

Men and supplies probably were coming out of Cambodia near Ha Tien by boat, landing north of the Three Sisters Mountains out of radar range, then proceeding quickly by land, trying to skirt the Nui Hon Soc radar, sensors, and artillery before they could be fired at. Once they were safely to the south of Hon Soc and north of Rach Gia, the enemy took to the sea again and crossed the bay to land on the desolate Kien An coast. While we were busy concentrating on stopping land infiltration, previously heavily used, the enemy was making an end run around us by water. The trip with

Tai to Thu Sau outpost started me on a search for enough evidence to corroborate my conclusions and convince Tai and corps that we had to shift our tactics to adjust to the enemy's tactical changes.

Three months later, armed with more conclusive evidence, I succeeded in persuading corps of my analysis, and air and naval units, along with land forces, were reoriented to counter the seaward infiltration. Water targets detected and engaged at night increased soon after. But, except for finding some floating wreckage, bodies, and scattered supplies, it was hard to gauge our effectiveness. Considering the vast and remote areas we were operating in and the nature of what we were trying to accomplish, that wasn't any surprise. All we could do was to continue, hoping that the volume of men and supplies funneling into the Delta through Kien Giang would be decreased.

At the end of March, I received a very concerned phone call one evening from John Vann's secretary. Vann had made a helicopter trip to our vicinity in mid-afternoon and was long overdue on his return. Since it was already after dark, my immediate response was limited. First I asked Tai to alert all districts to report information of any helicopter in trouble or downed. Next, I contacted the U.S. Navy Patrol Base at Rach Soi and requested that all patrols check the area.

A call from the navy at Rach Soi a little after dawn said that a patrol boat checking the small island of Hon Tre had found Vann's helicopter on the beach and the corps deputy senior advisor fast asleep in the village chief's house. Vann was annoyed that his escape to relax and enjoy the serenity of the hidden paradise was rudely interrupted. He called me later from Can Tho and thoroughly chewed me out for initiating the search. After I defended my actions and criticized his, he softened and recommended that I visit the island myself. I did so some months later.

The island was a tropical Eden as yet untouched by the violence and sorrow thirty miles away. The villagers and their chief were friendly, gentle, and courteous. The village was located on a picturesque beach at the base of a sheer mountain wall flanked by green jungles. Sunrise bathed the village in a soft golden hue, while sunset behind the mountain slowly altered the colors of the sky as blinking lanterns spread along the darkening beach below. I spent the night with the village chief and his family, as Vann did, and I found it difficult to leave and return to the realities of the war in the morning. During dinner with the village chief, I asked him if the VC ever came to the village. When he answered my question, I understood why the island retained its unique peace and seclusion. The islanders had had no trouble since two boatloads of VC had come to the island six years earlier to collect taxes. The villagers beheaded them all, then put the bodies into the boats that had brought them and towed the boats into the currents that would return them to the mainland.

The last part of March continued to be hectic. The VC launched a well-planned attack against Kien Luong District town. The sleepy cement-plant town was awakened when the attackers simultaneously hit all military targets, including the advisor's compound, the district chief's house, and the cement plant itself. As usually happened, the VC already were inside the defenses when the first mortars fell to announce the assault at 2:30 A.M. Tai and I arrived after 8 A.M. to investigate. The advisor's house on the southern edge of the town's defenses was hit hard, as was the defense headquarters compound next door. None of the advisors was hurt, but, had it not been for the group's immediate and rehearsed response, the results could have been tragically different. A B-40 round had blasted a hole in the wall two feet above the bed of the only man awake, a sergeant on radio watch in the kitchen. As the VC streamed through the team's small compound, the ensuing firefight moved from door to door and bunker to bunker. The path of the enemy's retreat was marked by dead VC bodies and by blood trails from the middle of the compounds, through the barbed wire, and into the flooded fields beyond. The team and their counterparts tried to act cocky, but they showed subtle signs of post-violence shock, which sometimes has a lingering effect worse than the actual experience.

The last days of March brought a spurt of enemy activity along the road from Rach Soi to normally peaceful Kien Tan District town and the Cai Son Canal which paralleled it. Night security positions on the perimeters of villages lining the canal and road either caught, or were caught by, several large VC groups reusing the old land infiltration routes. After skirmishes brought casualties to both sides, including families in houses nearby, the VC withdrew into patches of swamps and jungles to the north. One of the dead was the province intelligence officer, whose bad luck and bad intelligence put him on the road in his jeep at the wrong time and place. When two nervous ambush parties fired on each other, the operation ended. So, thank God, did March.

Chapter 12

At Da Dung Mountain

In contrast to March, April, 1970 passed quietly. After one Monday morning's flag-raising ceremony, each of which was now preceded by a painstaking inspection of all areas likely to hide a mine, Tai asked me to accompany him by jeep to Kien Binh District to help the district chief, Major Dang, celebrate a reported big victory the previous Friday. We would be going by road because security in the district had improved. The district senior advisor, Major Kone, had sent me a note earlier, saying that he wanted to talk to me about Friday's operation, as he wasn't sure it was all that much of a success.

The after-action report had claimed a lopsided victory with no friendly casualties, twenty-two VC killed, and fourteen weapons captured. The ratio of VC killed to weapons captured was unusually high and included three crew-served weapons, an extremely rare occurrence. I was eager to hear more about the operation, as we had received the report late.

Maj. Charlie Kone was a good soldier and the best district senior advisor I had. He was an old, grizzled rancher from Texas and prided himself on being the only remaining National Guard officer on active duty in the entire army. When he returned home to Eagle Pass, Texas, in June, he would be the last, after retiring with twenty years of active service. I thought a lot of Charlie and respected him, so I looked forward to hearing his droll, animated rendition of the operation's details.

Even though the road was supposed to be safe, Tai characteristically increased the odds and arranged for an extra-large security escort to travel with us. I was glad to have it because the road, when it branched east ten kilometers south of Rach Soi, passed through dense jungle the rest of the way to Kien Binh. Since much of the district was jungle and the town lay astride the land infiltration route from Cambodia into bordering Chuong Thien, I often wondered why the VC left the town alone and why little activity was reported throughout the district. Charlie Kone hadn't been able to answer either question, although he had his suspicions.

Charlie and District Chief Major Dang met us at Dang's house, and we all walked to the district headquarters, where the captured weapons were displayed. While the district chief briefed us using a map on his office wall, Charlie leaned over and whispered that he wanted to talk to me alone before I left; before lunch might be the best time. I nodded, not wanting to miss what Dang was saying. Knowing that Tai never minded if I went off on my own and left him alone, I excused myself when the briefing was over.

Charlie was sweating profusely as he always did and got Cokes from the propane refrigerator for us before talking. While he did so, I sat with the rest of the four-man team and inquired about things small but all-important. How was their health? How were things at home, and who was scheduled for R and R leave? When and where? Since most of the district advisors—the MATs, too, for that matter—lost a lot of weight on the job, health and morale, as well as their safety, were always among my big concerns. When Charlie joined us, he set his Coke on the floor and told the team interpreter to go to lunch.

Charlie stated flatly that Dang had faked the operation. Dang had been saving up the supposedly captured weapons for a long time. Perhaps Dang had rigged the whole operation because he—and maybe Tai, too—knew that they hadn't really been going after the VC for months. I asked about the real state of security in the district; it looked good on paper. Charlie shot back in his farm drawl that, while the figures looked good, the situation was shaky as hell. When I asked if he thought Dang had an agreement with the VC, Charlie took a long, slow drink of his Coke. He finally acknowledged that, while he hadn't intended to bring that up now, it sure was beginning to look that way. Dang went on every operation, but they all ended up being just long, quiet walks in the sun. Except for the staged production on Friday, there hadn't been too many shots fired in the district lately. I asked for the details about Friday.

Charlie crunched his empty Coke can in his large hands, leaned back, and told the story. Dang had said that he had some dependable intelligence about the location of the district VC platoon and got the district intelligence squad and a company together and quickly moved out. Sergeant Pete, carrying the radio, and Binh the interpreter were with Charlie, and they all were with Dang and the intel squad when the action began. The lead people in the squad started shooting, and Charlie and Dang moved up to see what was going on. When they got to where the unit point was, the company, which was to their left, started firing, and it sounded like everyone was letting loose. Charlie wanted to get Dang to move in that direction, but Dang was on the radio. When he finished talking, he said the company was in heavy contact, and everyone should stay where they were. After it was all over, they joined up with the company, but Dang kept Charlie with him, out of the supposed area of contact. I asked if there were any wounded, and Charlie shook his head, adding that there was not a scratch on any body and not a drop of blood—theirs or anyone else's. The company was supposed to have left the VC bodies for their own to retrieve. All there was to show for the story was the weapons, and they looked like they'd not been used for a long time. There were no papers, no nothing, taken from the VC. It was all a bunch of baloney. When Charlie finished, I told him I'd correct the record in Can Tho but didn't feel there was anything to gain by confronting Tai with it now. He probably was in on the sham, anyway.

On the return trip, I thought about Dang's pretense. If the bastard really had an accord with the VC, I hoped it covered road travel and such a tempting target as the province chief. On second thought, maybe the VC would let us alone even without any collusion, because they had to be smart enough to know that it was in their best interest to keep Tai in the job.

General Nghi, the dynamic young commander of the 21st Division, capable but manipulative, sent for Tai to meet him one afternoon in mid-May, 1970. When superiors called, Tai jumped. Although the meeting was set fifty-five kilometers away near Ha Tien, south of the Cambodian border, Tai announced that we were going there immediately by road. Had the sector ship been available, I would have used it for the trip, but it had been canceled for commitment to the effort we were soon to learn about. The drive to Thuan Yen not only was long, but had to be made over a road with spotty security and hazardous conditions. As we rolled through the long stretches of desolate countryside past the small and infrequent outposts, it wasn't difficult to see why the road was often sabotaged and mined.

General Nghi's meeting had been called to plan details of the 21st Division's part in the second joint U.S.-Vietnamese attack across the border into Cambodia. The incursion was scheduled to start two days after the meeting, with division units striking quickly along the road from Ha Tien into the border sanctuaries from which the enemy had been operating with impunity. Tai was ordered to use province forces to surround and capture a VC stronghold called Nui Da Dung, or Da Dung Mountain, one kilometer across the border from Ha Tien.

It was late afternoon by the time the meeting was over. Tai had a day and a half to prepare before the attack. We arrived before dark in Rach

Gia, and Tai immediately put together a force of four militia companies. That evening, I had Major Holland form three advisor teams. Two would accompany the units, while the third was to operate at Tai's command post. What I thought would be a short operation turned out instead to be a tough, bloody one that took a week.

As I peered through my binoculars at Da Dung Mountain, I could hardly believe what I saw. The so-called mountain was an almost solid chunk of rock rising like an island out of the surrounding rice paddies. I measured it on the binocular lens reticle as three hundred meters across at its base and one hundred meters high. It had abrupt and sometimes sheer walls, and some scrub brush was scattered around the base to a height of about twenty meters. A few scraggly trees grew from higher crevices and on the top. What I couldn't see, but soon would learn about, was the inside. Instead of being solid, as it appeared, the rock was honeycombed with a labyrinth of connected caves and small crevices where the enemy could move, fire, and rapidly change location. The better-trained, better-equipped and better-supported 21st Division units skirted and rolled past Da Dung toward their inland targets and left the formidable natural fortress to be taken by Tai and his lighter, ill-prepared forces. Tai's command post was already set up in similar but smaller caves inside the rock hill up on which I now crouched, staring through my binoculars and wondering how the job could be done.

Both of the rocks were considered holy places, and the caves were used as Buddhist shrines. The command post was in one such cave, which the tables, maps, and radios shared with a large statue of Buddha, urns, flowers, burning joss sticks, and candles. When Tai arrived, I asked what his plan was. He answered in a flat tone, without his usual flair, "The general said capture Da Dung, so I will attack." His voice trailed off. Maybe we would be lucky, he said, and the VC would go away when they saw the division go behind them to their rear. I didn't want to be sloshing around in hip-high water under the mountain, and I surely didn't trust to luck, so I suggested that Tai let me first see if I could get some air strikes on the mountain before the troops attacked. He agreed. I sent the request and asked for napalm, if possible, because of the rock's impregnability. Twenty minutes later, we had six sorties on the way. Helicopter gunships from U.S. Navy ships cruising off the nearby coast, eager to get in on the action, also were being sent.

For the first time during my experience in Vietnam, I had no problem identifying the target to the pilots. The strikes engulfed the rock. Then came the Navy gunships. The helicopters aimed their rockets and machine guns at the crevices and holes and received return fire as they swung past. At least we now knew we weren't "lucky." The VC had not been frightened away by the quickly passing division.

Cautious probes by the troops after the air strikes were immediately turned back by heavy fire from the rock. When Tai turned the units around and tried from the far side, they received additional fire from a second, smaller rock to their rear. My first inclination was to tell Tai just to surround the goddamned rocks and let the enemy sweat it out.

The next day's activity was a repetition of the first day's: air strikes, this time with all-napalm loads, and the troops again repulsed. On the third day, we decided to put an air strike on the smaller rock and have the gunships cover the troops as they moved toward it. Four soldiers were wounded during the final assault, but when the unit got to the smaller rock, the enemy had disappeared. I went to see it late in the afternoon and developed a keen appreciation for the difficulty that lay ahead with Da Dung.

As the days went by, we tried everything available to wear down or eliminate the rock's defenders. Every airplane and helicopter returning from other targets and still having some armament left unloaded it on the rock. It got so we didn't have to ask to have them sent, they just came by and reported in on the radio. The heat was oppressive, and the long climb to the crest of the rock above our command post to witness and record the strikes left me exhausted and drenched in sweat.

Tai got permission from the division to move one of their supporting 155-millimeter howitzers to the road beside the rock. For an entire morning, we adjusted the cannon's fire into all the caves and crevices we could see. During lulls in the firing, the VC fired back, as if to let us know that we were wasting our time. I both hated them and couldn't help admiring the raw courage and determination that were the real roots of our problem.

Near noon, we stopped firing to let an "Early Word" psywar broadcast plane from the U.S. 10th Psychological Operations Company at Binh Tuy make pass after pass over the mountain playing a taped message promising amnesty to the defenders if they would lay down their arms. As I had expected, the plane was fired on, so we resumed the shelling. Tai began shouting excitedly that he could see a white flag of surrender near the top of the caves. When my binoculars revealed that it was only a light patch of granite uncovered by the shelling, the firing continued.

I requested and received large smoke pots. We dropped fifteen of them from helicopters onto the rock to screen a planned attack under the smoke's cover. They just bounced off and fell into the rice paddies. After the fifth day, we were no closer to our objective than we had been on the first. On the seventh day, we decided to try a sneak night attack on Da Dung. Moonrise was going to be late, and enemy fire had been slackening over the past few days. Two companies would assemble after dark in a thick jungle clump on the rock's east side and try to make it across the narrowest open area, which was about one hundred meters from the edge of the jungle treeline to the base of the mountain. Our plan was to try to establish a foothold at the base which the defenders couldn't shoot at without exposing themselves. If they did, our units still in the jungle would fire back and try to keep the VC inside, giving the troops at the base a chance to work their way around the rock's side.

Throughout the day, we kept up the appearance of normal activity and hoped that the enemy would think the coming night would be quiet like the others. The silent attack began at 11 P.M. and proceeded without a hitch until the point unit was halfway to the base of the rock. Whether something happened to alert the VC or they just detected the delicate ripples in the rice paddies made by moving troops, the rock suddenly erupted with gunfire. The second company preparing to leave the edge of the treeline fired back blindly, trying to quench the muzzle flashes flickering from the dark, evil hump. When the company caught in the paddy struggled back to the cover of the trees and took count, twenty-four men were missing, including the company commander. One of my captains was missing, too. I checked with the radio operator and found that it was Capt. Bob Stiles, a good officer and fine young man. As periodic bursts of firing rang from the rock throughout the night, I waited and prayed that Stiles somehow would show up. He hadn't by midmorning, so I sent the report that he was missing. Again I prayed as I watched the floating forms in the paddy being riddled over and over again by the VC in the rock.

All during the day, things were still and quiet, both around the mountain and in the command post. We decided to try a small probe from the east, on the back side of the mountain, in the morning when the sun would be at the probers' backs and in the eyes of the enemy. To everyone's surprise and relief, the rapidly moving and dodging squad made it to the base of Da Dung without a shot being fired. Better yet, as the squad worked its way around the base of the rock to the south side, they found Captain Stiles, the Vietnamese company commander, and ten men hiding in the boulders and bushes. When the command post radio received the news, I let out a shout of thanks. Immediately after, I relayed the news to Can Tho so that the previous message to Stiles's family could be stopped or corrected.

We all rejoiced quietly when Stiles returned to the command post. As he told the story, tears rolled down his cheek. During the first terrible moments of firing, he rushed to the base of the mountain, carrying the wounded company commander. Then he returned into the dark, flooded field amid the bullets to carry one more wounded man to the slim margin of safety in the brush at Nui Da Dung's edge. They stayed hidden in the rocks and brush throughout the night and the next day, while the VC above them shouted obscenities and continued to pump bullets into the bloated, floating corpses below.

Other units followed the probe to the rock without incident and, when they finally reached the caves, found that the enemy had withdrawn. To account for our fourteen dead, there were only scattered piles of unidentifiable charred bodies, twelve rifles, and one destroyed machine gun. Before I returned to Rach Gia, I waded alone through the waist-high water on the route taken by the attacking companies and stood at the base of Da Dung, looking up at its commanding walls. We probably got off cheap, I thought, although fourteen families wouldn't agree.

Back in Rach Gia, I recommended Captain Stiles for the Distinguished Service Cross, our second highest award for valor. I would be gone before the answer came back. Months after I left the province, Lt. Frank Howard wrote that Captain Stiles's award had been downgraded to a Silver Star. Since we were advisors and not assigned to an American troop unit, I wasn't too surprised. Although Stiles deserved the Distinguished Service Cross, few if any advisors were accorded that honor, no matter what the circumstances. Perhaps if the two men Stiles carried to safety under fire had been Americans, he would have gotten the Distinguished Service Cross.

Chapter 13

Hon Soc, B-52s, and Chickens

Major Holland came to the province operations center one Saturday afternoon to find me. In low tones he asked if I could come outside for a minute. I followed him to the courtyard, and he continued. We had just received a radio message that a courier was en route from Can Tho and could speak only with me. The plane was due to land at Rach Soi in about forty minutes.

The plane was already parked when I drove the jeep onto the airfield; a young captain was pacing back and forth beside it. He saluted, asked if I was Colonel Metzner, and glanced at the name tape on my shirt to make sure before he continued. In rehearsed fashion, he told me I could divulge everything he was about to reveal except the source. The Vietnamese were not to know the source. I replied that I understood, and he went on. He was from a U.S. Signal Corps radio intercept unit, and they'd been monitoring VC radio messages regarding Nui Hon Soc. Since Hon Soc was the largest of the Three Sisters Mountains, where the U.S. radar and sensor monitoring detachment was located with the Vietnamese artillery unit, he had my immediate and total attention. The VC had been moving into position for about ten days to attack Nui Hon Soc, and the order was intercepted last night telling them to execute the attack tonight. I looked at my watch. It was 2:35 P.M. I asked if he had any other information or details. He didn't. Before he returned to the plane, he reminded me again not to divulge where the information came from. Before I started back to Rach Gia, I switched on the jeep radio and told the office to contact the sector ship, have it finish the trip it was making, and then have it stand by for me at the helipad.

Tai was at his house and looked disgruntled when I insisted on seeing him. After I told him the information, he just sat and looked at me. When he asked how I knew the information was correct, I told him that it was extremely reliable but that I could not reveal the source. He obviously didn't like it that I couldn't trust him with the source. While he still sat contemplating, I continued that the team helicopter was coming to take us to Hon Soc in about twenty minutes, and we could be there and back in an hour. We had to convince them the attack was coming and to get ready. He still didn't answer and sat looking as though he hadn't heard anything at all, with his thick lips hanging open; I began to get visibly irritated. Finally he got up and walked toward the telephone, saying he'd tell the operation center to radio the information to Hon Soc. Bolting out of my chair, I yelled at him that we couldn't do that, as it would tell the VC that we knew. It would be better if the Hon Soc units were alerted and ready, so we could catch and punish the VC. When he just stood motionless, I turned my back on him and retrieved my pistol belt and hat, stating that I would go alone to tell the Hon Soc commander that I was bringing the information from the province chief. Tai gave me a mechanical handshake and said to go and tell him that.

As the helicopter swung toward the steel-matted pad nestled in the boulders on Hon Soc's crest, I leaned out and looked for anything out of the ordinary beneath the surrounding ridges. But I knew beforehand that there would be none. The young American captain commanding the radar detachment was waiting to meet me. I told him of the courier's message as we walked to the operations bunker to meet Major Canh, who commanded the two territorial companies stationed on Hon Soc to protect the site.

The major met us outside his operations center holding his handsome eight-year-old son by the hand. Father and son never were far apart, and today the boy was dressed in a small version of his dad's uniform. Inside the heavily sandbagged bunker, I said that Tai had sent me and related the intelligence information. When I finally convinced Canh that there was no mistake and that the attack would occur tonight, he answered that they would be ready.

At my request, the three of us, followed by the boy, walked through the artillery positions; the large, crowded family living area; and the maze of defensive positions, surrounded by tangles of barbed wire. As we passed the tall flagpole, I noticed that a small American flag fluttered beneath the large yellow and red Vietnamese flag. When I pointed to it, the captain smiled and said sheepishly that one of the sergeants had had his wife send it. I thought it looked very good up there. Suddenly I felt tired and depressed, and during our walk I had considered staying with them and sending the helicopter back without me. But I had concluded that that would be dumb and wouldn't accomplish a thing. As I waved from the departing helicopter, I suffered profound guilt watching the two commanders and the boy slowly walking up the path to the operations bunker.

Climbing the six flights of stairs to the rooftop club in the new consolidated quarters took great effort, and I was exhausted when I reached the top. The sun was beginning to set when Major Holland arrived and joined me at one of the tables overlooking the city. I was preoccupied and couldn't get the small, fluttering flag and the people on Hon Soc out of my mind. When Holland finally asked about my visit and I was in the middle of telling him, the team of night-patrol gunships that I had had him request earlier passed over the city on their way to fuel at Rach Soi Airfield. Suddenly I pushed Holland, telling him quickly to go back to the office and, over the radio, ask the command and control ship if one of them could take me someplace before dark. I would explain later to the pilot. Holland squinted his eyes at me and said slowly that if I was going where he thought I was going, that was stupid. I urged him to hurry and do what I told him to. Maybe it was stupid, but I had to go.

The gunship team was nicknamed "Fireflies" because of the large searchlights attached to their ships' undersides and because they operated at night. Since it was almost dark, the entire flight came to the helipad, and the gunships orbited above as the command and control ship landed for me. I explained to the pilot and asked that the team do its patroling at the southern end of Kien An district and the coastal fringes of the U-Minh Forest, so they could reach Hon Soc quickly if we needed them. I also told him to keep the gunships far away when he took me to Hon Soc. As we headed for the mountain, I watched the flashing navigation lights of the gunships moving toward the Kien An coast and felt very alone but strangely calm. As I instructed, the pilot radioed ahead to the radar detachment that he was delivering the mail, and the captain was on the helipad to meet me. I told him that I was adding one more gun for the night, as we hurried up the path and the command and control ship lifted off into the darkness.

Propping my gun in the corner of the operations bunker I had picked to squat in, I settled down for a long night. Major Canh had had his cot placed beside the radios, and his son was already asleep on it. The captain brought in his sleeping bag and revealed two warm cans of beer for us when he unrolled it. By ten o'clock, he was fast asleep, and the only sound to keep me company was the background static of the radios. Because of the mosquitos, I couldn't have slept even had I not been expecting something to happen. The last time I looked at my watch it was 2:45 A.M. I must have dozed off shortly thereafter, because, when the major shook my arm, the first dim light of dawn was creeping through the bunker entrance. It had been quiet all night; nothing had happened. My back, hips, and knees ached from the damp mud floor and cracked loudly when I stretched. As the major handed me a canteen cup half full of hot tea, he silently mouthed the words "No VC." I tried to impress upon him that the information was good and that he should continue to take it seriously and be very cautious. He patted my arm and walked out with his son.

Tai never mentioned Hon Soc after that, and I didn't know if he knew that I spent the night there. Four days later, Hon Soc was attacked, and signal intelligence confirmed that the VC were already in the caves beneath its crest in force the night I was there. The VC didn't get to the radar or the guns, but they were inside the wire and firing as they ran through the family living area before they were discovered, most likely because security had reverted to a loose "normal." Thirty-two family members were killed or wounded, and most of the huts were burned to the ground. Only six province soldiers were wounded, and twelve VC bodies were recovered, all inside the wire. All the Americans and the major and his son were safe. Tai wasn't interested in visiting, so I went by myself. The fight had been fierce and fast, but, other than the bloody and burned family area, the site didn't look much different. Tai never said a word about the attack, and I felt he never really associated it with my earlier warning.

The number of B-52 bomber strikes available for use within the provinces had increased over the past year, and corps had urged us to take full advantage of them on appropriate targets. Precautions for use of these awesome weapons were stringent, as they should be, and approval and cancellation authority rested solely in American hands. Delivery accuracy of the high-altitude strikes was assured by new radar targeting techniques, but each province senior advisor requesting the strikes was personally bound by procedure accurately to define the precise limits of the target and scrupulously to avoid the most remote possibility of accidental civilian casualties from the devastating saturation bombings.

Both the province chief and province senior advisor were required to sign a mission request certifying the exact nature of the target, the accuracy of the map location, and the absence of civilians in the target area. The request had to be accompanied by a map of the area, upon which were drawn the precise limits of the target. (A strike by one B-52 covered an area three miles long and one hundred meters wide. A formation of three planes covered an area two miles long and five eighths of a mile wide.) While the agreement and consent of the province chief were required, the final decision rested with the province senior advisor. Before this time, I had avoided using the weapon because I never could trust the truth or accuracy of the intelligence upon which the selection of targets was based.

Tai submitted a list of twenty-two targets, which I reduced to five after comparing his list with those the district senior advisors ethically and morally could condone. The final test was scrutiny of my own conscience. Two targets were reliably verified base area locations in the U-Minh; two more were radar- and sensor-verified infiltration assembly and trans-shipment locations southeast of the Three Sisters Mountains, and the last was an enemy training and staging hideout in thick and impenetrable jungle southeast of Kien Binh, near the Chuong Thien border. Tai argued that his entire list should be bombed, but I remained firm, since even the slightest doubt on my part made a target unacceptable. Compliance with the requirement to preclude civilian casualties I achieved by personally inspecting the target from the air within several hours of the scheduled strike, then verifying by code that the area was clear of civilians.

The VC intelligence network was vast, stretching as far as Soviet trawlers near Guam, which sent radio signals each time the B-52s took off. The enemy knew that a lone helicopter making repeated passes over or near any target worth consideration could forecast a coming strike. Agents and returnees told of bases quickly being cleared or moved deep underground in such instances. Accordingly, I made my prestrike helicopter observations by having the pilot make one pass wide of the target, as though we were traveling out of the province; then, after an appropriate time lapse, circling and returning from another direction to land at the nearest district town. After another delay, hoping that the stop would make it appear we were visiting, we took off again, overflew the target, and swung back to land once more, after a pre-arranged radio message called us back. On our final departure, we crossed a different portion of the target. In all, that provided me five overflights to attempt scrutinizing the target with my binoculars. While I would have liked fifty, five permitted a decision.

Each prestrike flight was a lonely experience during which I prayed I'd see either evidence indicating civilian presence or a total absence of signs, and not something in between. On one such flight, I saw several sampans pulled up under the trees on a canal bank in the target area. Since the canals of the area were the only way to travel through the dense underbrush and both sides used them, I had the pilot rapidly cross several more times as I strained in the decreasing twilight to stare through the jungle crown with my binoculars for some indication that the sampans might belong to civilians. As we were about to leave and I had made the decision that sampans left in that desolate, known VC base could belong only to the enemy, two white specks moved from beneath the trees. I shouted for the pilot to swing back and make one more pass, and two scrawny white chickens saved the area from the obliterating rain of bombs.

The other target areas had no chickens, visible huts, undisguised cooking fires, animal pens, or sampans continuing to move along canals despite the helicopter's presence, and the strikes went in. Wherever I was when they did, the frightening, prolonged rumble and the earthquake vibration of the explosions made me pause and pray that death might come to the enemy and avoid the innocent. Friendly forces were required to make a sweep through the target within twenty-four hours after the strike. Other than some blood-tainted, water-filled bomb craters and some broken rifles, nothing else was found. As I viewed the utter destruction, I knew that little survived after the bombing, anything else buried forever beneath the mounds of mud surrounding the large holes.

Meanwhile, the enemy was not sitting idle or staying on the defensive. Three large outposts in the coastal low-mountain Binh Tri area south of Kien Luong simultaneously were attacked and partially overrun at 1:40 A.M. in early June, 1970. Tai and I listened to the frantic calls for help from the outposts over the province operation center radio and heard their reports that the supporting artillery fire from Kien Luong was ineffective because the VC were too close and already starting to come through the barbed-wire perimeters. I made several attempts to get Tai to gather forces for a night heliborne operation to land behind the attackers and relieve pressure on the outposts, but he wouldn't consider it. He protested that it was too late and we couldn't do it at night.

As the radio reports kept describing the outpost's worsening plight, I kept insisting that, precisely because it was late and at night, we should go in and surprise the enemy. If we waited until daylight, surely it would be too late. The Kien Luong district team close to the action radioed that it was doubtful the outposts could hold out through the night, and Tai rebuffed another of my pleas, so I took a calculated gamble. Away from Tai's hearing, I radioed Can Tho and requested the helicopters required to lift three companies to the Binh Tri area near the outposts, telling the lie that the province chief already had dispatched the companies to Rach Soi Airfield and they would be ready when the helicopters arrived. Certain that such a bold and rare move would be supported, I told a second lie. I informed Tai that helicopter units and gunships were on their way, hoping to force him into face-saving action, because the corps commander would be asking questions in the morning. When he appeared to be over his shock and anger, I pushed him to order the three companies to prepare and move quickly to the airfield at Rach Soi for the pickup.

After we hurriedly mapped out the landing zones and schemes of maneuver for the troops, I contacted the Kien Luong team in code to arrange and supervise the refueling and rearming of the helicopters at the district airfield. Then an excited, high-pitched voice broke in on our frequency in English, shouting that he was VC and would kill all Americans and government soldiers. I shook my fist in the air, calling him a VC sonofabitch and shouting that he'd better get off this goddamn frequency. Half the operations center duty shift was looking now and wondering what was going on, and half was laughing. I was so infuriated and frustrated that I just continued to yell, ordering him to get off the radio and stay off. If he didn't, I promised to come up there and kill *him*, not him me. Surprisingly, he got off, and I continued my message to Kien Luong.

The landings went in without problems under the direction of Major Holland and Tai's deputy for security, and the VC broke off their attacks after almost overrunning two of the three outposts. Tai received great praise from the corps commander for his quick, daring response, and he acted as if he deserved every bit of the credit.

In early July, I received a radio call from the Kien An district senior advisor, wanting to know when I would be coming to his location. He was anxious for me to hear a plan devised by the district chief, Captain Trinh, which he was convinced had a lot of merit. Next morning, I radioed the Kien An team to pick me up by boat from the village directly across from the mouth of the Big Tree Canal. Trinh greeted me with his usual broad smile and genuine enthusiasm, then ushered me to a chair and began to explain his bold, straightforward plan. I liked it, even though he was proposing a giant step.

If the province could be given authority to recruit ten additional territorial force companies, of which Trinh could guarantee recruiting six; and if corps could be persuaded to send one regiment from the 21st Division to operate for four months in Hieu Le District in the U-Minh Forest south of Kien An, Trinh could guarantee taking back and keeping control of Hieu Le District. Trinh had the precise locations of the ten new outposts plotted on the map and proposed a phased progression for their establishment, under protection of the regiment. Captain Trinh had been district chief of Hieu Le years before, and the people had contacted him and wanted the government back.

The ten outposts would be built along the canal and within one kilometer either side of the canal, where 95 percent of the people lived. Zones for the regiment to clear of the enemy would extend another three kilometers beyond. Both Trinh and I understood that he would be gambling his family's lives on the plan's success. When I asked if I could make a copy of the charts and the map overlays, Trinh sheepishly smiled and handed me a prepared packet that included all facts, figures, and timetables. As I left, he cautioned me that Colonel Tai wouldn't consider the plan, since he would see no profit in taking Hieu Le back from the enemy. I wondered how Trinh meant the word "profit." I answered that now I could only say that the plan looked good to me and that I agreed with him that we should take back Hieu Le if we could.

As the district senior advisor walked with me back to the boat dock, he asked me to do him a favor. Trinh was due to have been promoted to major a long time ago and deserved the rank. The reason he had not been promoted was that he was an ethnic Cambodian, a second-class citizen in the army's eyes. The district advisor was due to go home in three months and wanted to see Trinh made a major before he left. I promised I'd work on that and jumped in the boat.

I took Trinh's packet with me to the next CORDS meeting. When John Vann heard the plan, he didn't commit himself one way or the other but commented that he'd be in Rach Gia with the corps commander the following week for an update briefing by Tai. He told me to present Trinh's plan to the general after Tai's briefing, and we'd see what happened. I said I'd have to let it come as a surprise to Tai, because he'd never agree to springing it on his boss. Vann answered that that was how it would be. Before I left, I asked him to help me push for Trinh's promotion, which he promised to do.

The next week, Tai gave one of his usual smooth, theatrical briefings to Major General Thanh, the corps commander. He covered the details of the Nui Hon Soc radar site attack and the Binh Tri outposts night rescue. When Tai finished, and before the Corps commander could get up and start to leave, I stepped onto Tai's briefing platform, and Tai moved to the side, smiling with his oversized lips and wondering what was going on. I announced that I'd like to take a few more minutes to show the general and Mr. Vann an interesting plan Captain Trinh in Kien An had shared with Colonel Tai and me. I nodded with a smile to Tai, whose smile had turned to a puzzled frown as he took a seat to the right of the general. Tai kept blinking his eyes widely and then turning to smile at the general, as I used enlarged versions of Trinh's charts and maps to go through the plan.

General Thanh watched in impassive silence until I finished. Before he or Tai could say anything, Vann got up beside me and said he thought it was a workable plan and deserved earnest consideration. The general just smiled as he got up to leave, while I grabbed two copies of Trinh's packet from my chair and handed one to the general and another to Vann, with the comment that Tai and I thought they'd want to take the details with them. The general handed his packet to his aide, turned to Tai, and thanked him for both good briefings. He then strode toward the waiting jeeps, with Tai waddling close behind him. When the general's party was gone, Tai glowered at me without a word and hesitated before shaking hands. I feigned surprise and frowned back: Trinh *had* briefed him on the plan, hadn't he?

Tai got over being peeved about my surprise briefing and began taking much of the credit for Trinh's plan, as corps and CORDS started seriously to consider it. He was asked to elaborate on it in writing and later was called to Can Tho to consult with the corps staff about the recruiting potential for the ten territorial force companies and to discuss timing and other details. Tai called Trinh in to help in both instances, and I was relieved to see that Trinh had not gotten in trouble, as things were turning out.

Returning from one of my frequent visits to our widely dispersed teams, I received a radio call. Tai had been looking for me all morning and wanted to see me at his house as soon as possible. The matter had to be important, for Tai to be so anxious to see me, so I had Tong speed as fast as the mud road would permit. When we arrived, Tai was presiding over a large staff meeting which included many of his civilian officials.

Every other time I'd arrived when he was busy with a meeting, he acknowledged my presence with a wave and motioned me to sit and wait. This time, as I automatically headed for the couches, Tai jumped up when he saw me and quickly waddled toward me, looking anxious. Instead of the usual limp, dead-fish handshake, followed by a quick release, he grabbed my hand and held onto it as he pulled me over into a corner. He spoke softly telling me that he had just received word from President Thieu that he would be transferred to be the province chief of Vinh Binh. I was equally surprised and relieved. As I groped for the correct facial expression and words of regret to hide my pleasure at the news, he shattered my joy. He had asked Mr. Vann if I might go with him, and Vann had agreed. My phone call to John Vann to get off the hook and stay in Rach Gia was to no avail. I definitely was going with Tai, and the Vinh Binh Province senior advisor, Col. Dick Ellison, was to trade places with me here in Rach Gia. Tai and I were due in Tra Vinh, Vinh Binh's capital, in three days.

During the team's impromptu farewell gathering, they gave me a gift intended to bring good luck. As events would turn out, I'd need good luck in Vinh Binh. The province had the reputation of being a difficult can of worms, and I would be there with Tai.

Chapter 14

Sometimes You Lose

Tai waited until the afternoon before our morning departure in early August, 1970, to tell me that we would drive the long distance to Tra Vinh. He had arranged permission for my jeep and driver to leave the province so that we could make the road trip together. Resigned now to going, I was pleased at the prospect of traveling through places I'd not seen before.

When we crossed the Kien Giang border, the drive through mostly pacified An Giang Province became relaxed, and even Tong, my driver, stopped nervously watching the side of the road for trouble more than he watched the middle for traffic. Once across the wide Hau Giang arm of the Mekong River, our drive through Vinh Long Province was pleasant and uneventful but very hot, with a few passing rain showers providing some relief. About two hours later, about forty kilometers southwest of Vinh Long City, we began to see a noticeable change in the character of the land, people, and road. A short distance further, as we reached and crossed the Vinh Binh border into Cang Long District, the change became pronounced.

The mood of the countryside was disturbingly ominous. Silence and inactivity contrasted with the bustling activity seen all along the trip to that point. Hamlets became fewer and shabbier, and the people were tense and nervous as we passed. The paved road all but disappeared inside Vinh Binh and became a quagmire of muddy holes and ruts between small patches of surviving blacktop. After Tai conferred with the police and military escort that awaited us at the border, we bounced on, following

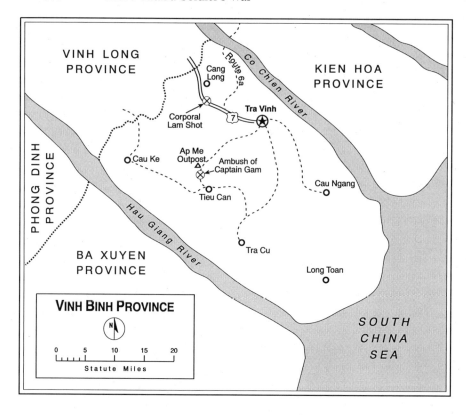

them at a speed reduced to a crawl by having to weave and sway around and through the muddy mess. After we crossed a long concrete bridge that was scarred and chipped from gunfire, the countryside, the road, and our speed improved. We were in Chau Thanh District. It was almost 5 P.M. when we arrived in the province capital of Tra Vinh, strained and tired. A ceremony awaited us before we could unpack and unwind, however.

A thick-set man whom I recognized as Col. Ton That Dong, the outgoing province chief, and Col. Richard Ellison, his province senior advisor, waited beside the flag-bedecked dais to greet us. Dong looked the part of the bully he was reported to be. He had a thick neck supporting a dullard's face and wore thick eyeglasses that accentuated slightly crossed eyes. Before Dong became the Vinh Binh province chief, he had served mostly in intelligence assignments. After mismanagement and oppression of the province's 60 percent ethnic Cambodian population, he was being sacked by the Saigon government. The Americans had long pressed for his removal.

The final straw that prompted Dong's departure came when the leading ethnic Cambodian Buddhist monks in Tra Vinh departed from quiet apathy and advocated open opposition to Dong's heavy-handed policies. Dong's response to the antigovernment demonstrations was to have the military move in and truncheon the monks before throwing them in jail.

Dick Ellison was as cool to me at our meeting as Dong was to Tai. I guessed that he long had urged Dong's removal and now was stuck going with him to Kien Giang. After a very long and boring speech which bordered on being a scolding tirade, Dong introduced Tai. Tai wisely kept his address short, finishing to the same polite applause given Dong.

Dick lived alone in a small villa near the province administrative center. The house was tended to by one cook, housekeeper, and mother hen called Chi Hai. She scuffled out to meet me, rattling off a string of welcoming remarks. Tong, my jeep driver, had told her that I spoke Vietnamese. Chi Hai was small, bone-thin, old, and wrinkled. She wore her graying hair pulled into a small bun, which made her bony face look more gaunt. She had no hips, and both feet were crippled and splayed outward, extending almost sideways. Her teeth were bad and beginning to rot, but her eyes sparkled when she smiled and, I was to find out, when she was mad.

Tong was given a place to sleep at the rear of the house with the U.S.-employed ethnic Cambodian security platoon, since he would not be returning to Rach Gia until Dick was ready to leave in a day or two. When the time came to say goodbye, Tong wiped tears from his eyes. He hesitated going during our long handshake, at the door, and while sitting in his jeep, until I gently shouted and waved for him to get going. He didn't even notice the paper bag I'd placed near the steering wheel. It contained some money and three cartons of his favorite cigarettes.

I kept a low profile until Dick left. Then I occupied my desk in the team office and signed the assumption-of-command order that the team adjutant had placed in the middle of my desk. The order was dated August 8, 1970. For the next two days, the team presented fact-crammed briefings which were organized and directed by my civilian deputy province senior advisor, Don Colin. Don was tall, large-boned, and heavy but not flabby. He had a full beard, wore thick glasses, spoke Vietnamese well, and turned out to be both an outstanding deputy and a great help to the province and to me.

Vinh Binh was slightly more than half the size of Kien Giang but had 90 percent as many people as Kien Giang. It had 5,880 more men under arms in province territorial forces than Kien Giang, a fact that suggested the province's security problem. There were seven districts, all except one accessible by an extensive road network. Long Toan District was on the fringes of a large mangrove VC base area along the South China Sea coast. Cang Long District, through which Tai and I drove when we arrived, was dominated by another large VC base area and was the province's biggest problem. The second biggest problem was the long-standing friction between the ethnic Cambodians and the government.

The Cambodians had settled the Delta long before the Vietnamese had moved south, beginning in the fifteenth century. The Cambodians were pushed out of most areas except Vinh Binh, where racial and historical animosities remained firmly rooted in cultural differences. The Cambodian culture stemmed from Indian civilization, while the Vietnamese was influenced mostly by the Chinese. Even the Buddhist religion they shared failed to help the two groups bridge their differences. The Vietnamese followed the Mahayana form, while the Cambodians adhered to the Therevada conformation. Although the VC tried hard to play on the differences, they had one big disadvantage in the eyes of the ethnic Cambodian population: the VC were Vietnamese. On the whole, the Cambodians in the territorial forces fought and defended their hamlets well.

Fanning the flames of trouble recently between the Cambodians and the government was the new national draft law. The Cambodians resented and resisted conscription of their youths to serve in the regular army away from their province, villages, and homes. The government was accusing the monks of hiding draft dodgers disguised as novice monks in the numerous temples and pagodas. The monks were steadfastly claiming that the young men were indeed monks and warning the government not to violate the sanctity of the temples to apprehend the young men. This tense deadlock Dong exacerbated and Tai inherited.

Conservative estimates placed thirty hamlets and 18 percent of the province population under firm VC control. As in other provinces, figures didn't mean much, as the bulk of the population was still on the political fence. The American province advisory team was sizable, with 157 military and 9 officer-level civilians. At the end of the first day of briefings, my personal interpreter came to me and introduced himself. Sergeant Long, whose name meant *dragon* in Vietnamese, was an educated young man who took his job as my advisor very seriously.

When I asked Dragon for an honest opinion about why there were no ethnic Cambodian interpreters on the team, he looked around to make sure nobody was close enough to hear, leaned near me, and said there would never be any, because it was not in the interest of the province staff for the team to have one. There were problems the government would prefer to hide. The AID advisor, Jeff Milligan, spoke Cambodian well and was trusted by the chief monks. He could help me. Before I left the office, Dragon called over another interpreter, Corporal Lam, and introduced him. Dragon recommended that if he ever was not available for some reason, Lam should be the replacement I called on.

When Tai held his important first meeting with the monks, I took Dragon along with me. En route, Dragon asked if I knew that Tai was ethnic Cambodian—one of the few who had risen to high government position despite his background. I had always suspected it because of Tai's appearance but never had given the matter much thought. Even though Tai spoke Cambodian, he used Vietnamese and a Cambodian interpreter when he addressed the monks. I knew he did so because he needed to act cautiously early in his new role, in order to protect his position with the government.

As Tai became involved in his own round of briefings, I traveled to visit the district teams. In the following weeks, I covered every foot of the large road network, bouncing and bumping along the monsoon-muddied roads, much to the dismay of Dragon, who insisted on coming with me. Cau Ke and Tra Cu were the most distant districts, but the trip to Cang Long was the one requiring the most vigilance. Military vehicles often were sniped at when they had to slow down to a snail's pace on the rutted and frequently sabotaged road. As we passed through the bad sections, Dragon and my driver Song urged caution. In response, I leaned way out of the jeep brandishing my large-barreled grenade launcher, hoping that the sight of it would discourage any would-be VC snipers. Months later, we were fired at twice. Long Toan was the last district I visited, because it could only be reached by helicopter. All the teams impressed me favorably, but Long Toan and Cang Long became special. Both teams' spirit and determined optimism was directly and wonderfully disproportionate to their isolation, the primitive living conditions, and the preponderance of VC control in their districts. I ended my grueling and arduous visits with buoyed spirits.

The province economy was on the upswing despite the large areas under VC control or influence, and Tra Vinh City had a surprising number of thriving commercial ventures. The province economy was primarily agricultural, with rice the main crop. As was happening in other parts of the Delta, the farmers were becoming more prosperous as each crop season went by. Of the 148,554 tillable hectares in the province, 133,000 were planted with rice, yielding an average of 1.7 tons per hectare.

U.S. advisors and the Agriculture Service were introducing new high-yield seed strains and demonstrating how the new seed, in conjunction with commercial fertilizers, could raise production. As of my arrival, pilot plots totaling 6,000 hectares were getting attention by producing first yields averaging 5 tons per hectare; one yield was officially recorded at 11 tons. The economic future looked bright, and Tai quickly saw how to take advantage of the budding prosperity. Not long after our arrival, I received reports of new province taxes which never were recorded or reflected in the budget.

A team of U.S. Air Force doctors and medical technicians worked with the province hospital staff. The team chief, a major and also the senior surgeon, came to my house one evening to ask a favor. They needed an interpreter to work part-time with the team and preferred one who could learn medical terms and was intelligent enough to help with supply requisitions and inventories. Dragon recommended Lam, who thereafter was assigned to work at the hospital four hours each afternoon. Lam took to the job well, and the Air Force medical team took to Lam.

Lam was a handsome, serious young man who worked hard and took pride in his new job at the hospital. In fact, he studied his medical vocabulary so intently that the other interpreters joked with him about it and called him "Doctor" Lam. That never seemed to bother him. One Saturday afternoon when he should have been off-duty, Lam came to the office while I was working on end-of-month reports and asked if he could use the team's bilingual dictionaries to finish a translation for the hospital. He introduced his beautiful wife and good-looking son, who sat quietly while he worked.

Almost three months had passed since our arrival in the province and, except for his initial visits to three districts, Tai had not ventured out of Tra Vinh. Instead, he called the district chiefs to come for meetings at his province office. But the war, a see-saw battle seemingly ending in a draw, continued to be fought out in the districts. Our biggest problems with the enemy were along the seacoast mangroves and in the two districts forming the land border with Vinh Long Province—Cau Ke and Cang Long. Cau Ke had our most competent district chief and Cang Long our weakest and least aggressive.

Most of my time was spent traveling to the districts, mostly to Cau Ke and Cang Long. While it wasn't difficult to stay alert on the road to Cang Long, where an occasional sniper shot would ring out, on the other lengthy and deceptively quiet trips, it took constant effort to stay on guard.

Tai still attended Monday morning flag-raising ceremonies but now clustered his assistants and staff around him, as if to say that if he was to be killed, most would join him. This was only another of the bizarre changes I'd begun to notice in Tai's behavior. He was keeping to himself more and more and was staying at home as much as he was in his office. In three weeks' time, he called me only twice. Once was to accompany him on a seemingly pointless trip to a small, isolated outpost surrounded by jungle and accessible only by boat. We stayed there only twenty minutes, during which time Tai made a show of looking over the flimsy defenses. I couldn't imagine why Tai would go to such a place, particularly when he was not going to the many places he should have visited. The whole episode was irrational, but so was Tai lately.

Tai's other invitation started out as a surprisingly pleasant experience. We went to a gala opening ceremony at the Tra Vinh community swimming pool, an old AID-sponsored project that had been closed for several years—since the filtration system broke down. After a showy entrance, we joined the city council and elders at an elaborate and formal dedication. Amid flags and banners proclaiming the town's appreciation, Tai made a speech with flashes of his old flamboyance. Looking at the inviting clear green water, I assumed that Tai had manipulated some budget money to fix the filter. At the end of Tai's speech, he started counting: "One, two, three." On "three" the mob of youngsters crowding the pool's edge all jumped in, screaming, laughing, and chattering. It was a happy sight, shared and enjoyed by the smiling guests and parents. As we left to the applause of the guests, Tai seemed to be his old self, and he waved and paused several times to laugh and point out some child doing a crazy dive into the water. Three days later, the pool was closed, and two children were dead. The filtration system hadn't been repaired, and the first child's body was discovered in the dirty, fetid water when other children stepped on him. The second body was found when the pool was drained. Tai reacted by becoming more somber and withdrawn.

The corps plan to speed the pacification of the Cang Long VC base area was centered around an ambitious effort to rebuild Route 6A, which pierced its center. Once the road was completed, the new commerce it generated would draw people to the area, under the protection of new government centers. Road work had stopped months before Tai and I arrived, due to VC sabotage, attacks on the work crews, and the inability of province forces to protect the widely spread corps engineer units involved. As a result, the project had been abandoned instead of postponed when the last rainy season came.

With John Vann's support, I began to pressure corps to resume the project soon after we arrived, and the decision was made to proceed again at the end of the rainy season. In addition to sending corps engineer units, a regiment from the 21st Division was assigned to shield the engineers by aggressive operations and was in the process of setting up its command post in the heart of the base area.

When I couldn't get Tai to drive to the incomplete and insecure sections of road construction to give encouragement and spur progress, I began going without him. I took the team's engineer advisor, Capt. Ted Sloan, with me. Sloan had to submit periodic reports on the project's progress, and I wanted to see for myself how the work was coming along. After several trips, I noticed that the regiment's command post was completed, so I stopped on the return leg to visit and introduce myself. I also wanted to find out when the regiment would start operations, because Sloan and I had been shot at several times during our inspections.

To my surprise and pleasure, the commander of the regiment turned out to be an old friend from my days in My Tho. Col. Huynh Van Chinh had been Captain Chinh an assistant division operations officer whom I had known six years earlier, when I was with the 7th Division. From the beginning of our talk, it was apparent that, apart from our past friendship, we were now on different sides. While there was no conflict concerning overall objectives when division units were sent to a province to operate, there were always conflicts over perceived scopes of authority and prerogatives. I asked Chinh if he had met with Colonel Tai yet, and he answered dourly Tai hadn't been to see him, nor had he invited him to visit. Seeing that I had better try to manipulate some kind of get-together, I lied to Chinh, saying that Tai was arranging a meeting and Chinh would hear about it soon. Chinh just grunted and chuckled.

When I arrived back in Tra Vinh, I went directly to Tai's house and told him that Chinh would like to meet with him in the next few days before all the regiment's units arrived in Cang Long. Tai just nodded and let me know that our meeting was over. Tai's secretary called me to the meeting several days later, during which plans and agreements were worked out between Chinh and the province deputy for security, while Tai sat in stony silence and seemed not to be listening. In the weeks that followed, Chinh aggressively pushed operations through the base area. Road repair and construction moved ahead at a slow but steady rate.

The long road to Cau Ke went through Tieu Can District, and I always stopped at the team compound to rest and visit before continuing on the remaining hazardous portion of the trip. This time, Maj. Craig Murray (this name is changed in the interest of the officer and his family), the Tieu Can District senior advisor, had a surprise for me. He had a new district chief, Captain Gam, who already was implementing team recommendations long disregarded by his predecessor. Tai hadn't told me, but I pretended that I knew about Gam's arrival and asked to meet with him. Captain Gam returned to the team house, choosing to do me the courtesy instead of making me go to meet him.

Gam was young and clean-cut. His boyish, disarmingly gentle voice expressed sincerity, anxiety, an admission of his inexperience, and acknowledgement of his need for the advice and support of his counterpart—all atypical for a Vietnamese officer under any circumstances, but particularly at a first meeting. When Gam left, Murray told me out of hearing of the rest of the team that Gam's obviously well-to-do mother had come all the way down from Saigon for his installation ceremony and proudly had sat beside his wife and two children until it was over.

Captain Gam later had confided that his rich mother had made him promise that he would be honest, work hard for the people, and not get involved in graft or corruption. That was very important for the honor of the family and himself. To help him stay out of temptation's way, she was giving him money each month to add to his small salary, to make certain that his wife and children were properly taken care of. My response was only an incredulous smile.

It was too late when we left Tieu Can to go on to Cau Ke, so I told my new jeep driver, Song, to turn south to Tra Cu. The population of Tra Cu District was predominantly ethnic Cambodian, like their energetic and competent district chief. I didn't go there often because the district was doing so well economically and militarily that VC units didn't like to go there, either. Each of my infrequent trips had been enjoyable, and this one was no exception. The district chief proudly displayed simple but fact-crammed charts outlining the ongoing progress of economic and social reform. One figure that caught my attention was the surprising number of tractors purchased by regional farm cooperatives. The staggering quoted cost of each investment spoke well for the present and future prosperity of the district.

Things started well enough the last week of November, 1970, with two well-executed province-level operations. Both were heliborne and were run by the deputy for security instead of Tai. The first attack was a rapid, pouncing raid on a VC engineer workshop in Long Toan District. We suffered no friendly casualties and found the engineer workshop near an old World War II Japanese airfield. In addition to capturing a variety of weapons, explosives, radios, grenades, mines, generators, fuel, boats, engines, and batteries, we took several more interesting items.

The most significant and thought-provoking was a large number of U.S. 105-millimeter artillery projectiles, which, I knew from past experience, almost certainly were destined to be used as mines. Although I wondered how the VC got such a large number, interrogation of our few captives drew a blank. The most intriguing item was a 500-volt lighting set, complete with sockets, bulbs, and wire and capable of lighting a vast area. The second operation was tactically similar and was conducted in Cau Ngang District, not far from the old airfield. It produced nothing except two badly maimed soldiers.

At 5 A.M. on a Sunday morning, tragedy struck Can Long District town. I didn't learn about it until it was over. The operations center duty advisor called to tell me that he hadn't been able to contact the Cang Long team since the routine 1 A.M. radio check. He added that he didn't notify me earlier, since it might be only a radio problem; nothing was happening with the Vietnamese at the operations center to indicate otherwise. He called me soon after to say he'd just been informed that the district headquarters and the troop compounds had been attacked and overrun by a large VC force sometime between 1 and 3 A.M. When Can Tho couldn't send the sector ship early, as I requested, I drove to Cang Long.

By the time I arrived, much of the bloody physical evidence of the disaster had been covered up or removed for burial, but enough remained to show clearly the extent of the early-morning horror. We pieced together the story from the shaken but still defiant district team. The team had made its usual check around 11 P.M., to make sure that the night ambushes and patrols were out, and then turned in. But all of the supposedly all-night ambushes and patrols returned to their families and beds near midnight.

Hard as we tried to make the Vietnamese understand that diligent, all-night security was the only way to prevent such disasters, they just never learned the lesson, despite recurring bloody examples. Even when they infrequently occupied night positions, they usually gave them away by lighting cigarettes, playing transistor radios, talking, and moving about. At Cang Long, the ambush units revealed their positions, and the VC followed just behind the returning groups, waiting long enough for the soldiers to go to sleep before cutting the wire and stealing into the compounds. The district team awakened to the sounds of the VC guns and grenades and joined the battle. When it was all over and they returned to the team house, three unexploded grenades sat on the floor inside the door. Luckily the grenades were the unpredictable, homemade VC type and not the more effective Chinese make, or their luck would have run out at the start of the fight.

The luck of the other compounds was all bad, predestined by the stupidity of the defenders. More than thirty women and children were killed in their beds, and the wounded had not as yet been counted. Over twenty soldiers had died, and more were wounded or missing. Thirteen VC bodies were still sprawled inside the compounds and in the wire, as though caught while escaping. Many of the flimsy huts had been burned to the ground, making identification of the dead difficult or impossible.

Tai arrived in his jeep long after I did and slowly inspected the gruesome sight. He then quietly walked alone around the untouched village opposite the compounds and disappeared without a word. John Vann also visited and added a string of expletives to our anger and frustration.

Less than a week after the Cang Long disaster, Captain Sloan needed an interpreter to go with him back to the district, to see what he could do to help rebuild the compounds. Corporal Lam was the only one available and went, after getting Sloan's promise to return in time for Lam's afternoon duty at the hospital. Lam made it back to the hospital that afternoon, but not in a way anyone wanted. Sloan radioed for a Medevac helicopter from the Cang Long team house. Three kilometers out of Cang Long, two sniper bullets obviously meant for Sloan struck Lam as he sat in the back seat of the advisor's jeep. The sector ship was diverted in flight to pick up Lam, when the estimated arrival time of the Medevac ship indicated that we could do the job quicker. When Lam was landed next to the hospital, the Air Force team rushed him into surgery and later gave me the encouraging initial word that they thought they could save him. Over the next two days, they reported gloomily that they were losing the battle. Lam's wife and son remained at the hospital all three days, and I could tell by their growing despair that things were not going well. Captain Sloan was on the hospital veranda each time I visited, and all that either of us could do was to make sure that Lam's son was fed and his wife encouraged.

Lam died, and his young widow and son took him home. I paid my respects on the second day of the wake, after arranging for money from the imprest fund to be given to Lam's widow and some lie to be recorded to cover the amount. Although the sum wasn't large, when added to the money the Air Force and province teams had contributed, it would see Lam's family through the difficult months ahead. When the time came to bury Lam, I walked behind the casket in the long, slow procession from his house to the cemetery. As final graveside services were conducted on the hot and humid December morning, a sudden breeze stirred and flapped the flag draping the cheap wooden casket. The relief the wind brought was quickly replaced by the stench of death which wafted from the casket over the crowd. The civilians present discreetly moved handkerchiefs to their faces. I and the other soldiers fought nausea to hold the salute we were rendering, as the casket was lowered into the grave. When the earth reclaimed Lam, the crowd drifted slowly away, leaving the two white-clad, grieving forms prostrate on the muddy, unmarked mound where their husband and father now rested.

Chapter 15

Deceptive Statistics

In February, 1971, we were informed by the province deputy for administration that Tai was being transferred. He was to be promoted to full colonel and assigned as military attach, in Phnom Penh, Cambodia. I went to Tai's house without an invitation, to say goodbye and wish him well. He seemed in excellent spirits. Several days later I attended a small farewell dinner he hosted. He disappeared quietly shortly after.

Several days after Tai's departure, Can Tho sent word that Tai's replacement was due at the airfield early the next morning. The little that corps could tell me about him was encouraging. Col. Chung Van Bong was coming to the province from commanding a regiment in the U-Minh Forest and had the reputation of being a tough but fair soldier. When Bong's helicopter landed and a group of province officers finished greeting him, I stepped forward to introduce myself and add my welcome. Without breaking his stride to his waiting jeep, Bong returned a quick, toothy greeting and handshake. Led by the welcoming delegation, the line of jeeps sped from the airfield into town. It was their show, and I didn't mind that I wasn't included. In fact, I felt good because Bong looked and acted tough and confident. And if he lived up to his reputation even partially, he would be what the province needed.

In the first few days during May, 1971, Bong gave every sign of being exactly that. He was barely cordial, all business. Tall but thin as a rail, he had a face that resembled a skull covered by skin stretched so tight that his lips never completely closed. Even when he talked, his lips had trouble reaching each other, and the invariably visible teeth gave the impression that he was always leering. This unnerved his staff and commanders and made them cautious when addressing or answering him. Bong's left arm was stunted and deformed, and the clawlike angle at which it was permanently fixed added to his forceful presence. When he spoke, his low, steady tone combined with an unblinking stare to compel attention and prompt reaction. Bong embarked on a series of staff meetings and tough talks with troop commanders. He quickly got things moving again in the province, after the inactivity caused by Tai's months of withdrawal.

Bong didn't just talk. He set the example and demanded an exact and efficient response to his orders, much as when commanding a regiment. It took only one or two briefings for the staff and me to learn that 7 A.M. briefings started when Bong arrived, which was 6:30 A.M. or earlier. When the briefings were over, he whisked away as quickly as he had arrived, and I rarely heard from or saw him again until he finished his office business— usually late morning to early afternoon. Bong's calls for me to meet him meant only one thing: we were going to inspect and instruct units and outposts. Colonel Chinh and his regiment had departed from Cang Long just prior to Bong's arrival, because the start of the rainy season halted the repair and completion of Route 6A. As Bong and Chinh were alike in so many ways, I wondered whether they would have cooperated or opposed each other.

As something bad inevitably followed the good, the bad came three weeks after Bong's arrival. The phone call from the operations center woke me at 1:45 A.M. I knew it couldn't be good news at that hour. Ap Me outpost in Tieu Can District was under attack, and the district couldn't get them on the radio. The operations center duty officer already had requested helicopter gunship support, which was on its way, so I drove to the center. While Ap Me was small and insignificant much of the year, it served an important pacification function protecting farmers during rice harvest.

The duty officer was briefing me on information received up to that time, when Major Murray, the Tieu Can district senior advisor, came up on the radio and asked about the status of the gunships. After the duty officer responded that they were on the way, I took the microphone and asked Murray what information he had had from the outpost before their radio went dead. He replied that they didn't sound too excited but that there was a hell of a lot of firing going on in the background. He still could see flashes in the sky from his location at the district headquarters. They'd been firing artillery one hundred meters outside Ap Me's perimeter wire, and that was about it. I told Murray to keep me informed of any new developments and to pick up control of the gunships when they arrived at his location. We'd be monitoring from province.

Twenty minutes later, Tieu Can called back, and Murray sounded excited. His counterpart had put a relief force together, and they were getting ready to go to Ap Me. The plan was to truck to the bend of the road and then proceed on foot. After silently cursing him for passing the information in the clear, I moved quickly to the map, located Ap Me, and saw that the outpost was next to the road about a mile and a quarter from the district town. The road went straight for the first mile to the northeast, then bent roughly north past the outpost, which was a quarter-mile beyond the bend. I immediately sensed ambush. I smelled it, knew it, felt it in my bones. The whole situation pointed to a perfectly baited ambush trap. Jumping to the radio, I grabbed the microphone from the duty officer, identified myself to Murray, and almost shouted, "Don't go! Convince your counterpart not to go. It's an ambush!" Murray answered that his counterpart had already gone and that he was leaving now to catch up with him. He would check in later on his backpack radio. I bellowed for him to catch his counterpart and tell him not to go. If it was too late to stop him and he wouldn't turn back, make him travel the last stretch off the road. Murray replied a quick "Roger," then silence. I just knew it was the classic sucker play but prayed I was wrong.

Fifteen or twenty minutes later, Murray's voice exploded over the receiver. They were being ambushed! He was gasping, and his transmission was broken, as if he were running, with shattering sounds of firing almost drowning him out. The shaken duty officer handed me the microphone, while Murray moaned that they were caught in a trap and the VC were attacking from positions west of the road. The district chief was hit, and Murray was apologizing that he had not been able to catch up with him. The gunship team leader broke in, telling Murray that the helicopters should be over him now. He could see the firing and asked if Murray could see or hear him. Murray gasped their location as thirty or forty meters east of the road, adding that the VC were on that side of the road now, too close for the helicopters to shoot.

I interrupted, telling the team leader to make a couple of dry fire runs to the west, sensing that the gunships probably couldn't identify the road but hoping that some passes by the gunships in that direction would make the VC turn. The team leader persisted in asking Murray to tell him where the friendly troops were, and to try to give him some kind of location fix. Murray screamed back almost hysterically that the VC were beginning to break off. The calm reply from the gunship continued to ask in which direction from the road and the outpost were the VC withdrawing. Murray just sobbed over and over that the firing was stopping and the VC were going. The pilot coached Murray to use the road as a reference and give him clearance to fire to the west of the road. Murray's response was unintelligible. The team leader tried several more times, with no response from Murray.

The voice of one of the district team sergeants finally came up, telling us that it was all over. They were moving back to the road. When he paused, I reminded him to stay in touch with the gunships until they were back at base and not to pass any results over the radio. The gunship commander droned that he'd stay with them until they were home safe, reminding them to stay in radio contact. I dropped the microphone on the radio table and sat down, drained of feeling except for the throbbing in my temples and the prickling between my shoulders.

The morning briefing went on as scheduled, and Colonel Bong remained unmoved when the Tieu Can ambush was covered. When the briefing was over, Bong asked me to follow and led the way to Tieu Can in his jeep—just him and his driver, no bodyguards or escort. When we arrived at the ambush site, a group of province and district officers were waiting. While Bong stared in stony silence, they recounted in low tones what had happened. I walked the blood-darkened mud road, stopping where VC AK-47 automatic rifle shells were scattered and trying to reconstruct the scene. The rice fields flanking the road were wet but not flooded, and, from the shell casings on the road and in the field to the west, it was evident that the VC had waited very near the road, then moved to the road to finish what the initial bursts had started. There were no foxholes dug in the paddies, which meant that the VC confidently had used only the darkness for concealment.

Bong motioned and called to me. We were going to district headquarters. The small town and district compound made a dark and gloomy contrast to the bright morning and chirping birds. The remaining occupants of twenty-four homes were preparing to bury their dead. I followed Bong directly to Captain Gam's house. The young district chief was already in his casket in front of the candlelit family altar. Bong put his hand on the shoulder of Gam's grieving widow and offered futile words of consolation. When he moved to the children, I stepped before the wife and whispered slowly and distinctly how very sad and sorry I was, too. She nodded acknowledgment through silent tears, and I walked over to the very young children and touched their expressionless faces.

When we left the house, we walked to the nearby district headquarters, where a district officer related the events of the night. The proud, well-trained, and efficient District Intelligence Platoon had led the relief force and took the brunt of the ambush. Captain Gam and his radio operator were behind the platoon, and half a territorial force company stationed at the district compound followed. After they dismounted from the trucks at the bend of the road, all were moving at a fast trot, and the district senior advisor and his sergeant were among the territorial troops trying to catch up with the district chief. When I had heard enough, I leaned over and let Bong know that I was going to talk with Major Murray.

Two days after our visit to Tieu Can, Bong asked me to arrange for a C-7 Caribou to fly Captain Gam's body and his wife and children from Tra Vinh to Saigon, so that Gam cold be buried at the family's ancestral home. Bong prepared and presided over an impressive military ceremony at the airfield, attended by top province military and civilian officials. Most of the advisory team also showed up. After his speech, Bong read a citation and pinned a Cross of Gallantry on the flag-draped coffin, as the widow broke down completely and had to be supported to keep from collapsing. When Bong started to pin the medal on the flag, I realized that I had to make a gesture, too, even if it was unofficial and beyond my authority. While the first of several other scheduled speakers began his eulogy, I walked briskly to the plane's cockpit window and called to the pilot to stall the takeoff for twenty minutes, until I got back. Urging Song to go to the office quickly, I barely made it into the jeep before he took off.

We bounced and skidded to the office door, and I ran to my desk and grabbed one of the boxes containing Bronze Star medals that were awaiting presentation to several members of the Cang Long District team. The coffin and family were already aboard the plane and the propellers were turning when we arrived back at the airfield. As I ran from my jeep, the crew chief waved his arms for me to hurry, so I speeded up, jumped on the rear ramp, and bolted inside. After taking two deep breaths, I stood at attention and shouted over the roar of the revving engines. Feigning to read from a blank piece of note paper, I recited: "On behalf of the army and the people of the United States, the President of the United States has authorized the Bronze Star Medal for Gallantry to be awarded to Capt. Nguyen Trung Gam for heroism and sacrifice to his country." The widow was crying uncontrollably, her head against the coffin, and she didn't understand a word of what I said. I pinned the medal on the flag near the Cross of Gallantry and placed the empty box beside the young sons, who were clutching her knee. As soon as I leaped off the ramp, it was raised, and the plane taxied into position for takeoff. Colonel Bong was already gone when I walked back to the jeep, and the rest of the crowd was leaving as I sat dejectedly in the jeep and watched the Caribou turn and level off in the direction of Saigon. Song gave a smile, patted my arm, and said, "Good."

With the first heavy rains of the monsoon season came the shocking news that Col. Dick Ellison, who had exchanged places with me in Kien Giang, had been killed. The plan of Captain Trinh to reoccupy Hieu Le District in the U-Minh Forest had been put into operation successfully some months before. Dick visited often during the early stages. On the day of Dick's death, his request for an additional sector helicopter was refused. He didn't want to tie up the only available one for his personal use. So he drove to the junction of the Big Tree and Trem Trem canals and had the Kien An district team meet him and take him in their high-speed boat down the Trem Trem to the new district town. I often had done the same, for similar reasons. The VC evidently saw him pass, set up an ambush, and waited for his return. Dick and the sergeant from Kien An who was driving the boat were killed, and Dick's first sergeant was wounded.

At the time, I didn't think about the circumstances that had caused Dick and me to change places, but later I thought about such quirks of fate. Every soldier has to come to grips with, and learn to live with, thoughts of death. The smart ones keep the shadow of death in perspective and try to do nothing stupid to skew the odds. But the time usually comes—normally when the hazards are long past—that some emotional price is paid. In my case, that price habitually was exacted in dreams.

Colonel Bong took me with him by Vietnamese Air Force helicopter to visit his old regiment and attend the division's anniversary celebration. I suspected that he missed the neat and orderly life he had exchanged for province chief's unsteady control. Bong's previous headquarters was an ingenious artificial island suspended over the surprisingly clear water of the flooded central U-Minh Forest. The most gratifying part of the experience was learning that we were in Hieu Le District, Kien Giang Province, and that Bong's regiment was the covering force assigned to protect Captain Trinh's successful return to his people.

On the flight back to Tra Vinh, we passed through heavy black rain clouds, and my thoughts turned to the three weeks remaining until my scheduled return home. It was the end of June, 1971. My orders were to attend the War College in August. I felt only mild pangs of regret at the thought of leaving, as I was very tired and needed a change. During three tours, I had spent five of the previous seven years in Vietnam.

As the weeks and then days until my departure passed, I kept busy traveling and writing my end-of-tour report. I worked until late, determined to make the final report clear and meaningful.

One of the many significant and prophetic changes I wanted to emphasize in the report was the increasing number of tractors replacing manpower and water buffaloes in the rice paddies of the province. I considered that change profoundly symbolic as well as substantive. The sight of the large machines churning up the paddies day and night, for two and three plantings instead of one, reinforced my contention that economic progress was a major factor, if not the central one, in moving the people to increase their support for the government. The recent economic boom had baffled and frustrated the VC. There was no way they could stop it. When they tried to delay, disrupt, or double-tax progress, it clearly hurt the people and was resented. In sum, whatever the VC did that was antiprogress exposed the lie that the VC were interested in the people's welfare.

My final report started out with the deceptively encouraging statement that the number of VC-controlled hamlets in the province now stood at three, in contrast to thirty when I arrived. The paragraphs that followed emphasized the ways that statistic misled, rather than the encouraging aspects. I wanted to get the attention of those who instituted and relied upon a system that produced such deceptive statistics. Part of that system was the American-derived Hamlet Evaluation Survey (HES) questionnaire, which was the basis for determining who controlled the hamlets. Unfortunately, the questionnaire dealt primarily with subjective observations that could be readily manipulated, and overlooked many issues which actually determined whether or not the government controlled a hamlet. Regardless of real, substantive progress and honest, encouraging answers to the questionnaire, any vulnerability of the hamlet people to VC influence or pressure after the sun went down meant at best that government control was spotty and at worst that the VC was in control. To underline the point, I included a list of "secure" hamlets that neither province officials nor I would be reckless or naive enough to spend the night in.

There was measurable improvement, surely, and I documented it with conviction rather than pride. People everywhere were risking getting off the political fence and committing themselves to the government's side. However, they did so only becase it was in their best interest economically to do so and the other side had no better alternative to offer. Programs instituted or energetically supported by the United States—Land to the Tiller, Village Self-Development, People's Information, public health, education, and every other aspect of economic development, social reform, and local self-determination—hit on crucial and decisive issues. These were the programs pushing the people to make the choice, many times for the sake of their children rather than themselves. While guns and security still were essential, the most powerful weapons were the social and economic changes replacing centuries of oppression, indifference, and empty promises. The decreasing number of late-night calls from the operations center and the lessening of artillery fire rumbling out from the darkness reinforced my cautious optimism.

When my report was finished, I added a separate handwritten note to John Vann. I didn't want its controversial subject matter to pass through channels with my report to Saigon. In the note, I argued that the fixed outpost system inherited by the Vietnamese from the French, which we perpetuated, wasn't the way to provide the kind of security so vital to pacification in the rural areas. In many ways, the small, mud-walled forts hindered in providing effective security and played into the hands of the enemy. Most government units did not operate effectively outside the outposts after dark and ceded the night to the enemy. In most instances, the outposts protected only the soldiers and their families, fixed their location for the enemy, and provided targets for the VC to attack when it suited them. With the units safely buttoned up behind their walls after the sun went down, the VC could move easily to and within the hamlets. And, since the people in the contested areas already knew this, the VC didn't always have to come to remind them. The solution to the vexing problem was radical, equally vexing, and sure to be resisted adamantly by every level of the Vietnamese military and civil government, if it ever was proposed: raze most of the outposts and force the units to seek survival by adopting the tactics of the enemy. Without fixed mud walls to protect them, the units would have to move often at night, set up patrols and ambushes, and make the night their ally in order to survive. If our side did that, we would restrict the VC's night freedom of movement and deny them the advantages of surprise and unrestrained access to the people in the villages.

The idea was not new and had been suggested by others before me. I now was firmly convinced that we'd never achieve effective security at night in many parts of the country without some such radical change in tactics, and I wanted to add my voice to the small chorus. The single most persuasive argument against such a drastic change in thinking was that the people initially would perceive that demolishing the outposts meant abandonment by the government. No doubt, the VC would work hard to intensify that perception. When I read over my note, I almost tore it up and threw it in the wastebasket. I knew down deep that the outposts were here to stay, no matter how ineffective and vulnerable they were. And, while I was convinced that the idea would eventually work if tried, I also knew it wouldn't be tried because it entailed radical change. There went an American again, trying to create change—which was not the way Vietnamese culture worked. I went ahead and attached the note, as a mark of conscience if not wisdom.

After the morning briefing on my last day, I said good-bye to Colonel Bong. With his toothy smile and a handshake, he wished me well before whisking off in his jeep. Earlier, as I prepared to leave, I had felt troubled and irritated that my replacement hadn't even been identified. I calmed down in the knowledge that Bong and my civilian deputy, Don Colin, would keep everything firmly on track after my departure.

After dinner, the head of the province council paid a surprise farewell visit. While I greatly appreciated the old man's thoughtful gesture, he added honor to it by giving me a nicely wrapped gift. It was easy to see that the small blue-and-gold ceramic elephant was old, probably a family possession. That made it all the more valuable to me. We sat and talked about many things, some consequential for the province, others personal and important only to us, as we had done several times before. I sensed that he was letting me know that what we had been involved in together was correct, and I thanked him. When he finally got up to go, I was astounded to discover that we had talked for an hour and a half in Vietnamese. My vocabulary obviously had expanded much more than I had realized.

My interpreter, Dragon, insisted on going with me to the airfield. When it was time to go, I got a very tearful and bony hug from Chi Hai, during which I slipped an envelope with two months' pay into the pocket of her black pajamas. As she stood wiping tears from her eyes at the front gate, we continued to wave until Song turned the jeep off the main street toward the airfield. Tractors were making waves in a number of fields outside town as the helicopter climbed and turned toward the Co Chien River.

As I ate my last breakfast in the one of the small soup shops near the entrance to Tan Son Nhut Air Base and watched Saigon awaken, I knew that I was where I belonged, doing what should be done. Leaving to attend schooling that would guarantee me a promotion made me feel ashamed.

Chapter 16

Peace without Honor

Throughout my year at the Air War College in Mont-
gomery, Alabama, the dreams and hopes of the people
of Vietnam stayed in the forefront of my mind. In my
research papers and seminar discussions, I argued the
moral legitimacy of the war and attempted to place the
struggle, including the heavy cost in human suffering, in
proper perspective. In January, 1972, I was invited to
return to the Province Senior Advisor program. Before
the letter from the army chief of staff arrived, I already
had made up my mind to return to Vietnam. When I accepted the assignment, my classmates kidded me that I
was a missionary now, rather than a dyed-in-the-wool
military man. In fact, they were close to correct. As I embarked on my fourth tour, I concealed—because I was
sure nobody would understand—the feeling that in reality I was not leaving home, I was going home.

Starting when I walked into the terminal building
at Tan Son Nhut Airport in Saigon, I saw many signs
that American involvement was winding down. The line
of American soldiers waiting to board the jet for home
dwarfed the small cluster of arrivals, and both groups
were silent. Downtown Saigon no longer had the large
crowds of noisy, free-spending American soldiers, and
the bars lining Tu Do Street were quiet and subdued.
Some already had been converted into sandwich stands
and snack parlors, while others were closed, awaiting
some similar transformation.

In the early spring rains, the faces of the girls standing
in the doorways of the almost empty bars were as gloomy
as the dark skies. It was the same kind of day as that on

which I left a year earlier, but I didn't mind. Although something about the changes in the city bothered me, I was back and felt comfortably calm.

My assignment was to return to Rach Gia. Colonel Dong, the dull-witted former bludgeoner of Cambodian monks in Vinh Binh, was no longer there. Instead, the new province chief was Colonel Chinh—the same Chinh I had known in my initial assignment with the 7th Division eight years earlier and again in Cang Long two years ago. The bad news was that John Vann was dead. Vann had been sent to II Corps in Pleiku to be the corps senior advisor. He was killed when his helicopter crashed near Kontum, about the time I was graduating from the Air War College. Vann's replacement in Can Tho was Wilbur Wilson, who had been Vann's assistant before Vann went to Pleiku. Wilbur and I had gotten along well, even though some disliked him for his hard and unbending demands for progress. In his early sixties, he was a crusty, square-jawed, retired colonel from the old "brown shoe army." He walked ramrod erect and had a sharp tongue that caused both offense and amusement—but communicated wisdom and insight. Recalling Wilbur's strength and character, I was pleased that I'd be working for him.

A two-day stopover in My Tho was authorized. The town looked the same, making it difficult for me to realize that eight years had passed since my first arrival. Visits with Det, now a major stationed at Dong Tam, and with Dao only reinforced the time distortion. The impression continued when the plane landed at Rach Soi Airport in Kien Giang, and my old friend Mr. Hoi hurried across the parking ramp to greet me. He laughed when I said that it was good to be back and that I felt like I'd come home. On the way to Rach Gia in his International Harvester Scout, Hoi told me all the news and added that Colonel Chinh would welcome me at a party at his house that evening.

After I unpacked, I walked around the well-kept front garden of this new house beside the sea. Settling into one of the lawn chairs grouped under the palm trees in the yard, I watched a beautiful sunset over the familiar Gulf of Thailand. When the unchanged routine of evening artillery fire echoed across the bay from the Kien An coast, I remembered the bloody beds and lined up dead that I saw with Tai at the Thu Sao outpost. A cold chill swept over me, the combined effect of the sombre memory, the wind rising in the dark, and the expectation of things to come.

Chinh gave me a warm welcome and, by his tactful handling of all the guests, it was clear that he had made the transition from regimental commander to province chief without difficulty. Bud Moreland, my predecessor, left early the next morning after a brief good-bye, and I quickly moved to the business of getting briefed and reacquainted. Wilbur Wilson had mentioned in Can Tho that the team had developed a negative, pessimistic attitude. The majority of the team felt frustrated and underutilized, because much of the province Vietnamese leadership was competent, inspired, and doing well independently. Since none of the young team members had past experience to measure against, they couldn't compare and recognize the great advantage they enjoyed.

The province leadership indeed had improved significantly on both the military and civilian sides, undoubtedly helped and motivated by a new CORDS program to identify and eliminate corrupt and incompetent individuals. Many of the same old weaknesses still existed, however. All were related to inexperience and poor leadership at the village and hamlet levels. Twenty-eight separate programs now made up the Annual Province Community Defense and Local Development Plan, and a high priority was being given to producing effective local government and generating local revenues to finance a portion of the plan. Problems were to be expected with low-level administrators trained marginally or not at all. Many military units, too, had inept or unwilling leaders. Arbitrary quotas, unrealistic deadlines, and overly optimistic goals reflected a desire to show progress, but things were moving too quickly for the struggling village officials. Apathy, greed, indifference, and corruption also continued to alienate segments of the rural population. In short, plenty of challenging work existed for the team to do in helping the province leadership correct these persistent problems. On the positive side, the economy was growing, and security had improved appreciably in every area of the province except in good old Kien Binh District. Province forces under Chinh's leadership appeared to be strong and motivated enough to maintain the balance of power as things now stood.

Apparently moved by the conclusion that the insurgency was being defeated, Hanoi had decided to change to big-unit, direct intervention during their disastrous Easter, 1972, offensive, almost five months before my arrival. The simultaneous infusion of North Vietnamese Army cadre to direct the war in the provinces had created open dissent and conflict with the VC southerners, a fact not lost on the rural population.

The Easter offensive started a series of government reactions which strengthened the ability and resolve of province forces to cope with the intensified local action. As the regular divisions deployed to meet the North Vietnamese Army's large-unit invasion, province forces were reconfigured to fill the void. Some territorial companies were formed into battalions, and selected local platoons were upgraded in weapons and training to take over the missions of territorial companies. With the exception of a few cases in which village-level desertions and operational disasters resulted, the net effect for security was positive. At the same time, the VC were experiencing serious strength and morale problems.

The first district I visited was the new one, Hieu Le. Trinh called my attention to his recently awarded major's insignia when he met me at the helicopter. His plan to take back his old district had worked, although, viewing the small, isolated bastion of government presence in the middle of the foreboding and hostile U-Minh Forest, it was difficult to see why. His canal-side village was one street wide, one hundred meters long, and consisted of mud huts with thatched roofs.

My other district visits were not noteworthy, except for Ha Tien. Going to Nui Da Dung produced a strong emotional impact. I watched the rock mountain from beside the old command post hill for a long time and wondered if the VC were back. If events followed their usual course, they were; no way would I have walked toward the domineering rock across the flooded rice paddies in that morning's apparent calm.

Compared with my first assignment in Kien Giang province, pacification and the shooting war were going well. Instead of waiting for the other side to act first, Chinh wisely conducted continuing province-level operations. He ordered the districts to do likewise, both to keep the enemy off balance and to avoid the erroneous assumption that all would go well if left alone.

I now took time to study in detail the province pacification plan, as I had not been able to do in the past. The size of the plan and its complexity were staggering, with programs and subprograms reaching down into the villages and hamlets. Over the past year, monthly team reports had chronicled steady, verifiable progress. As I sifted the statistics, a most significant conclusion emerged. Increasingly the population was seeing that the government's efforts, however bumbling at times, represented the best hope of a decent future for both adults and children. The schools, dispensaries, roads, bridges, land reforms, and economic programs demonstrated that the government was trying to bring about change for the better and provided a vision of what could be. When the VC destroyed the evidence of progress, they destroyed their credibility by revealing that they were not truly interested in the welfare of the people. In contrast, when the government moved quickly to alleviate the suffering and destruction caused by the enemy's offensives, the people reaped tangible benefits from the effort.

The rapid growth of the economy had produced a widespread rise in the standard of living. As this occurred, it heightened expectations and made the thought of a return to previous conditions intolerable. The net result was a steady increase in government support throughout the province. The lesson was apparent. If even the destitute people of Hieu Le could rally to the government's side, then rice instead of rifles, and education and medicine instead of fear, pain, and misery ultimately were the means of ending the war.

Problems more critical to the future turn of events in Vietnam were beginning to take shape far removed from the Delta. The Paris Peace Talks brought a first glimmer of hope for a just and lasting peace, with freedom for the long-suffering people of the South. I feared, however, that a war-weary United States, in its wish to disengage and pull out quickly, would fail to insist on adequate safeguards for continued freedom in the South. Experience had convinced me that Hanoi's promises could never be taken seriously. Denied a complete takeover on the battlefield, they were sure to continue seeking it at the conference table. I thought of Colonel Lien's conclusions in "Would There Be Another Dien Bien Phu?"

I also worried about the reaction of the people in the South, particularly in the ranks of the armed forces and in the hamlets. I saw three varieties of hope emerge, each in a different segment of the population. The lowest classes displayed a naive and almost blind hope; the middle ones a cautious, reserved hope; and the educated upper classes a faint hope held carefully in check by fear born of bitter previous experience.

When rumors of progress toward settlement leaked from the Paris talks, the VC reacted with a predictable maneuver. In October, 1972, they launched a concerted effort to grab all the land they could, hoping to convince outside decision makers that they had legitimate claim to the territory taken. The timing of the enemy's land grab was premature, however, and the only lasting results were more blood and suffering. Tong and I were on the road from Kien Thanh District town to Minh Luong village when hundreds of people streamed in panic across the road from the rice paddies and jungles to the west. Breathless, crying women clutching young children and struggling, exhausted old people surrounded the jeep and told us that the VC had overrun and occupied Hoa Quan village. I immediately radioed the operations center to see if the Vietnamese at that location had gotten the report. They hadn't. I instructed the operator to send the principal AID advisor to my location with imprest funds to set up temporary shelter and feeding facilities and to round up his Social Welfare and Refugee Service counterpart to accompany him.

The deputy for security arrived soon after the AID advisor and immediately launched an operation to regain control of Hoa Quan. The battle which followed ended at dark, and Chinh and I accompanied troops into the deserted village by sampan shortly after dawn. The scene that greeted us was a tragically familiar one. Much of the village was burned to the ground. Police, People's Self-Defense Forces, village territorial soldiers, and council members had been held hostage in the village temple and shot when the VC withdrew before dawn. The survivors and returning villagers reported that the VC had been enraged that the village security forces had resisted and that the people had fled.

In rapid succession, other bloody attempts were made to occupy and hold villages and hamlets. Soc Son village near the capital was overrun and occupied until Chinh (with me in tow) personally led a relief force up the road from Rach Gia and ousted the VC in a day-long fight. Hieu Le District town was attacked, but the enemy quickly was pushed out of the section they penetrated by the dependable Major Trinh. The final spate of activity was an assault against a small Catholic village named Thanh Hoa, off the Kien Tan-Rach Soi road. Attacking again in daylight, the VC surprised and occupied Thanh Hoa; took the priest, village council, and some elders hostage; and held them in the village church, digging in around it when the villagers ran away.

Now ensued three days of stalemate, which saw air strikes on the unpopulated jungle tree line from which the VC had come, artillery fire around the outer periphery of the village, and meter-by-meter advances on three sides of Thanh Hoa by Chinh's troops. At last the VC disappeared into the night. This time, for whatever reason, the hostages were left alive.

The last of the attacks was not a land grab, but a savage, old-style night attack on the outpost protecting Hieu Le's southern flank. Chinh and I arrived the next morning to view the carnage, inflicted in an apparent effort to vent frustration or send a message to the previously successful defenders of Hieu Le. Men, women, and children all had been shot, most at close range, and the skulls of many of the wounded had been crushed with rifle butts. Of the forty territorial soldiers manning the outpost, seven survived.

As the Paris Peace Talks continued, the Vietnamese prepared to see the political struggle intensify before and after the truce that was rumored to be coming. The first phase was nicknamed by the Americans "the battle of the flags." Saigon ordered that paper and tin national flags should be nailed on the door of every house and that cloth flags should be flown from flagpoles, so that any truce commission would recognize clearly all areas of government control. The VC reacted by entering isolated hamlets and villages, tearing down the flags, and substituting the colors of the National Liberation Front. That caused Chinh to return, tear down the VC flags, and help the people paint—instead of nail—the government flags everywhere.

The annual 1972 Christmas and Tet truces were anticipated with mixed emotions, but caution, frustration, and distrust predominated. Sadly, Wilbur Wilson died of a heart attack while home on leave in Washington, D.C., on December 19, 1972. Wilbur was buried in Arlington Cemetery beside his old friend John Vann, and the CORDS staff in Can Tho published a memorial booklet containing some of his well-known sayings. I laughed remembering Wilbur as I read:

Don't do what I say, do what's right!

Of course we'll muddle through, but we've GOT to raise the level of muddling.

There you go, thinking again, weakening the team.

The FIRST thing we've got to do is abolish stupidity.

When you get something from these provinces, Jesus Christ, don't just copy it down. Some of these goddam guys are semi-literate.

We've got to get these little guys out from under the shade trees.

Leadin' lieutenants is easy. Keep 'em so goddam busy they can't think about what they're always thinking about, which is girls.

We can only tolerate a certain level of incompetence around here.

I agree. Targeting the enemy units is a GREAT idea! But nobody's ever been able to do it.

I know how to improve communications in the Delta. Take the goddam Signal Officer out and shoot him.

Of course I chew out captains, that's what captains are for, f'gawdsake!

Tet 1973 passed quietly, and I assumed that it was because the VC correctly sensed that the people felt unfriendly toward them, did not want their kind of control, and did not want even a hint of violence during a religious time traditionally reserved for family reunions. With the announcement of the truce agreement from Paris in January, 1973, VC units concentrated their land-grabbing attacks throughout Kien Binh District and succeeded in temporarily occupying three hamlets.

Contrary to my earlier fears that war-weariness and visions of peace might sap the will of province forces, they fought like tigers and threw the VC out of the hamlets, along with the North Vietnamese Army soldiers who now accompanied them. As their reward, the troops received outward expressions of respect and appreciation from the villagers. For their efforts, the VC and North Vietnamese gained only the hostility and bitterness of the villagers, who returned home to find the usual death and destruction.

For months I had been witnessing what I had begun to notice earlier in Vinh Binh. The population's attitude was changing. The enemy not only was losing credibility and support, but also was being refused willing and even forced cooperation. What I was seeing was the long-awaited turning point of the war. I fervently hoped that it had not come too late.

The cease-fire agreement at Paris gave Hanoi and Washington what they wanted. Within the framework of continued American support to the South, American forces were to phase out and leave, unbelievably permitting all North Vietnamese forces to remain in place. The one exception to the American evacuation was a small military contingent, assigned to the Defense Attaché's Office as part of U.S. Embassy in Saigon, which would be overseeing the continued flow of arms and supplies to the South Vietnamese as prescribed in the cease-fire agreement. The implied threat of U.S. intervention by air from Thailand and elsewhere was supposed to keep the enemy's forces in check.

I felt confident that the South Vietnamese Armed Forces could hold their own if we properly supported them. However, some things worried me. Replacement of government war supplies was to be made on a one-to-one basis, when they were used up or destroyed. We would be bound morally by the terms of the agreement, while Hanoi didn't have morals. Hanoi had to be caught violating the truce, and we wouldn't be here to catch it.

Many in the American government still were more distrustful of the South Vietnamese than of the North Vietnamese. To stack the odds further against the South, half of the International Commission for Control and Supervision (ICCS) of the truce was made up of representatives from Communist countries, and the commission was bound to unanimous consent in all decisions.

When I received advance notice of the phase-out of the province team, I sat dejectedly in my office until late, studying the message and wondering how best to accomplish it when told to do so. Although the notice gave no firm dates for the beginning of the move or for the final exit, it was clear that it was to be accomplished much more quickly than I had anticipated. The district teams were to be phased out first, starting with the most remote and vulnerable; and all American teams, along with all Vietnamese units, outposts, and rural offices, were to be instructed and alerted to receive and evacuate the U.S. and Vietnamese prisoners expected to be released as stipulated in the cease-fire agreement. Since we continually received reports of large and small VC prison camps in the U-Minh Forest, we remained alert and ready to receive the returnees. They never materialized!

Tired and depressed, I told Tong to drive me home. It was already dark, and as we passed the lighted tennis courts near the house, Colonel Chinh waved and called for me to stop. He told me to go and change and come back quickly to play, because he had a surprise for me. Over his shoulder I glimpsed his surprise: a pretty lady in a tasteful tennis dress was sitting and watching the foursome playing on the court. After quickly gulping down some dinner, I jogged back to the courts.

Chinh introduced me to Madame Pham Thi Cam Nhung and said his surprise was that I was to play a set against her. I sat next to Chinh while the match in progress concluded and leaned across him to make polite conversation with Cam Nhung. When I asked where she was from, she returned a beautiful smile and shook her head to show she spoke no English other than the greeting we had exchanged when Chinh introduced her. Using Vietnamese as best as I could I found out that she lived in Saigon and was on a business trip. Chinh and she had been schoolmates long ago. Suddenly the match finished and Chinh waved us onto the court.

Starting with the first ball she powered past me, Chinh's real surprise

and my humiliation on the court began. The pretty lady was as commanding on the court as she was off it. She whistled her serves and volleys past
me, making me run back and forth desperately trying to reach her accurately placed strokes. When she decided to finish my struggles, she fired
the ball where I had no chance of reaching it. Chinh and the others were
having a wonderful time enjoying my agony until I held up my hand and
my racket, walked to the net to shake hands and gasped with a sweaty
smile that I'd had enough. She graciously smiled back and started to leave
the court, until one of the better players ran up and asked her to continue
with him.

When I sat down heavily beside Chinh, he handed me a towel and hu-
morously asked how I had enjoyed the game. The pleasant joke was that
Madame Cam Nhung was the national women's tennis champion. As I
watched her dominate her next victim and the one after that, I didn't feel
too bad. In fact, I felt very good. When I said good-night and walked back
to the house, I was light-hearted for the first time in years. By the time I
went to bed, Cam Nhung's smile had replaced the phase-down message in
my mind, and I slept peacefully.

The next day was Sunday, and Cam Nhung was on the courts again
when I returned for lunch in the early afternoon. Since she was flying back
to Saigon that evening and I didn't know when I would see her again, I
boldly asked her if she would have dinner with me the next time I visited
Saigon. Her smile gave the answer before she said yes and told me how to
get a message to her. As my face unexpectedly flushed, my heart was beating rapidly.

The ringing of church bells to celebrate the signing of the 1973 cease-
fire agreement was followed immediately by gunfire, as the enemy blatantly
violated the truce. Washington did not react, but Chinh did, instantly and
aggressively. The fact that we were now denied the support of U.S. air
strikes and helicopters delayed the retaking of VC-occupied hamlets and
greatly increased our casualties. While the soldiers seemed no less determined, they obviously were more cautious, and I couldn't blame them. After
surviving to this point, nobody wanted to be on the final casualty lists
during what all hoped was the beginning of the end of the long shooting
war. The retaking of Soc Son dragged on into a bloody stalemate, however.
Later we found out the reason they hung on more doggedly in Soc Son.
The enemy force was predominantly North Vietnamese.

Chinh called for a Vietnamese Air Force (VNAF) helicopter to take us
to Soc Son to see what was going on. When we circled the village itself,
an extremely large VC flag was flying from the flagpole in front of the village office, and several dozen people scurried for cover.

During my hundreds of hours of flying over the countryside, that was
only the second time I had seen the enemy from the air. I watched intently,

and my eye caught sampans on a canal leading into the village. When they saw the helicopter, they quickly pulled to the bank, and their occupants scrambled under the scant cover of banana trees lining the shore. The pilot must have seen them, too, for he banked to circle the area. Chinh was busy talking to his units over his radio when the pilot shouted and pointed to the canal. Chinh glanced at the figures still moving cautiously from tree to tree, finished some directions over the radio, and shouted to the pilot that they were VC and to shoot them. The door gunner began firing his machine gun at the darting forms but didn't even come close, because the pilot kept turning for a better view. I heard Chinh cursing and turned to see him leaning out the door, firing his pistol while he shouted for the pilot to go lower and slower, and to stop maneuvering. The pilot couldn't hear with his helmet on, and, by the time Chinh unstrapped his seat belt and crept forward to slap the pilot's shoulder hard, the darting figures had disappeared.

Chinh directed the pilot to return to the village center, and this time—the wrong time—the pilot followed Chinh's instructions and slowly hovered at about one hundred feet. An explosion of shots immediately burst from directly beneath us, as we hung almost motionless and in a position that prevented the door gunner from firing back. Chinh had his radio headset back on and was talking into the microphone, as the continuing fusilades made my legs twitch involuntarily. I leaned over and gave Chinh's knee a sharp rap and, when he bolted around to look at me, I pointed to the ground and in rapid succession made a gun gesture with my forefinger and thumb followed by slicing my hand across my throat.

After what seemed an eternity, the helicopter swung away and climbed. Chinh took off his headphones and said disgustedly that we were going to Long Xuyen. The Corps commander had called a meeting. On the twenty-minute flight to Long Xuyen, my thighs, buttocks, back, and head began to ache from the tension of the close call. Chinh had his eyes closed and looked like he was sleeping.

As Chinh jumped from the helicopter, I motioned and waved for him to go on to the meeting without me and called that I'd join him later. I wanted to inspect the underside of the ship for damage, since it didn't appear that the crew was going to do it. There were five bullet holes in the tail boom, two through the cabin floor beneath where we had been sitting, and a gouge in the tail rotor. When I called the holes to the attention of the Vietnamese pilots, they looked at them without interest, shrugged, and went back to talking or napping.

After the meeting, I told Chinh about the bullet holes, adding that the control cables go through the tail boom; if they were damaged, they could fray and snap in flight. I didn't want an accident to finish what the VC tried to accomplish back at Soc Son. Chinh answered with a grunt but looked at the holes when we got back to the ship and talked to the pilots. The copilot consequently removed several panels in the tail boom and inspected the cables and controls before we took off. If someone hadn't checked, I already had decided to ask for a ride back with the corps senior advisor and accept any consequent loss of face.

The order to phase down and close out the team came in mid-February, 1973, and included a timetable. Most military advisors had to be out by the third week of February and all by the end of the month. The district teams were to go first. Otherwise I had discretion as to the remaining order of departure. The decision to close out the district teams first and the loss of U.S. Army helicopter support caused major problems for those remaining. The number and frequency of situation reports required increased as our ability to comply dwindled. As the team grew smaller, the few of us who remained found ourselves exclusively in the reporting business.

With Chinh's approval and the civilian Air America helicopters sometimes provided, I repeatedly traveled to all the districts vacated by the advisors and tried to get relevant information from the resentful district chiefs, who felt abandoned in the pullout. Only Trinh in Hieu Le remained open and candid with me. Long evenings were required to put responses from the others into proper perspective and make the information coherent. A most frustrating and difficult time for me personally was made worse by guilt over the fact that our job was being ended ignominiously before it honorably could be concluded. Chinh remained understanding, close, and open, but others in the province headquarters reacted with shock, concern, sadness, some bitterness, and, finally, a disturbingly quiet resignation.

During the final two weeks, General Tarpley, the corps senior advisor, and Tom Jones, a retired colonel with CORDS in Can Tho, recommended to the Defense Attaché Office remaining in Saigon that, because of my experience, I stay on with them. The answer came back that all authorized positions already had been assigned. And, in typical army fashion, most officers assigned were coming from the States and had little or no previous experience in Vietnam. Resigned now to my approaching final departure, I continued team phase-out and reporting with a very heavy heart.

The province farewell party was a tennis round-robin tourney followed by a catered dinner set up on the courts. I appreciated the thoughtfulness of whoever had arranged the event that way—probably Mr. Thanh, the province deputy chief for administration. It was an evening of fun and constant activity which left little time for sentimentality, except during short speeches at the end. Mr. Thanh presented me with a ceramic set of ancient oriental figures named Phuoc, Loc, and Tho. They graced most Vietnamese homes and were supposed to bring the recipient health, prosperity, and a long life. I finished my farewell speech by wishing all present, and the Republic of Vietnam, those same good wishes.

When the party finished, Chinh and I went to his house as we had arranged earlier. I wanted us to be alone when I gave him the last of my monthly assessment and recommendation letters. The letter was long, and I had been charged with emotion when writing the six-page, typewritten farewell, but as expected, Chinh read it with his old stolid, expressionless face:

> This letter and our talk regarding it will be the last of our many discussions about the war, your people, and the future. I thought about what the future holds for Vietnam as I traveled around during Tet and watched with a warm heart the many happy and hopeful faces of all the beautiful children. That experience brought back clearly to my mind what I heard often in the past from many Vietnamese people including farmers, soldiers, and government officials. They all said, in essence, "We are making our sacrifices today to ensure a peace with freedom and happiness for our children in the future." In so very many families only the children remain, waiting for that world of peace and happiness that their parents sacrificed to obtain for them. The cost paid by the good and brave Vietnamese people in suffering, tragedy, and death is enormous.
>
> The sacrifice and cost paid by my country is also great. Fifty thousand Americans died to attain a future that will include peace with freedom for your beautiful land. As a soldier who has spent almost one-fifth of my life and nearly half of my army service in Vietnam as your comrade-in-arms, I can say with emphatic sincerity that my government has pursued that ultimate goal with honor and integrity. You will recall that when I first returned to Kien Giang, I said that because I know you, I also know you are an outstanding, competent leader who really didn't need an advisor. With that in mind, I write this letter to you not as your advisor but as the personal friend, trusted ally, and comrade-in-arms which I consider myself fortunate to have been since we first met nine years ago in 1964.

Throughout the letter, I recalled needs we had often discussed at length: for the government to continue improving the lives of the people if the people were to support the government; for developing leadership and integrity in the lower ranks of the province forces; for good civil administration; and for keeping corruption from burdening those on the lowest rungs of the socioeconomic ladder. In closing, I reemphasized that the side that gets the support of the people ultimately would win. When he finished reading, Chinh simply stood and thanked me for everything. We shook hands and said good-night, pretending that my departure was merely one of many such farewells.

Tong, my driver, waited until the last afternoon to invite me to his house for dinner. Even though I had a busy schedule, I accepted for several reasons. We had grown very close, and a refusal would have been an affront. By going too, I could avoid an awkward last dinner with my constantly tearful housekeeper. As it turned out, I merely traded her tears for Tong's, even though we would be together for another ten days on our drive to Saigon.

On the way back to my house, I remembered that I hadn't said good-bye to Mr. Hoi. When I prepared to leave, Hoi drew me aside, where his wife couldn't hear, and asked me to buy him a pistol in Saigon and send it to him. His request surprised me, and I wondered how he intended to use the gun—in defense, or on the family if the worst happened? I agreed to send the weapon, and we said our last good-bye. As I left, my heart was heavy.

Chinh, a few of his military staff, the three remaining U.S. civilian team members, and some of our Vietnamese employees were waiting at the airfield in Rach Soi to see me off. A bottle of sparkling wine was passed around to fill paper cups for a last toast, and I quickly thanked them all and said good-bye. Tong loaded my bags and footlockers on the Air America helicopter, while I made sure he understood my instructions for meeting me with the jeep the next day at the CORDS compound in Can Tho. When the loading was finished, I turned, snapped a final salute to Colonel Chinh, and jumped aboard. It was February 26, 1973.

Chapter 17

Beginning of the End

Many thoughts and emotions filled me on the flight to Can Tho. I was not so much sad as uneasy and resentful at leaving things unfinished, and I tried to find comfort in the thought that a glimmer of hope remained for the future, even though a long and difficult period must lie ahead. I'd given my best effort and felt disgust and shame at the fact that the truce had stacked the odds in favor of the enemy.

As the canals and rice paddies slowly passed beneath me, I strained to recognize familiar landmarks and silently repeated their names when I did. With the names came faces—American and Vietnamese faces of those I'd shared with and learned from. Nameless children and old people, too, returned with surprising, clarity bringing both pain and comfort. Although these faces formed the background for unfolding events, they were what the whole sad, blood-soaked effort had been about.

While waiting on the Can Tho Airfield parking ramp for a vehicle to take my belongings to the transportation office, I remembered sitting on my footlocker and getting drenched by a monsoon cloudburst in almost the same spot when I first arrived in 1964. It seemed inconceivable that eight and a half years had passed.

Ten days remained before my scheduled flight from Saigon, and I was in no hurry to go. I was given a comfortable room in the guest house and relaxed in the pleasant, resortlike surroundings. Although previously I always had enjoyed the luxury of the CORDS compound whenever I spent the night, now the stark contrast between its self-indulgent comfort and the dust, dirt, and squalor beyond the gate made me feel self-conscious and guilty. Suddenly I wished I was already on the plane and out of the country.

The long drive to My Tho was—as I had hoped—pleasant, unhurried, and filled with small but enjoyable experiences. Memories as well as miles sped by when we reached Dinh Tuong Province and as we rolled down Highway 4 and through the districts, especially Cai Lay. When finally we reached My Tho, bidding Dao and his family farewell was difficult and painful; telling Det good-bye was painful and tearful. Sleep came late and then only because Dao poured extra-large drinks.

When I finally located Cam Nhung's apartment in Saigon the following morning, her neighbor told me that she was at work. She was on the faculty of Marie Curie French High School and would not return until late afternoon. While waiting in a nearby park, I knew I wanted much more time to know her. The feeling intensified as I returned to her apartment. With Tong waiting in the street below, I ran up the five floors to her door, taking the steps two at a time. As I knocked, my heart was beating heavily, more from anticipation than from exertion. When she opened the door and I saw her lovely smile, I knew that I loved her and had to find some way to keep her.

I was never happier or more relaxed than during the next seven days. We spent afternoons at the Circle Sportif and ate quiet dinners at secluded rooftop restaurants. Encouraged by her responsiveness and by the fact that I only had a few days remaining, I asked her to marry me. She turned away from me with tears streaming down her face. Earlier we had told each other that we both had been married previously and divorced; she had three children. Now, as we professed our love for each other, I understood clearly that, if leaving her country to go with me was a frightening thing to contemplate, leaving her beloved children behind would break her heart. Suddenly, I wanted all of them and told her that I would find a way for all of them to follow me as soon as possible after I left.

Feeling depressed and confused, I returned to the poolside bar at Bachelor Officer's Quarters (BOQ) Number One. It was the wrong place to go. While sitting beside the pool, trying to think how arrangements could be made for the children to follow later, the revelry around me, reminiscent of the last days of Pompei, only reminded me that time was growing short. When a pot-bellied old civilian contract employee threw his young bargirl date into the pool beside me, I dumped my drink on the grass and retreated to a small restaurant nearby that was visited by few Americans. Since it was the quiet I needed most, I told the waiter to bring a glass of whatever was available. The scene at the BOQ was foreign to the values of the culture that kept drawing me back to Vietnam. I loved Cam Nhung all the more because she held those values so dear. Several drinks later, I walked back to the BOQ steadier in mind and heart, if not steadier on my legs.

Next morning, when I returned to my room at the BOQ from out-processing, a note was taped to my door. Brig. Gen. Ralph Maglione, the assistant defense attaché, wanted to see me at nine the next morning. Although the appointment might have been set for any number of reasons, I had to struggle to keep calm, hoping that some change had come about which would permit me to stay on. It was difficult that evening not to tell Cam Nhung about my hopes. If the appointment turned out to be about something other than my staying, I didn't want to add more disappointment to the melancholy mood we were in.

The Defense Attaché Office (DAO) was already functioning in the Military Assistance Command, Vietnam (MACV) headquarters building, as MACV completed its phase-out. Maj. Gen. John Murray, the previous MACV deputy chief of staff for logistics, was the new defense attaché, and Brigadier General Maglione was his assistant. Because of the limit on military staff who could remain, I found the bustling corridors of the DAO offices filled with civilians. Following the signs to General Maglione's office reminded me how thankful I always had been to be assigned out in the field rather than being stuck in a staff job. Now I was imploring the Almighty that the appointment with the general would result in such an assignment. It did. The job was to be chief of liaison to the Vietnamese Joint General Staff (JGS). I would manage a team of U.S. civilians in offices located in the JGS compound.

I couldn't remember being happier in my life. During dinner, Cam Nhung smiled her beautiful smile the entire evening, and we even threw caution to the winds and attempted to dance to the small, out-of-tune orchestra. Such carefree days were numbered, though, for us and for all of Vietnam.

Tong would have been happy to stay with me in Saigon, but I gently pushed him on his way back to Rach Gia. He wept openly as I gave him some money and the pistol I had bought for Mr. Hoi. I instructed him to deliver it personally and to tell Mr. Hoi that I hoped he'd never have to use it.

When I finally moved into my office in the JGS operations building on March 31, 1973, the day of the deadline for U.S. troop withdrawal, my first task was to continue to interview and recruit retired military and ex-AID advisors to fill the section's positions. When that was completed, we began around-the-clock monitoring and reporting of daily Vietnamese operational activities. Vietnamese Army interpreters were assigned as part of each duty shift. I also was in charge of an American army major who, with our section's chief interpreter, maintained a protocol office in a separate building occupied by the offices of the chief of the JGS, Gen. Cao Van Vien.

I had weighty and time-consuming adjunct responsibilities as well. I was to monitor and support the psychological operations of the Armed

Forces Political Warfare Directorate, which was commanded by a three-star general. I was to perform required liaison activity with the headquarters of the Vietnamese Army, Navy, and Air Force; and I was the designated DAO representative to the Embassy Task Force for Psychological Operations. Initially the job promised to provide the opportunity I had hoped for to help in the war that continued despite the cease-fire. But soon, due to General Maglione, it turned into a frustrating experience.

A 1970 Ford sedan was provided for my use, to make sure that I could respond quickly when called. Because the war intensified rather than slackened during the so-called truce, the military members of the DAO toiled seven days a week and were on call at all hours, even though the Vietnamese with whom we worked, except for low-ranking duty officers, did not work on weekends. Eventually I moved into the old MACV general officers' compound. I continued to court Cam Nhung in the little free time I had.

The section's monitoring and reporting shifts at JGS worked smoothly, and activity soon became routine. The enemy's truce violations grew from small, local incidents to large-scale infiltration of weapons, supplies, individual replacements, and eventually entire units; and the Vietnamese Armed Forces moved, repositioned, and operated against the threat. General Maglione began pressing me to obtain prior notification of all intended friendly actions. I tried to explain to him that such confidential information might be given to me only after I had established the trust and confidence of the lower-level staff officers I worked with, but he didn't want to hear that kind of "negativism." What I wanted to ask, but in the face of his stubbornness and impatience did not, was how he expected those lower-ranking officers to divulge sensitive information to me without the approval of their bosses, who were the principal contacts of Maglione and General Murray.

Help came from an unexpected source. My translator, Ms. Chinh, had worked in various assignments throughout the JGS headquarters for a number of years and was trusted and respected. She received her translating assignments from my secretary, Pat Eichen, so I enlisted Pat in my effort. I told Ms. Chinh openly about the need for advance notice of operations and, with Pat's help, convinced her that relaying the information was in the best interests of both our countries. Moreover, it would be treated confidentially. With surprising alacrity, Ms. Chinh put me in contact with two officers. Colonel Tam was the assistant chief of staff for operations, and he agreed to twice-weekly informal conversations covering what was happening throughout the country and what reactions to enemy moves might be considered. Lieutenant Colonel Khanh was Tam's chief of operational planning, and, because he was the real workhorse of the plans section, he turned out occasionally to be a dependable and valuable source.

Once Tam and Khanh discovered that I had spent more than six years with the 7th Division and out in the provinces, they became friendlier, and I had easier access to them. Still, they had to get the approval of their boss, Brigadier General Tho, before they could release any information to me. Tho, Maglione's principal contact, was a sharp young officer who I knew couldn't help wondering why Maglione was dealing through me instead of talking directly with Tho himself.

After two months on the job, I was promoted to full colonel. Two weeks earlier, Cam Nhung had consented to marry me. My application for permission to marry was approved by U.S. Army Pacific headquarters at the end of April, 1973, and we set the date for mid-May. Pat Eichen, my secretary, was particularly happy for us, as she and Cam Nhung had grown close. We invited Pat to be one of our witnesses at the simple civil ceremony. When it was over, we held a reception at the Continental Palace Hotel. My heart swelled with love and pride when I went to Cam Nhung's apartment to take her to the reception. She looked more beautiful than ever. More happiness was added to the day when I saw Det and Dao with their wives in the reception line. Dao was now a brigadier general and a division commander, and Det was looking healthy and rested.

The months following our marriage were happy times. Since I was almost forty-nine years old, I had about given up hope of having a family; the unexpected and happy acquisition of the children, in addition to Cam Nhung, gave me new and wonderful experiences. Each giving of love brought a bountiful amount back in exchange. We were permitted to move into a house trailer at what formerly had been the U.S. Military Assistance Command general officers' compound on Tan Son Nhut Air Base. The children—two boys, ages thirteen and eight, and a girl, age twelve—quickly stole the hearts of the other officers living there. Only General Maglione was discomfited by my newly acquired family living in the compound and served notice that I should be looking for new living quarters to rent outside the compound.

Shortly after Cam Nhung and I returned from a hurried trip home to meet my family, the situation throughout the country worsened, as did my relations with General Maglione. After tentatively testing American resolve and reaction, the North Vietnamese stepped up their truce violations and, predictably, became bolder when there was no retaliation. Having made a mockery of the Paris cease-fire agreement by substantially reducing funds to aid the Vietnamese armed forces, on June 30, 1973, the U.S. Congress passed the War Powers Act, formalizing congressional oversight of the president's use of troops overseas. Despite Defense Department attempts to honor what should have been a solemn international agreement to keep the needed ammunition, equipment, and spare parts flowing, in order to give the Vietnamese a fighting chance to defend themselves, the critical supplies were dwindling. The mood at the embassy and at DAO worsened, as attempts to communicate the inevitable consequences to our lawmakers were rebuffed. At the same time that the Vietnamese were becoming cooler and more distrustful, the U.S. military chain of command pressed for more information, more facts, and more reports to justify keeping the needed supplies flowing. In response to those pressures, General Maglione pushed me harder to get warning of Vietnamese counteractions from the increasingly reluctant and resentful Tam and Khanh. My relations with senior JGS officers deteriorated further as I had to deliver General Maglione's requests and notices to their homes in the evening or while they played tennis or relaxed on weekends. I was not permitted to know the reasons that prompted my urgent visits to the Vietnamese generals, for DAO had withheld my access to all sensitive information because I was now married to a "foreign national."

While DAO focused on the crucial issues of getting ammunition convoys to Phnom Penh through the gauntlet of enemy fire along the Mekong River, increasing the antitank capability of the increasingly outgunned Vietnamese Army, and getting enough spare parts and fuel to keep the planes flying and the tanks and trucks rolling, my time was less profitably employed. I was attending sterile Embassy Psychological Task Force meetings, where philosophical debates were conducted on the hidden meanings of pronouncements out of Hanoi; or checking on the adequacy of assistance—more and more consisting of advice rather than material—to the Political Warfare Directorate; or delivering those unappreciated messages to the Vietnamese. I tried to keep my frustrations from Cam Nhung but found it difficult.

One Sunday, we sneaked to My Tho and visited Colonel Bong, my previous counterpart as province chief of Vinh Binh, who now was the Dinh Tuong province chief. The reunion lost its appeal when I stopped by to see the civilian province advisor and he informed me of the magnitude of Bong's greedy and oppressive corruption. Only a pleasant dinner overlooking the Cuu Long River saved what turned out to be a long and disappointing trip. When we returned, Dao invited us to the anniversary review of the 18th Division he commanded in Thu Duc, north of Saigon. The trip provided a chance both to get away from the office and to see that Dao hadn't changed. He was whipping the division into shape and was eager to get into action against the North Vietnamese Army. I had a feeling he wasn't going to have too long to wait.

Near the end of 1973, at a time when my section didn't need more tasks to keep us busy, a team from the U.S. Support Group headquarters in Thailand came to show us how to keypunch all enemy incidents of the last six months on computer cards. Someone in Thailand had the idea that putting the bulky data into the computer would enable our side to predict trends and patterns. After accomplishing the three-week job, I awaited some worthwhile results. But we heard nothing. The Thailand-based headquarters, which was commanded by an Air Force four-star general, was supposed to direct punitive strikes against North Vietnamese units openly violating the "truce." That retaliation never took place, and the Support Group supported only itself—one more example of the American penchant for useless "layering" of unnecessary control mechanisms.

Cam Nhung and I began a frustrating and futile month-long search for living quarters. When landlords learned that Cam Nhung was married to an American officer, they tried to exact, as a condition for renting to us, concessions that would reap them black-market opportunities. Had they known beforehand her inflexible honesty, unbending integrity, and moral courage, they would have saved themselves the effort. As it was, all they got was a tactful lecture about greed and dishonesty, along with pointedly critical remarks about lack of appreciation for America's sacrifices for their country.

As Cam Nhung dejectedly returned to the trailer each day after her futile house hunting, she'd pass General Maglione playing paddle tennis in the compound. Because she looked so tired and because, like all the Defense Attaché Office officers, he liked and respected her, he asked me if she was still teaching in the French high schools. When I said she was not and detailed the problems she was encountering in house hunting as a result of her staunch refusal to be ensnared in a black-market arrangement, he completely surprised me. He told me to tell her not to look any further and to see him in the morning. When I did, the general phoned the embassy and arranged for us to move into one of the two-story houses in downtown Saigon leased by the U.S. government. Later, her charm, grace, loyalty, and support for our efforts prompted a remark in my efficiency report about what a great asset she had been to our liaison efforts with the Joint General Staff.

Two months before my year at DAO was to expire, I applied for and was granted a six-month extension of my tour. Even though I was frustrated over my inability to help with the burgeoning problems of the war within the truce, I needed the additional time now to work out a plan to make sure that we would have no trouble getting the children out of the country when we left.

Rare, happy weekend moments with Cam Nhung and the children contrasted with progressively gloomy reports of the escalating fighting and my depressing field trips. While the trips got me out of the office and away from the tensions of DAO and General Maglione, they also brought me face to face with the stark realities of the military deterioration in the countryside.

The first journey to anti-armor training at Quang Trung Training Center near the outskirts of Saigon left me unconvinced that the outgunned foot soldiers would overcome their fear of the increasing numbers of tanks being introduced into the South by Hanoi sufficiently to get close enough to score hits with the missiles we provided. Subsequently, when I flew to the 5th Division headquarters near Lai Khe, northwest of Saigon, enemy mortars fell close by at midday. Although the division commander initially seemed unmoved by the explosions, soon after he expressed his frustration at not being able to go after the well-protected source of the firing—or do much else, for that matter—because his tracked and wheeled vehicles were immobilized by a shortage of gasoline and spare parts.

The situation in the central highlands north of Kontum also was becoming precarious, as NVA units reportedly were working their way eastward in what the JGS suspected was a flanking move to cut Route 19, the vital artery linking Pleiku with Qui Nhon and the coast. Since approval for each trip had to be obtained from General Tho, as a courtesy we invited him to send a staff officer with us. This time, Tho sent Colonel Tam along.

As our plane approached Pleiku, I thought about John Vann's and Lien's deaths and remembered my unpleasant half-year in the same area. For the first time in revisiting familiar places, I was uneasy and wanted to get the visit over with and return quickly to Saigon. Colonel Tam had to check in at II Corps headquarters for permission to proceed north to Kontum, and I waited for him in the hallway, having no inclination to go see my old office or the nearby vacated American compound. When he returned, he informed me that the Corps commanding general was providing a helicopter to take us to Kontum.

As we boarded the VNAF helicopter and I took my seat, I automatically reached around to fasten my seatbelt. There wasn't any. Tam and the other officer from corps had none, either. Half of a set was lying on the cabin floor. When we took off, I received an answer to my silent question about what good half a seat belt was. The crew chief picked it up and used it to fasten shut the right cabin door, because the latch was broken. I glanced at the opposite door. Sure enough, the other half of the belt was holding that wildly vibrating door shut, too. As we swung toward Kontum, I hoped the crew had enough spare parts to maintain the engine in better shape than the cabin.

The regimental commander briefed us at his command post on the road north of Kontum. Strong enemy units, confirmed as North Vietnamese, were exerting constant pressure and had succeeded in punching units across the road to the east. The regiment was spread thin and had been deployed following orders to place first priority on preventing enemy movement south toward Kontum and Pleiku City. The regiment commander seemed to understand the significance of an enemy move to the east. By bypassing Kontum and Pleiku, the other side would be in position to swing south and cut

Route 19 to Qui Nhon and the coast. But the commander was sticking with his latest orders and was hard pressed to defend both the east and the south. Since the entire corps area was large and friendly units available within it were meager, the Kontum situation foreshadowed other serious problems there in the future.

On the return trip to Saigon, we encountered violent thunderstorms over the mountains, and the small plane bounced like a skiff in a hurricane. The lights of Saigon twinkling through the rain in the distance were a welcome sight, and I breathed a sigh of relief when we landed.

The warmth of our house and Cam Nhung's welcome made me forget the long, dismal trip. She worried when I made each trip and pampered me when I returned.

That night I couldn't sleep as lightning flashes illuminated the room. Thoughts of the children sleeping contentedly nearby made me wonder whether in the morning I should mention the emergency family evacuation plan I had been given the day before. I decided not to, because there still seemed to be time, and Cam Nhung would worry too much.

My last trip was to see Dao. His 18th Division was approximately fifty miles northwest of Saigon, and the general was being pressed hard by the North Vietnamese. JGS headquarters had told him I was coming, and he was waiting for me outside his heavily sandbagged command bunker when the Air America helicopter landed. After we shook hands, his eyes bulged in the old, familiar way, and he shouted over the noise of the helicopter engine, "Brother, have the pilot take off and come back for you later. If the helicopter stays here, it will draw enemy fire." I nodded that I understood and asked the pilot to return for me in an hour, but not to land unless he saw me outside the bunker waving. As Dao led me inside, the low rumble of explosions not far away underlined his concern. I had not expected to find that his command post was within range of enemy artillery.

We spent only a few minutes in personal conversation before he started the briefing. The corps commander was due to visit shortly, and Dao wanted to finish with me before he arrived. Dao did the briefing while his staff sat and listened. The more he described his situation, the madder he got. As he paced up and down in front of the map with his hands alternately hanging by the thumbs in his pockets and waving at or slapping the map, I recognized the old, fiery Dao from Chuong Thien:

Colonel Metzner, the Communists have me at a disadvantage in every way. My soldiers want to fight and they do well anything I ask them, but the truth is, we are on the defensive. We are rationed to four artillery rounds a day for each gun and about a hundred rifle bullets for each soldier each month—*each month!* The North Vietnamese have an unlimited supply. My soldiers are being killed and wounded because they enemy's artillery can reach us from beyond our guns' range, and I cannot even move my guns and tanks close enough to fight and fire back because we get so little gasoline.

He hadn't taken his eyes off mine, and now he pointed in the direction of a very close volley of explosions: "Communist artillery units have hundreds of observers in the coconut and rubber trees and fire ten, twenty, fifty rounds at anything that moves. My soldiers remain strong, and their spirit is high, but courage alone cannot stop steel."

I was listening silently and without expression, but inside my heart was wrenched with anger and frustration. When he launched into a scathing tirade against the corps commander, calling him unsupporting, dense, and uncaring, I was amazed. For him to say this openly in front of his staff meant that he had their absolute loyalty and support and that he was not overstating the seriousness of the situation.

When he finished, Dao hung his thumbs in his pockets and stared silently at the floor. "I understand everything clearly, general," I said firmly as I slowly got out of the chair. "And my report will contain everything exactly as you've told me." That was my official response in front of his staff, but as he waited with me for the helicopter outside the bunker, I slammed my fist into my hand. "Damn it, my friend, I'm sorry, really sorry that this is what we've come to. I don't know what encouragement I can give you." As the helicopter landed on the road, Dao cut me off, speaking tersely through clenched teeth: "I know it is bad and not as we hoped. Give us only what we need to fight with, and we will do the dying and get the job done."

Then he gave me his old piercing smile and shook my hand, sending regards to my wife and telling me to take care of myself. I smiled back and added that I wished for God and Buddha to be with him. He returned my wave as the helicopter took off, then turned and briskly strode into the bunker.

Dao's parting words, "Give us only what we need to fight with, and we will do the dying," rang painfully in my ears as our support continued to fade. And I felt a terrible shame in my heart as I looked over the beautiful countryside that, judged from the helicopter's altitude and speed, looked deceptively peaceful.

Chapter 18

Final Farewell

Pat Eichen, my secretary, stuck her head in my office to tell me that an American Catholic priest, a Father Devlin, was waiting in the outer office to see me. I was immediately impressed by the imposing figure who limped forward to shake my hand. Almost a foot higher than I, Father Joe Devlin was broad-shouldered and large-boned but lean as a rail. His crew-cut grey hair and weather-beaten, square-jawed face framed a disarming smile above the white collar of his short-sleeved black shirt. While crunching my hand in his large, powerful grasp, he apologized for bothering me but said that he needed help.

When we sat across from each other at the coffee table in my office, he crossed his legs and I saw what caused his limp. His right shoe had a sole and heel built up about three inches. He was working with a community of refugees near Phan Thiet and came to Saigon now and then for his personal supplies. This morning the manager at the commissary had told him that he wasn't authorized to shop because he wasn't in Vietnam at the invitation of our government. Even though the priest was an American citizen, the commissary manager had quoted regulations when refusing to issue the authorization. I phoned the manager and got the same answer he'd given Father Devlin. The fact that the priest was engaged in a humanitarian cause, undoubtedly welcomed and appreciated by our government, made no difference. The manager sympathetically offered a solution, though. He would issue a temporary privilege card if we could get a letter of authorization from the defense attaché. I called General

Murray's office and talked his secretary into making an appointment for Father Devlin that evening.

Pat kept the coffee coming while "Father Joe," as he wished to be called, answered my questions. He was a Jesuit teaching at a Midwestern college when he became touched by the plight of the Vietnamese people and the suffering the war had brought. He felt unchallenged and unrewarded in his teaching duties and asked his superiors for permission to seek a flock to shepherd in Vietnam. The Catholic Charities Office in Saigon replied that they could use him, and he ended up ministering to a group of several thousand war refugees mostly Catholics, about ninety miles east of Saigon on the coast. Before we parted, I made him promise to contact me so he could meet my family and have dinner with us the next time he came to Saigon. Father Joe returned five or six times and on each occasion had dinner with my family. He, Cam Nhung, and the children took to each other immediately. On each visit, the friendship grew.

Three and a half months remained before the end of my tour of duty at DAO, and I wasn't even close to a solution to the problem of how to get the children out of the country. I had dismissed any thought of applying for another extension because of my worsening relations with General Maglione and my concern for the safety of the family, in view of Washington's total disregard of Hanoi's escalating truce violations. While I still prayed, I'd just about given up hope of a miracle.

General Murray periodically was called back to Washington to testify before congressional committees. Pleading for sufficient ammunition and spare parts to give the Vietnamese a decent chance to defend themselves, he also reported in specific terms the blatant North Vietnamese violations of the Paris agreement that made resumption of the promised help necessary and justified.

Each time he returned after being rudely rebuffed, General Murray's frustration and irritation spread among the DAO staff. We momentarily had reason to cheer when he lost his temper on one trip, after being provoked by an antagonistic reporter. In response, he referred to the law makers on Capitol Hill as political bloodsuckers. We hoped that his angry slip wouldn't cause him to be removed and replaced by someone less sensitive to the immoral abandonment in progress.

Both in Washington and in Vietnam, grim events and forecasts of more to come seemed unending. Growing numbers of planes, tanks, trucks, and other equipment sat idle either because they were being cannibalized for parts to keep others going or because there was no fuel to operate them. A sapper attack against the large gasoline storage facility at Nha Be, near Saigon, destroyed much of the country's remaining reserve stocks. Ammunition stockpiles also were dangerously low. The already gloomy atmosphere at DAO headquarters plummeted after a VC ambush deliberately murdered an American truce officer assigned to the Joint Casualty Resolution Center during an agreed-upon investigation of a reported aircraft crash site, seeking remains of U.S. crew members missing in action.

Each time reports mentioned Phan Thiet as one of the locations where security was deteriorating, I thought about Father Joe and his band of refugees and wondered how he was getting along. His total dedication to his "flock" and his lack of care for himself had begun to take their toll. Although it was difficult to imagine his becoming thinner, when I had seen him last, his clothes had hung more loosely, and his gait had been slower and more labored than usual.

On his most recent visit with my family, Father Joe had gathered us all together after dinner and formally blessed us. At the close, he asked that divine favor grant that we meet again. Although that prayer would be answered, Father Joe's selfless service to others would lead soon thereafter to his disappearance.

My final plan to get the children out of Vietnam centered on securing their American citizenship at the same time that Cam Nhung was natualized. A letter of inquiry to the Immigration and Naturalization Service had brought an explanation of how spouses of servicemen assigned overseas could become naturalized during the period of overseas service. Application could be made for children to be granted citizenship at the same time. Two such procedures were scheduled before we were due to leave Vietnam, one in Guam and the other in Honolulu. I chose Honolulu. United States citizenship alone wouldn't assure the children's exit from the country, however, because Vietnam recognized dual citizenship. The boys in particular would be in danger of detention, due to pressing demands for manpower in the Armed Forces. Vietnamese government officials had become unsympathetic to American requests for assistance. I had to find a way to avoid the possibility of the children's being detained.

I decided to have their names changed and then obtain U.S. passports reflecting the new Americanized names. If that could be accomplished, I would schedule our return from Honolulu with a stopover in Hong Kong and apply at the Vietnamese Consulate there for temporary entry visas. The justification given for the visas would be that I wanted my family to accompany me into Vietnam, as if for the first time, as dependents authorized by the U.S. government.

If all went well up to that point, as we proceeded out at Tan Son Nhut Air Base for our final departure, I would keep the children out of sight when I presented our passports and visas to the immigration authorities and police. My application to appear for examination and naturalization came back approved for a hearing on May 14, 1974.

What began as an exciting journey for all and a much-needed vacation for Cam Nhung and me turned out to be one long exercise in frustration and suspense. We had to overcome unexpected delays and trouble at every turn. Cam Nhung and I were remarried on American soil. She and the children became U.S. citizens. Cam Nhung took the name Alina, and the children became Howard, Helen, and Hilton. Our passports were issued in the very last minutes of the afternoon before our departure. The passports were stamped with temporary entrance visas by the Hong Kong Vietnamese Consulate during our brief stopover there, and we returned to Saigon at the end of May, 1974, tired but happy that we had accomplished our objectives. A little over two months from now, my assignment would be over.

Time sped by, despite General Maglione's continued urging that I convince the increasingly withdrawn Joint General Staff to confide in us their secretly planned moves to counter Hanoi's mounting pressures. I made one last trip, as advance liaison officer to the aircraft carrier USS *Kittyhawk*, cruising off the coast. Key members of the JGS followed me to the carrier the next day to witness a firepower demonstration. The demonstrations went off with precision and were duly impressive. While watching them, however, I couldn't help thinking that the bombing passes and strafing runs would have been more appreciated and useful had they been made in support of Dao's beleaguered units not far away. Since I now doubted that the strength of the mammoth warship ever would be used to help those who were invited to witness its harnessed potential, both my stomach and my heart ached.

Father Joe made the trip to Saigon for a final dinner with Alina and me a week before our departure. His refugee village was under increasing pressure from the VC, and he now had a new concern for his flock. In addition to ministering to their spiritual needs, he had to supervise their security and protection. Alina and I had grown to love the old saint, and we were deeply concerned for his safety. Trying to keep the conversation light, I joked that he worried me because he had to be the tallest target in the country and, with his game leg, probably was the slowest, too.

He answered that he wasn't worried, because he had his own weapon now. It was a .45-caliber pistol, the gift of a departing AID advisor. He'd been practicing with it and was a pretty fair shot. We all laughed about his being a "pistol-packing padre," but the fact that he was carrying a gun meant that his situation was more worrisome than he had let on. The children went to bed after giving Father Joe extra-long hugs, and we talked until late, delaying our farewells until the last minute.

Alina and I walked with him to his new means of transportation, parked in front of the house—an aged three-wheel motorcycle that he'd convinced the Pittsburgh police's traffic department to contribute to his cause. As his white plastic pith helmet bounced down the dark street and out of sight, Alina cried, and I whispered a prayer for his safety.

Our last day in Vietnam, August 5, 1974, dawned to a mixture of bright sunshine and scattered heavy monsoon clouds. Takeoff time was 11 A.M., and I wished that we didn't have so much time to wait. Alina kept busy preparing breakfast, checking on final packing, and fussing over the children. The giant step of leaving her country, culture, and family—all so loved by her—was only hours away. I couldn't imagine the trauma, or how she would survive it, if the children were detained at the last minute. All I knew was that I was going to get them all on the plane, even if it took bribery, threat, or kidnap.

Alina's mother, father, and five of her brothers and sisters came to the house early and tried to help with last-minute chores. Since they only wanted to be together with Alina and the children for as long as they could, I stayed out of the way and kept busy on my own. Finally I had to begin moving everyone out of the house and on the way to the airport. Gently but resolutely gathering Alina and the children into the sedan, I waved for the family to follow in two borrowed cars. Although the children kept up an excited chatter, Alina and I were quiet as we drove through the bustling city, she squeezing my hand tightly. One brief but heavy monsoon downpour fell as we turned onto Cong Ly Boulevard. The blurry scene turned my thoughts back to the rain-dappled rice paddies, wind-lashed palm trees, and groups of soldiers huddled beneath them. A sharp pang of sadness started to pry at the composure I had vowed to keep firmly in place, so I forced my thoughts back to the present.

One of the people from my section met us and ushered us into the airport VIP lounge, where Pat Eichen, Ms. Chinh, others from the section, and several interpreters welcomed us with a surprise farewell party. Alina's family came in shortly after, and we all tried to join in the fabricated gaiety that I welcomed as a diversion for Alina. The chief interpreter from General Vien's office, Sergeant Minh, pulled me aside and said in a half-whisper that he'd come to help me process through the police and passport checks.

Minh often had helped me before, and I was sure he meant that he wanted to help me again with the final hurdle, if needed. I patted his shoulder, thanked him, and expressed appreciation for his good idea. After a few minutes, it struck me that it was indeed a *very* good idea, and I decided to let Minh interpret for me as if I understood no Vietnamese when we presented our passports for final check.

When the time came, I told Alina to stay at the party with the children and went with Sergeant Minh to the series of checkpoint booths in the terminal. I tried to look disinterested, but my heart was pounding as Minh put on a wonderful act while I stood silently by. He escorted me to the passport desk and coolly stated that I was the advisor to General Cao Van Vien, and the general had sent him with me to expedite my processing.

When there appeared to be the slightest hesitation, Minh became irritated, inquired about the delay, and looked at his watch. He repeated the act as we went from the passport desk to the police security check and through customs. When one of the policemen commented about the deep rows of ribbons on my chest, Minh smiled and proudly—but excruciatingly slowly—explained each of the Vietnamese awards to him, starting in 1964 and stressing that the last one he was pointing to had been personally awarded by General Vien, after the prime minister himself had signed the decree. That seemed to do it. All forms were signed and stamped, and the policeman stood up and leaned over to shake my hand. I thanked him aloud in English, then mumbled under my breath fervent thanks to the Lord.

Minh had even gotten a pass to take the sedan to the boarding area through a side gate, a courtesy reserved for real VIPs. With a little luck, the children never would be seen by the police. Back at the party, corks were still popping, and Alina was bravely dividing her time between my office crew and her quiet family. I gently squeezed her shoulder and whispered that everything was all right. We would go to the plane in the car.

When the loudspeaker announced time to board, Alina's artificial gaiety vanished, and she moved to the circle of her family for the emotional final moments. I passed slowly through my office staff and the interpreters, thanking them for all they'd done over the past year and a half. They had been consistently loyal, understanding, and dedicated. My stomach felt hollow and I felt sick, but I smiled and tried to stay cheerful and unruffled.

The family, Pat Eichen, two of the old retired army NCOs from the duty sections, and Sergeant Minh went with us to the car in front of the terminal, while the others stayed to finish the champagne. As Alina hugged her mother and father, then each sister and brother, they all broke down and started to cry softly. As soon as the car turned out of sight of the waving group, Alina put her head on my shoulder and shook with sobs. The police guard at the gate started to hold up his hand to stop us, then waved us through and saluted when he saw the pass on the dashboard.

As we climbed the plane's loading ramp, we stopped after every two or three steps to turn and wave at the figures signaling to us from the terminal observation deck. After a last pause and wave at the top, Alina stiffened to regain her composure and entered the plane with her head held high. The children already had scurried to their seats ahead of us.

The closing thud of the jumbo jet's door had a symbolic finality that brought mixed feelings of relief and regret. The noise caused Alina to reach out for my hand, while she strained for one last glimpse of the observation deck. When the plane began to taxi and the terminal no longer could be seen, she leaned her head back and closed her eyes. As I looked past her out the window, four old, propeller-driven Vietnamese Air Force fighter bombers rolled by and began to climb into the black, rain-laden clouds. A pang again stabbed at my heart as I leaned over to watch them go, and I said audibly, "Good luck to all of you."

Alina whispered, "Did you speak to me?"

"No." I touched her hand. "I just said one last good-bye."

Epilogue

President Nixon resigned four days after we left Saigon. Watergate and its conclusion in August, 1974, served only to hasten America's inevitable abandonment of the people of Vietnam. President Thieu merely accelerated the final collapse when, in 1975, he ordered the troops to pull back before advancing Communist forces in the Central Highlands. That effort quickly turned into a panicked, bloody rout. The dark chapter ended when Hanoi's tanks smashed onto the grounds of the Presidential Palace in Saigon on April 30, 1975, only hours after the last Americans had been plucked by helicopter from the roof of the U.S. Embassy. In the end, all the suffering, hopes, and sacrifices, all the blood and death, had been for nothing.

The day that Saigon fell, I numbly returned home through a gray and frosty New England morning to try to comfort Alina. In the months and years that followed the Communist takeover, she and I pieced together the events that followed the imposition of the new order. We learned not from the press, which complacently confirmed its prediction that no blood bath of revenge would befall the conquered masses, but rather from those who risked the unknown dangers of the sea rather than endure the spiritual and physical stranglehold of the new rulers.

True, there was no blood bath such as that which took place in neighboring Cambodia. "Reeducation camps" were quickly constructed in the jungles, swamps, and mountains, however. From the moment of the Communist takeover, thousands of people at every level disappeared, never to be seen again, because they were considered a risk. Their crime was that they cherished a wish for freedom and in some way announced or acted upon that wish. Even now, after ample testimony to the suffering imposed on countless South Vietnamese by their northern kin, some well-meaning but deluded voices continue to insist that America interfered in an internal struggle involving people who couldn't comprehend the value and true meaning of freedom. Some even add that the results are none of our business and that we shouldn't be concerned. If, through calculated sickness, starvation, and a systematic destruction of spirit as well as body, death came to so many former allies who trusted us, is that within the bounds of a peace with honor? Not as far as I'm concerned.

Dao rotted in a Hanoi prison for seventeen years. Characteristically, his 18th Division was the last unit resisting to the end against overwhelming odds in the final battle at the crucial road junction of Xuan Loc outside Saigon. We sadly heard that he had died in prison in 1985, but that was a false report. In April, 1994, through a mutual friend, we learned that Dao had survived and was in New York City, where we joyfully contacted him.

At last word, Colonel Tai remains in Vietnam after years of imprisonment in Hanoi. Dragon and his sons and Sergeant Minh from the JGS got out by boat and corresponded with us from Virginia. Dragon spent three years in a jungle prison after he was captured; Minh was lucky enough to avoid being apprehended. I heard that Madame Dao and the children made it to the refugee camps of Malaysia but dropped out of sight after that. In early 1985, Det got word to us through one of his sons who had escaped earlier, that he was alive and living in Can Tho. My rapid response to him went unanswered until 1988, when we learned that he also had escaped and was with his son in Hawaii. After we had struggled for almost ten years to get Alina's family out by every legal, diplomatic, and humanitarian means we knew, they were unexpectedly released in April, 1985, the tenth anniversary of the fall of Saigon.

Pat Eichen, my secretary at the JGS, volunteered to accompany an evacuation airlift of small Vietnamese children from Saigon during the hectic last days of the war. She was killed with most of the others, when the U.S. Air Force transport plane crashed into the rice paddies beyond Tan Son Nhut Airport. Father Joe made it out safely a day or so later and gave us the sad news. While working with the large Vietnamese refugee community in San Jose, California, he came to visit us several times. Characteristically for Father Joe, that kind of involvement wasn't enough. He felt there was a greater service he could and had to perform: working with the refugee camps for boat people in Malaysia. Several refugees with whom Alina and I talked long after he departed told of a tall, thin, gray-haired

Catholic priest who walks with a limp as he moves tirelessly through the beaches and camps, bringing compassion to the suffering and order amid the chaos.

The others? Chinh, Phuc, Mr. Hoi? Unbroken silence shrouds their fate. I still ask those who have escaped about them, but no one knows. I still nourish a slim hope that some made it to the impenetrable jungle and mangrove base areas vacated by the enemy, where groups of resistors keep alive the hope for freedom. Some of the refugees who escaped by boat have even made the equally long and dangerous return trip to join those holdouts.

While the war was lost and, with it, the freedom sought by the people of Vietnam, advisors did make substantial contributions to people's lives. The efforts of teams I served with saved many lives that otherwise would have been lost to violence, disease, or hunger; and we were only a few of many.

Certainly we made mistakes, in both the idea of what the role of an advisor should encompass and in the ways by which each of us attempted to bridge the wide gulf of cultural differences we faced. But few of our failures were the consequence of negligence or a lack of dedication, sacrifice, or effort.

Advising was new to us. To my knowledge, only three such experiences existed previously in all of U.S. military history: in China during World War II, in Greece after that war, and during the Korean War. Only the Chinese experience was wide in scope, and no guidelines or accumulated wisdom were passed on to future advisors.

In Vietnam, we learned as we stumbled along. By the time each advisor was beginning to learn how to function effectively, his year was up and he went home. Usually an advisor left with little or no time to pass on to a replacement what he had learned. Again, as John Vann accurately had put it, we didn't have twelve years' experience in Vietnam, we had one year's experience twelve times over.

While advisors at all levels accomplished many noteworthy things— some officially recorded but most known only to the people they benefited—I believe that the Vietnam advisory effort generally was ineffective. The vast cultural differences alone were enough to scuttle the effort at the lowest and most critical levels. That any thing at all was accomplished is a tribute to the advisors' tenacity. When Washington and Saigon failed to recognize and come to grips with the fact that two divergent conceptual and operational worlds were engaged in collaboration, advisors in the field were left pretty much to their own devices. What they needed was some clout, but in most cases persuasion was the main tool we had available to use with counterparts who didn't want to—or couldn't—change in the first place.

Often, though, we were fooled into believing that we were succeeding.

This was because our Vietnamese counterparts delicately balanced the need to assure survival after our departure with the need to encourage and prolong our involvement so they could reach that point of self-sufficiency.

In the end, U.S. decisionmakers chose to rely on brute force alone to win the war, disregarding the critical need to guarantee that the end result would be humane, just, and long-lasting. A high-priority pacification program engineered by advisors with some clout might have provided just such a guarantee. Time finally ran out, accelerated by war-weariness and a philosophy that justified abandonment, surrender of honor, and denial.

Looking back, I suppose that, more than most advisors, I was lucky. I was moderately effective, at least in two out of three cases. A good part of that effectiveness was due to the luck of the draw that paired me with Phuc and Dao. Second, I believed that I had not brought many answers to problems with me, so I had to keep stealing workable ideas wherever I could find them, even from the enemy. Too, I was relatively successful at camouflaging my ideas so that they appeared to be Vietnamese ideas. In every action, I tried to communicate that I was there simply as one round-eyed member of a Vietnamese team working to help the Vietnamese people—knowing in my heart that such a chore would be difficult in a culture that placed little emphasis on concern for others who were outside the circle of immediate family. I worked very hard at keeping my word, being dependable, and becoming trusted. Luckily, I was there long enough to establish something close to that kind of reputation; my abnormal length of service was a key factor contributing to my effectiveness.

Finally, I held firm to my conviction that my conscience had to be the final judge of all that I did and how I did it. I let it clearly be known that cultural differences could not alter or change my moral or ethical responsibilities. I include these thoughts here in the hope they may be of help to others at some time.

What was the significance of the establishment of CORDS? Given the problems of the Vietnam War in general and of pacification in particular, it's difficult to see how any real progress was made toward pacification before CORDS was created. Specifically, CORDS pulled together, under one undisputed authority, all the complex, competing, and often redundant U.S. civil and military pacification programs. Even more important, perhaps, CORDS was able to leverage some coordinated direction of the fragmented and marginally effective efforts on the Vietnamese side.

Several CORDS initiatives which supported my efforts to influence actions on my level were the reintroduction of language training, extended tours for key personnel, availability and control of Mobile Advisory Teams, and, last but not least, superiors in Saigon who understood the interdependence of pacification and military action and who tried to influence policy accordingly.

In spite of the sad final outcome and the emotional scars left by our futile, costly effort, I still firmly believe that our Vietnam cause was an honorable one and that most of those who gave of themselves in Southeast Asia and were touched by the people there feel the same way. If the stilled voices in the hamlets could speak, I believe they would testify loudly that they keenly appreciate the effort. Although we cannot take pride in the part our precipitous abandonment played in the final outcome, there is much to respect in the way America's young sons responded earlier when sent to prevent that very outcome. Father Joe Devlin, in an editorial published in the *Ogden (Utah) Standard Examiner* before before the dishonorable fall of Vietnam, gave a much more eloquent testament to that than I ever could:

Returning Vietnam Veterans Earned
Gratitude of People of S.E. Asia

(Editor's Note: As the U.S. participation in the nation's longest war winds down, a former Ogdenite points out vividly the fact that our returning veterans have earned the gratitude of the people of America and Vietnam. The author is the Rev. Joe Devlin, S.J., Catholic priest at a remote Mekong Delta mission.)

For the returning veterans, there are no proud songs.

The visible presence of war on television, the fury and tragedy of battle have taken away all the calmness from American judgment.

Vietnam, in the American dictionary, is an obscene word. And so the veteran comes home, an enigma to his own, who call him "cruel and ugly." But to the Vietnamese, the American GI is a man of awe and respect.

To an American airport he comes, this man of sacrifice and danger. He will be greeted and welcomed by his wife and children. No flags will be flying.

At a nearby airport gate, perhaps the heroes of the sporting world will be greeted by thousands of fans. Enigma? Who is? The soldier? Or the American people?

"The evil men do lives after them. The good is oft interred with their bones."

My Lai we all remember. Drugs we know. But how many know the orphanages helped by the American military man, the schools they supplied, the poor children . . .

The soldier helped out where he could because his empathy for people told him it should be done. He asked for no broadcasts, no praise, no blaring trumpets.

Like the mountain climber, he climbed his own mountain because "it was there."

For every cheating soldier who dealt with the black market, a thousand were here who did charitable works.

For every My Lai, there were a thousand other hamlets lifted to a better life.

And for every man exposed to dope, a thousand lived an ordered life. Despite it all, he is "branded" first in war but last in the hearts of his countrymen.

But not last in my heart.

I have been a constant and critical observer of the U.S. Armed Forces in Vietnam. I watched them in their barracks, in their outposts, in their ships, and in their choppers.

I was present at their briefings, watched them at menial tasks in the camps and in the fields—the young GIs, the sailors, the non-coms, the pilots, the doctors, the officers, the chaplains.

America never had finer representation, not in the halls of ivy nor the halls of Congress. They were the American image of our way of life, and what a witness they gave!

Together we went, the armed soldier and I, speeding down a canal, bending heaven and hell to get a little dying girl out of the middle of the Mekong and to a U.S. Navy doctor.

We were a team. As when three of us fought to keep a little boy's life-breath flowing until the Medevac could finally get there with his big bird.

We saw trips off the flight deck by night to save a little boy and Navy gunships converted into mercy carriers, threading the needle by night to carry off injured civilians in our village.

Gunshot wounds. Booby trap injuries. Crippled children. The works. The Americans took care of them all!

Shades of Tom Dooley? Rather shades of a deep American compassion and an inbred desire to help the needy and the underdog.

They came in conquest, this army from the United States. But they remained to be conquered by an army of orphaned kids, the needy, lepers, and missionaries.

You can learn a lot about popularity from the children of a land. Little naked children would stand in an open hut and say "My, my." (The Americans, the Americans.) Most likely they'd reach out their hands for candy.

To them, he wasn't "cruel," he wasn't ugly. They might not know of their native buffalo, but everyone, everywhere knew the American from over the sea.

San Francisco, Ogden, Hoboken all spelled magic Camelot to the Vietnamese.

I saw only a little of what Americans have done here. I multiply what I saw by the thousands—the saving operations of life and limb, the refugees, the lepers, the mountain-people cared for. It was a volume of many-splendored deeds told once but not twice.

The world will wait long before occupying armies ever again behave so circumspectly. One great heritage he leaves behind: "From the soldiers of the Armed Forces of the United States to the people of South Vietnam, bought and paid for by American blood, to you we bequeath Freedom."

Indeed, he cast a giant shadow.

And so he goes, and for his going this eastern world is a little bit less good.

Like the "passing of Arthur," his going is the end of an epoch, an emptiness that will not be filled.

Down deep in the Scriptures, we reach for some words to describe him.

"Erant gigantes in diebus illis."

In those days, giants walked the earth. And good men, big men, once walked the land of Vietnam.

The little ones they sought to help are still here. The giants are gone, their flag is gone, but their memory and spirit still hovers over the land.

"Good-bye, you great big generous lugs. Indeed, we shall remember!"

Index